ACADEMIC PRECOCITY

Thank You!

Camilla P. Benbow

Julian C. Stanley

5 July 1985

Volumes based on the annual Hyman Blumberg Symposia
on Research in Early Childhood Education
JULIAN C. STANLEY, GENERAL SERIES EDITOR

ACADEMIC PRECOCITY
Aspects of Its Development

Revised, Expanded, and Updated Proceedings of
the Tenth Annual Hyman Blumberg Symposium
on Research in Early Childhood Education

Edited by
CAMILLA PERSSON BENBOW
& JULIAN C. STANLEY

THE JOHNS HOPKINS UNIVERSITY PRESS
Baltimore & London

© 1983 by The Johns Hopkins University Press
All rights reserved
Printed in the United States of America

The Johns Hopkins University Press, Baltimore, Maryland 21218
The Johns Hopkins Press Ltd, London

Library of Congress Cataloging in Publication Data

Hyman Blumberg Symposium on Research in Early Childhood
  Education (10th : 1980 : Johns Hopkins University)
  Academic precocity, aspects of its development.

  "Revised, expanded, and updated proceedings of the
Tenth Annual Hyman Blumberg Symposium on Research in
Early Childhood Education."
    1. Mathematics — Study and teaching — United States —
Congresses. 2. Gifted children — Education — Mathematics —
Congresses. 3. Mathematical ability — Congresses.
I. Benbow, Camilla Persson. II. Stanley, Julian C.
III. Title.
QA13.H95   1980   371.95   83–48063
ISBN 0-8018-2990-9
ISBN 0-8018-2991-7 (pbk.)

To the memory of Professors Halbert B. Robinson (1925–1981) and Dean A. Worcester (1889–1982), innovative and effective proponents of improving the pace and level of education of intellectually talented youths. Professor Robinson's last publication appears in this book. Professor Worcester is especially remembered for *The Education of Children of* Above-Average *Mentality,* 1956.

Contents

Contributors

CAMILLA P. BENBOW is the associate director of the Study of Mathematically Precocious Youth, an associate research scientist in the psychology department, and an assistant professor in the sociology department at The Johns Hopkins University, Baltimore, Maryland 21218.

JOHN F. FELDHUSEN is the director of the Gifted Education Resource Institute and a professor of educational psychology at Purdue University, West Lafayette, Indiana 47907.

LYNN H. FOX is the coordinator of the Intellectually Gifted Child Study Group and a professor of education in the Evening College and Summer Session of The Johns Hopkins University, Baltimore, Maryland 21218.

JOHN F. LUNNY is the supervisor of mathematics, Charles County, La Plata, Maryland 20646.

RICHARD F. McCOART is a professor of mathematics at Loyola College, Baltimore, Maryland 21210.

KAREN MEZYNSKI is a doctoral student in psychology at Vanderbilt University, Nashville, Tennessee 37203.

WILLIAM B. MICHAEL is a professor of education and psychology at the University of Southern California, Los Angeles, California 90007.

SUSAN PERKINS is a doctoral student in clinical psychology at Boston University, Boston, Massachusetts 02215.

LYNN DAGGETT POLLINS is a doctoral student in education at Duke University, Durham, North Carolina 27708.

HALBERT B. ROBINSON, now deceased, was the director of the Child Development Research Group and a professor of psychology at the University of Washington, Seattle, Washington 98195.

JULIAN C. STANLEY is the director of the Study of Mathematically Precocious Youth and a professor of psychology at The Johns Hopkins University, Baltimore, Maryland 21218.

JOYCE VAN TASSEL-BASKA is the director of the Midwest Talent Search, School of Education, Northwestern University, Evanston, Illinois 60201.

Preface and Acknowledgments

On November 14, 15, and 16, 1980, a symposium was conducted at The Johns Hopkins University to discover what had been learned during the first decade of work by the Johns Hopkins Study of Mathematically Precocious Youth (SMPY). Was SMPY's identification procedure, the annual talent search, effective? What were the mathematically precocious students like in high school? Do the educational facilitation procedures utilized by SMPY, which are mostly accelerative, have long-term beneficial results? How adaptable are SMPY's methods to other settings? These and many other questions needed to be answered. The results obtained by SMPY were evaluated by its staff members and several leading professionals in the field of education of gifted children. Findings and conclusions are contained in the twelve chapters of this book.

This is volume 10 of the Hyman Blumberg Symposium series, for which Julian C. Stanley is the general editor. It is also number 7 in the Studies of Intellectual Precocity (SIP) series. All previous volumes in the series except the one noted were also published by The Johns Hopkins University Press: *Mathematical Talent: Discovery, Description, and Development,* 1974; *Intellectual Talent: Research and Development,* 1976; *The Gifted and the Creative: A Fifty-Year Perspective,* 1977; *Educational Programs and Intellectual Prodigies* (published by SMPY), 1978; *Educating the Gifted: Acceleration and Enrichment,* 1979; and *Women and the Mathematical Mystique,* 1980.

We greatly appreciate two main sources of income that made it possible to conduct the symposium. The National Science Foundation provided major support (SED 79-20868) for the project. In addition, income from a sizable endowment to Johns Hopkins from the Amalgamated Clothing Workers of America (ACWA) in 1969 that created the Hyman Blumberg Symposium on Research in Early Childhood Education helped finance this venture.

Extensive discussion periods were an integral part of the symposium. In addition to the authors in this book, Professor Ellis B. Page of Duke University and Assistant Professor Sanford J. Cohn of Arizona State University in Tempe served as discussants and greatly stimulated thinking about critical issues. Assistant Provost Robert N. Sawyer of Duke University spoke about how his Talent Identification Program (TIP) adapted the SMPY model and computerized some of its procedures. A revised version of his presentation was published elsewhere (Robert N. Sawyer and Lynn M. Daggett, "Duke University's Talent Identification Program," *G/C/T* (22, 1982), pp. 10–14).

Numerous individuals helped make the symposium a success and assisted in the preparation of the manuscript for this volume. We are especially indebted to Richard S. Broadhurst, Thelma V. DeCarlo, William C. George, Susan L. Meyer, Lola L. Minor, Susan Perkins, Lori S. Plotkin, Mildred Schwienteck, Barbara S. K. Stanley, and Paula M. Zak. We owe special thanks to Lois S. Sandhofer, SMPY's administrative assistant, who helped organize and manage the symposium and expertly typed the many revisions of the manuscript. Without her total dedication throughout, the project would have been much less successful.

We are also especially grateful to the Spencer Foundation; funds from it enabled Professor Julian C. Stanley to form SMPY in 1971. Generous, continuous support by that philanthropic organization has made it possible for SMPY to enter its second decade.

We are also thankful for grants obtained at various times from the Robert Sterling Clark Foundation, the Geraldine R. Dodge Foundation, the Camille and Henry Dreyfus Foundation, and the Educational Foundation of America.

Dr. Steven Muller became president of The Johns Hopkins University shortly after SMPY began. He has been ever supportive and helpful. Over the years we have also been helped greatly by other administrators, notably Vice-President George S. Benton and Provost Richard P. Longaker.

With a generous grant from the William H. Donner Foundation, SMPY is able to help hundreds of the mathematically ablest students in the nation, those who before their thirteenth birthday score at least 700 on the mathematical part of the College Board's Scholastic Aptitude Test (SAT). Only 4 percent of college-bound male twelfth-graders and 1 percent of college-bound female twelfth-graders do that well.

ACADEMIC PRECOCITY

1 Introduction

JULIAN C. STANLEY

The Study of Mathematically Precocious Youth began officially on September 1, 1971. Its origins went back at least thirty-three years, however, to the time when as a young high-school teacher of science and mathematics taking a summer "tests and measurements" course at the University of Georgia I became enchanted by intellectual talent. It also owes much to Galton (1869), Terman's *Genetic Studies of Genius,*[1] Hollingworth (1942), Pressey (1949), Worcester (1956), and Hobson (1963).

Its more immediate instigators were Doris Lidtke, Joseph Louis Bates, Jonathan Middleton Edwards, Carl Swanson, and Sam Nocella. Doris told me in the summer of 1968 about 12-year-old computer prodigy Joe. Johns Hopkins Dean Swanson admitted him as a regular freshman in the fall of 1969; only 13 years old until that October 20, he performed outstandingly, earning his B.A. and M.S. Engr. degrees at age 17. Jon heard about Joe and insisted on being admitted to Johns Hopkins in the fall of 1970 at age 13. He did well, too.

As international vice-president of the Amalgamated Clothing Workers of America, in 1969 Sam was instrumental in giving Johns Hopkins a $110,000 endowment with which to start the Hyman Blumberg Symposium on Research in Childhood Education. From time to time the symposia have helped SMPY report orally and in book form the progress of the many remarkable youths it has discovered and assisted educationally.

The stage was well set in early 1971 when the newly created Spencer Foundation of Chicago solicited proposals. One of the foundation's interests was intellectual talent. Having recently seen the potentialities for research and development in the area of mathematical reasoning ability, I submitted a proposal to President H. Thomas James and Secretary (now Vice-President) Marion M. Faldet. It was approved initially for five years, with a grant of $266,100. This generous support, followed by renewal grants for three, two, and three years, enabled us to create what is now a vast, far-flung set of educationally facilitative special opportunities for young students who reason exceptionally well mathematically or verbally. For a detailed rationale of SMPY see Stanley (1977).

1

From the first talent search in 1972 (450 participants) to the tenth in 1983 (15,479), and from the first fast-paced mathematics class in 1972 (22 students) to the residential summer program for 1,000 students in 1983, there are many milestones worth noting. That is why, with assistance from the National Science Foundation, the Blumberg Fund, and the Spencer Foundation, SMPY organized an overview symposium in November of 1980 at Johns Hopkins. What had been accomplished during the first eight years? What were appropriate guidelines for the future? This book is the augmented and updated result of the symposium's deliberations. The main focus of the volume is on mathematical talent because not until the seventh talent search, in 1980, was verbal talent sought explicitly. Nevertheless, the backgrounds of the participants at the symposium and of the authors of this volume vary widely. The supplementary or complementary backgrounds help guard against provincialism and bias.

Nearly all of the participants in SMPY's first three talent searches who had scored fairly well had graduated from high school and entered a postsecondary institution by 1977. They were systematically followed-up. Even though most of these students had been touched rather lightly by SMPY's educational-facilitation efforts (mainly through its newsletter, the *Intellectually Talented Youth Bulletin* — the *ITYB*), studies of them revealed definitely positive influences. As chapters 4–8 and 11 show clearly, influence on educational pace and level was quite strong when SMPY worked directly with some of the ablest young people found in the talent searches.

Though tempted to summarize the papers, I shall leave the savoring of their contents to you. See the concluding chapter of this volume for relationships among the chapters. These reports point SMPY in the direction of the twenty-first century, because by 2001 participants from that first talent search in 1972 will be only in their 40s. Having been born near the end of World War I, I cannot expect to see much (if any) of the new century. Dr. Camilla P. Benbow is vastly younger, however, so to her will probably go the privilege of learning via long-term follow-ups how SMPY's identified, acclaimed, and educationally facilitated young students perform professionally and behave personally as adults. Other persons, such as Dr. Lynn H. Fox, will also be observing the outcomes of various programs.

Perhaps some of the talent-search participants will spark grass-roots movements on behalf of intellectually talented youths. At least, many "ex-prodigies" (see Wiener 1953) may be able to help their own children use their abilities better. Programs based on unusual ideas tend to die when the zeal, fervor, and even fanaticism which characterized their original progenitors wither in transition. We believe, however, that SMPY's principles, practices, and programs are robustly exportable, not like a delicate wine on the hill at San Marino which will not travel well even to Rimini nearby.

Across the country many successful replications and adaptations testify to the power of the simple models SMPY developed by working directly with youths who reason extremely well mathematically. For example, at Duke University during the academic year 1980–81 Assistant Provost Robert N. Sawyer, supported strongly by Provost William Bevan, conducted Duke's first search for verbal and/or mathematical talent, closely following the SMPY model, in the following thirteen states: Alabama, Arkansas, Florida, Georgia, Kentucky, Louisiana, Mississippi, Missouri, North Carolina, Oklahoma, South Carolina, Tennessee, and Texas. Nearly 9,000 students, chiefly 12-year-old seventh-graders, participated. In 1982, Iowa, Kansas, and Nebraska were added.

In the fall of 1980 former SMPY Assistant Director Sanford J. Cohn began a talent search in Arizona, using Arizona State University at Tempe as his base for trying out the SMPY approach. In 1981 he extended the program to California and Washington. In 1982 Oregon and parts of Canada were added.

Dr. Joyce Van Tassel-Baska at Northwestern University, using elements of the SMPY model, conducts an annual search in the Midwest for mathematically apt youths. Educators in the Minneapolis–St. Paul area of Minnesota perform similar screening in order to form fast-paced mathematics classes. There are other laudable efforts here and there, including Eau Claire in Wisconsin, Omaha in Nebraska, and Berkeley in California.

As of the seventh talent search, conducted in January of 1980, however, SMPY relinquished the important service activity of screening to an agency under the provost at Johns Hopkins, the Center for the Advancement of Academically Talented Youth (CTY).[2] CTY conducts the talent search each year, looking for mathematically, verbally, and/or generally talented seventh-graders and youths in higher grades who are of seventh-grade age. In 1980 it added New Jersey to the group of political entities involved in the fourth through sixth talent searches, which included Delaware, the District of Columbia, Maryland (the sole state in the first three talent searches), Pennsylvania, Virginia, and West Virginia. CTY is also taking over the educational facilitation of all but the most mathematically able of the talent-search participants. Currently the staff of SMPY works only with students who before their thirteenth birthday score 700 or more on SAT-Mathematical (SAT-M). These students receive a great deal of individual counseling and educational facilitation.

Three Youths Move Ahead Especially Fast

The progress thus far of three of SMPY's ablest protégés helps reveal the great educational strides the intellectually most advanced young students can make when they are allowed the curricular flexibility they sorely need. By considering these extreme "radical accelerants," one can readily infer that milder acceleration is appropriate for a considerable percentage of youths (see George, Cohn, & Stanley 1979).

One of the earliest intellectual "finds" under the original Spencer Foundation grant occurred during the fall of 1971; this was a sixth-grade Baltimorean named Colin Farrell Camerer, who had been born on December 4, 1959. Having come from a state that had an earlier cut-off date for school entrance than Maryland, he was one of the oldest students in his grade, although undoubtedly the ablest. Colin was cooperative and ingenious, and so were his parents, so over the ten years – until the fall of 1981 – he went through to a Ph.D. degree and an assistant professorship before his twenty-second birthday. Had his pace before being identified initially as highly talented intellectually continued, he would have earned only a bachelor's degree by June of 1982. How did Colin move so fast and so well?

First, of course, it was established by careful use of difficult tests that Colin had the potential to accomplish far more than age-in-grade school curricula require. Then he was encouraged to skip the seventh grade in order to become one of the younger students in the eighth grade, rather than one of the oldest in the seventh. Also, he took for credit the regular introductory computer science course in the Johns Hopkins day school at age 13 and made a final grade of A. His easy success in the eighth grade and in the college course emboldened him to take many more accelerative steps. He skipped grades seven, nine, ten, twelve, and (by entering college with sophomore standing) thirteen. This allowed him to complete his B.A. degree in quantitative studies at Johns Hopkins in five semesters (rather than the usual eight) shortly after his seventeenth birthday. He did this through a combination of college courses taken for credit while still in high school, Advanced Placement Program (AP) examinations, and heavy course loads in college.

Yet, despite his academic speed he found plenty of time for extracurricular activities: varsity wrestling and the television academic quiz team in high school, varsity golf in college, much writing for the college newspaper, and tutoring of several other mathematics prodigies. Also, during the second semester of the academic year 1976–77, Colin, already a college graduate, worked as a factotum for a weekly newspaper on the Eastern Shore of Maryland until it was time for him to enter the University of Chicago's Graduate School of Business that fall while still 17 years of age. Two years later, at age 19, he had earned the M.B.A. degree. By December of 1981 he had completed the doctorate there in social science aspects of finance. In September of 1981 he became a 21-year-old assistant professor and statistics specialist in the Graduate School of Management of Northwestern University. All of this was done with much zest and gusto, quite unlike the public image of the student "pushed" too fast academically by anxious, overly ambitious parents.

Colin seems to have a highly promising future, as at each point in the past he did. Success and, as Zuckerman (1977) put it, cumulative educational advantage breed more success and cumulative advantage. Of course much depends on continued level of aspiration and many other personal and environmental factors. In social science one cannot hope that prediction at the individual level will be as precise as, for example, predicting the melting point of a bar of pure copper under known conditions of temperature and pressure. In the aggregate, however, high scorers on the College Board's Scholastic Aptitude Test at age 12 can accomplish vastly more than low scorers given the same opportunities.

A second example of the superb accomplishments by highly talented youths which are eminently feasible is the career thus far of Chi-Bin Chien, the American-born son of parents who grew up in Taiwan and completed their bachelor's degrees there. He first came to my attention via his father, a professor of physics at Johns Hopkins. Shortly after his tenth birthday, Chi-Bin scored nearly as high on the verbal part of the College Board's Scholastic Aptitude Test as the average Johns Hopkins student did as a 17- or 18-year-old twelfth-grader. He scored a little higher than their average on the mathematical part.

With much help from extremely facilitative parents and some from SMPY, he skipped grades six, seven, nine, ten, eleven, and thirteen, graduating from one of the country's most outstanding high schools at age 12 with sophomore standing in college because of the Advanced Placement Program examinations, on which he had scored splendidly. In May of 1981 Chi-Bin, who was born on November 3, 1965, became (by seven months) the youngest recipient of a baccalaureate in Johns Hopkins's 105-year history. He broke the record set in 1887 by 16-year-old Charles Homer Haskins, who went on to fame as a medieval historian and dean of the Graduate School of Arts and Sciences at Harvard University.[3]

Chi-Bin took his B.A. degree in physics with the following honors and awards: general and departmental honors, Donald E. Kerr Memorial Award for the outstanding bachelor's degree recipient in physics from Johns Hopkins that year (shared with another student), SMPY award for being the youngest graduate in the institution's history, Churchill Scholarship to study biophysics for a year at Cambridge University, and National Science Foundation three-year fellowship with which to work toward a Ph.D. degree at the California Institute of Technology after he returned from England.

A third SMPY protégé to make truly spectacular educational progress thus far is Nina Teresa Morishige, the American-born (on June 5, 1963) daughter of immigrants from Japan. Her accomplishments already seem virtually superhuman: she won the Oklahoma high-school piano contest as a tenth-grader; plays the flute excellently, and also the violin; was elected president of Oklahoma Girls' State (the mock political gathering) at the end of the eleventh grade; skipped the twelfth grade and came to Johns Hopkins as a mathematics major minoring in piano at the Peabody Institute, a division of Johns Hopkins; arrived with full second-year standing because of the five Advanced Placement Program examinations she had taken in one week and on which she had scored superbly; took 50 percent to 100 percent "overloads" of difficult courses in order to complete her B.A. degree in mathematics by May of 1982 at age 18 in a total of four semesters rather than the customary eight; won a Rhodes Scholarship with which to study for two years at Oxford University, being one of the youngest winners in the competition's seventy-eight-year history; and also won a Churchill Scholarship to Cambridge University, but had to decline it because of the Rhodes Scholarship. In her "spare time" Nina taught some of SMPY's fast-paced mathematics classes and served as a mentor-by-mail in calculus to six mathematically brilliant young students across the country.

We know of quite a few more as remarkable in their own ways as Colin, Chi-Bin, and Nina, but mention of the precocious achievements of these three should provide some idea of the progress readily possible for extremely able students when curricular arrangements are sufficiently flexible. None of these three cost their schools or parents a great deal in time or money. They were amazingly cost-effective in, for example, earning their bachelor's degrees in four, five, or six semesters instead of the usual eight. They also eliminated a total of ten years of schooling below the college level, and of course avoided much boredom and saved conscientious teachers concern about their special educational needs.

It will be fascinating to follow the progress of SMPY's "radical accelerants" as they go through life. One must not create a *reductio ad absurdum* expectation, as many have done for the Terman group, that each will become as eminent as Einstein or Newton. A number of them are likely to become first-rate scholars, researchers, or practitioners in their vocations.

We encourage educators and parents everywhere to consider carefully how far curricular flexibility of the kinds described in this book can take young people (most of them, of course, not nearly as able as Colin, Chi-Bin, and Nina) educationally and personally at minimum cost and with only slight disruption of the schools' usual educational processes. This need for and importance of curricular flexibility for intellectually talented students is perhaps one of the most salient findings of SMPY. It is implicit in all the chapters in this book, and explicit in most of them.

Notes

1. See Terman (1925), Cox (1926), Burks, Jensen, and Terman (1930), Terman and Oden (1947), Terman and Oden (1959), Oden (1968), Sears (1977), and Sears

and Barbee (1977). These pioneering works are still a basis for present-day research, development, and service to intellectually talented persons.

2. CTY was originally called the Office of Talent Identification and Development (OTID).

3. For further details about the youngest graduates of Johns Hopkins see Stanley and Benbow (in press).

References

Burks, B. S.; Jensen, D. W.; and Terman, L. M. 1930. *The promise of youth: Follow-up studies of a thousand gifted children.* Vol. 3 of *Genetic studies of genius.* Stanford, Calif.: Stanford University Press.

Cox, C. M. 1926. *The early mental traits of three hundred geniuses.* Vol. 2 of *Genetic studies of genius.* Stanford, Calif.: Stanford University Press.

Galton, F. 1869. *Hereditary genius.* London: Macmillan.

George, W. C.; Cohn, S. J.; and Stanley, J. C., eds. 1979. *Educating the gifted: Acceleration and enrichment.* Baltimore: Johns Hopkins University Press.

Hobson, J. R. 1963. High school performance of underage pupils initially admitted to kindergarten on the basis of physical and psychological examinations. *Educational and Psychological Measurement* 23 (1): 159–70.

Hollingworth, L. S. 1942. *Children over 180 IQ, Stanford-Binet.* Yonkers-on-Hudson, N.Y.: World Book.

Oden, M. H. 1968. The fulfillment of promise: Forty-year follow-up of the Terman gifted group. *Genetic Psychology Monographs* 77: 3–93.

Pressey, S. L. 1949. *Educational acceleration: Appraisal and basic problems.* Bureau of Educational Research Monographs, no. 31. Columbus, Ohio: Ohio State University Press.

Sears, P. S., and Barbee, A. H. 1977. Career and life satisfactions among Terman's gifted women. In *The gifted and the creative: A fifty-year perspective,* ed. J. C. Stanley, W. C. George, and C. H. Solano, 28–65. Baltimore: Johns Hopkins University Press.

Sears, R. R. 1977. Sources of life satisfactions of the Terman gifted men. *American Psychologist* 32 (2): 119–28.

Stanley, J. C. 1977. Rationale of the Study of Mathematically Precocious Youth (SMPY) during its first five years of promoting educational acceleration. In *The gifted and the creative: A fifty-year perspective,* ed. J. C. Stanley, W. C. George, and C. H. Solano, 75–112. Baltimore: Johns Hopkins University Press.

Stanley, J. C., and Benbow, C. P. 1982. Using the SAT to find intellectually talented seventh graders. *College Board Review,* no. 122 (Winter), pp. 2–7, 26–27.

_____. In press. Extremely young college graduates: Evidence of their success. *College and University.*

Terman, L. M. 1925. *Mental and physical traits of a thousand gifted children.* Vol. 1 of *Genetic studies of genius.* Stanford, Calif.: Stanford University Press.

Terman, L. M., and Oden, M. H. 1947. *The gifted child grows up: Twenty-five years' follow-up of a superior group.* Vol. 4 of *Genetic studies of genius.* Stanford, Calif.: Stanford University Press.

_____. 1959. *The gifted group at mid-life: Thirty-five years' follow-up of the superior child.* Vol. 5 of *Genetic studies of genius.* Stanford, Calif.: Stanford University Press.

Wiener, N. 1953. *Ex-prodigy.* New York: Simon and Schuster. (Paperbound edition is available from M.I.T. Press, Cambridge, Mass.)

Worcester, D. A. 1956. *The education of children of* above-average *mentality.* Lincoln: University of Nebraska Press.

Zuckerman, H. 1977. *Scientific elite: Nobel laureates in the United States.* New York: Free Press.

2

Adolescence of the Mathematically Precocious: A Five-Year Longitudinal Study

CAMILLA PERSSON BENBOW

Abstract

SMPY's first set of longitudinal findings are strong indicators that SMPY's identification measure is effective in selecting students in the seventh grade who achieve at a superior level in high school, especially in mathematics and science. Questionnaire data obtained from 1,996 students who as seventh- or eighth-graders had scored better on the SAT than a random sample of eleventh- and twelfth-grade females were analyzed. Relative to the comparison groups SMPY students were superior in both ability and achievement, expressed stronger interest in mathematics and sciences, were accelerated more frequently, and were more highly motivated educationally, as indicated by their desire for advanced degrees from difficult schools. Sex differences were found in participation in mathematics and science, performance on the SAT-M, and the taking of and performance on mathematics and science achievement tests. The majority of the students felt that SMPY had helped them educationally while not detracting from their social and emotional development. The SAT-M score of an intellectually talented seventh- or eighth-grader has much predictive validity.

The Study of Mathematically Precocious Youth officially began with hopes of finding youths who at an early age were able to reason extremely well with simple mathematical concepts, "students who even before taking or completing the first year of algebra would reason mathematically much better than the average male twelfth grader does" (Stanley 1977). SMPY then studied these youths further, helped to

9

facilitate their educational progress, and disseminated its findings, e.g. in Keating and Stanley (1972), Stanley (1973), Stanley, Keating, and Fox (1974), Keating (1976b), and Stanley, George, and Solano (1977). In order to identify mathematically talented students, the concept of a talent search was devised (George & Solano 1976b). Six separate talent searches have been conducted by SMPY (Benbow & Stanley 1980). This paper focuses on longitudinal findings and evaluations of the first three, which were held in March, 1972, January–February, 1973, and January, 1974. The purpose of the paper is to characterize at high-school graduation those students who scored highly enough in these talent searches and trace their educational development.[1] Some of the special findings from this study are presented by Michael in chapter 3 (manifestation of creativity), by Benbow, Perkins, and Stanley in chapter 4 (longitudinal evaluation of accelerated mathematics classes), and by Fox, Benbow, and Perkins in chapter 7 (sex differences) in this volume.

Talent-Search Results

In the first three talent searches seventh- and eighth-grade[2] students in Maryland were eligible to participate if they scored in the upper 5 percent (March, 1972) or the upper 2 percent (January–February, 1973, or January, 1974) nationwide in mathematical ability on a standardized achievement test. As part of the talent search they took the College Board's Scholastic Aptitude Test-Mathematics and also, in 1973, the Scholastic Aptitude Test-Verbal (SAT-V) (Angoff 1971). Results have been discussed by Keating (1974, 1976a). In general, the average participant, who tended to come from a home where the parents had been rather highly educated, scored well and at a level better than or equal to that of a random sample of high-school juniors and seniors. Although both sexes scored about the same verbally, boys performed much better mathematically than girls. This sex difference was especially evident in the upper ranges of mathematical ability (Benbow & Stanley 1980, 1981, 1982a). It was particularly significant that this sex difference was observed in the seventh and eighth grades. Up to that time these boys and girls had received similar formal instruction in mathematics (Benbow & Stanley 1982b). Elsewhere Benbow and Stanley (1980) have shown that differential course-taking cannot account for the observed sex difference in mathematical ability.

Longitudinal Follow-Up Procedure

The students selected to be followed up by SMPY after high-school graduation had to have scored at least 390 on SAT-M *or* 370 on SAT-V during the talent search. If in 1972 the student had met the score criterion on a test of scientific information (i.e., 75 points or better out of 150 possible points on the sum of Form A and B scores on the Sequential Test of Educational Progress [STEP] General Science Information Test, Series II, Level 1a [first year of college]), he or she was also included in this study. This level of performance selects for a group of students who as seventh-or eighth-graders scored as well on the SAT as the average eleventh- or twelfth-grader does.

Selected through the use of these criteria, 2,188 talent-search participants received through the mail an eight-page follow-up questionnaire (see Appendix 2.1) along with an offer of monetary compensation ($5 or, in some cases, $6) as an incentive to complete the questionnaire. The questionnaires were mailed to students at a time when they would have been graduated from high school if they had not accelerated in their education since their participation in a talent search. The questionnaire reached the students and was usually completed by them while they were freshmen in college. Because the students were sampled from three talent searches held in 1972, 1973, and 1974 and because both seventh- and eighth-graders were eligible to participate in the talent searches, the follow-up questionnaires had to be sent out in four different waves: in December, 1976 ($N = 214$, Cohn 1980),[3] 1977 ($N = 594$), 1978 ($N = 881$), and 1979 ($N = 499$). After six weeks had passed, the students who still had not completed the questionnaires were sent a reminder letter including an additional questionnaire. Six weeks later a postal card reminder was sent. Finally, to bring the response rate up, each unresponsive subject was telephoned (sometimes several times).

The response rates for each wave of the follow-up were 94 (Cohn 1980), 90, 93, and 90 percent, respectively, of the total sample. Omitting persons we were unable to locate the response rates become 98 (Cohn 1980), 94, 96, and 93 percent, respectively. Combining the waves, the overall response rate exceeded 91 percent of the total sample of 2,188 students. In the analyses, there were 1,996 students, 38 percent of whom were females.

DATA ANALYSIS

The data were coded, keypunched, and verified. For the first and second waves of the follow-up they were entered onto the computer by means of the SOS computer package (Shesko 1975). For the third and fourth waves the data were entered through the use of the Filgen and Qgen computer system (The Johns Hopkins University Computing Center). The statistical analyses, performed by using the SPSS program (Nie et al. 1975), were done separately for the first wave, the second wave, and the combined third and fourth waves of the follow-up.

SAT Scores at Time of Talent Search

Mean SAT scores of the follow-up groups at the time of the talent search can be seen in table 2.1. As expected, mean scores are much higher than the average from SMPY's six talent searches due to the additional selection criteria. The group's mean SAT-M scores were also far superior to the means of a national sample of college-bound seniors (ATP 1979a). On SAT-M, boys in each wave scored significantly higher than the girls (by at least twenty-eight points), whereas girls scored higher on SAT-V — significantly so for the second wave.[4]The effect size for the sex difference on SAT-M in the talent search was medium, while for the difference on

TABLE 2.1. Mean SAT Scores of Talent-Search Participants and College-Bound Seniors

	First Wave[a]		Second Wave		Third and Fourth Waves		National Sample of College-Bound Seniors	
	Mean	Standard Deviation	Mean	Standard Deviation	Mean	Standard Deviation	Mean	Standard Deviation
				Talent Search				
SAT-M								
Males	567	91	549	74	526	76		
Females	505	58	510	58	498	61		
t of mean	5.1		6.7		6.9			
difference	$p < .001$		$p < .001$		$p < .001$			
SAT-V[b]								
Males	—		443	86	400	65		
Females	—		468	86	411	74		
t of mean			-3.1		not significant			
difference			$p < .01$					
				High School				
SAT-M								
Males	691	75	693	72	695	67	493	121
Females	652	72	643	68	650	75	443	109
t of mean	3.5		7.9		10.6			
difference	$p < .001$		$p < .001$		$p < .001$			
SAT-V								
Males	596	100	602	82	590	88	431	110
Females	594	115	612	83	592	91	423	110
t of mean								
difference	not significant		not significant		not significant			

SOURCE: Edmund C. Short, "Knowledge Production and Utilization in Curriculum: A Special Case of the General Phenomenon," *Review of Educational Research* (Summer 1979): 237–301. Copyright 1979, American Educational Research Association, Washington, D.C.
[a] Taken from S. J. Cohn, "Two Components of the Study of Mathematically Precocious Youth's Invervention Studies of Educational Facilitation and Longitudinal Follow-Up," Ph.D. diss., Johns Hopkins University, 1980.
[b] SAT-V was administered only in the 1973 talent search. Thus SAT-V scores were available for the 1973 talent-search eighth-graders, all in the second wave of the follow-up, and for the 1973 talent search seventh-graders, all in the third wave of the follow-up.

SAT-V it was only small. Thus the sex difference on SAT-M was considered important, but the difference on SAT-V was not.

SAT Scores in High School

From their reports, by the end of high school the boys' and girls' mean scores on SAT-M had been raised an average of 155 and 145 points, respectively, from the time of talent-search participation (see table 2.1). Thus the sex difference found on SAT-M at the time of talent-search participation increased during the high-school years by about 10 points. (For further discussion see Benbow & Stanley 1982a.) Both boys and girls in the follow-up scored approximately 200 points better than their respective sex norm group of college-bound seniors (see the lower half of table 2.1). This indicates that the students maintained their superior mathematical ability.

On SAT-V males improved by 159 points and females by 144 points in the second wave of the follow-up. For the third wave males increased by 190 points and females by 181 points (see table 2.1). Thus the initial sex difference on SAT-V favoring girls diminished, and for the second wave it was no longer statistically significant. Both on SAT-M and SAT-V the boys improved significantly more than the girls (see Benbow & Stanley 1982a), unlike in some other studies (e.g., Shaycoft 1967) where it had been found that members of the sex with the initial advantage improved their scores most through high school.

Because the students were selected initially on the basis of their high mathematical ability, it was expected that they would score less well on SAT-V than on SAT-M because of statistical regression toward the mean. This was true both for the talent-search and for high-school results (see table 2.1). In high school the students' mean scores on SAT-V were approximately 170 points above the mean for a national sample of college-bound seniors, compared to the 200-point superiority on SAT-M. This difference held up when percentile ranks were compared. Again, on SAT-V the students maintained their initial superior ability.

MATHEMATICS COURSE-TAKING

The mean number of semesters of mathematics taken in grades eight through twelve is shown by group in table 2.2. Boys reported taking approximately 9.2 semesters, while girls reported approximately 8.4, significantly different beyond the .001 level. The effect size, *d,* equalled approximately .33. Thus the effect was considered small and not important (see Benbow & Stanley 1982a). Boys and girls received mainly *A*s and *B*s, with the girls obtaining slightly better grades (see Benbow & Stanley 1982a).

Approximately 66 percent of the boys took at least one calculus course, compared to 40 percent of the girls (see table 2.2). Furthermore, many

TABLE 2.2. Reported Mathematics and Science Course-Taking in Grades 8–12 (by Wave and Sex)

	First Wave		Second Wave		Third and Fourth Waves	
	Males (N = 133)	Females (N = 69)	Males (N = 310)	Females (N = 221)	Males (N = 785)	Females (N = 478)
Total mathematics						
Mean number of semesters	9.4	9.0	9.3	8.1	9.2	8.5
Standard deviation	2.3	1.8	2.5	2.6	2.6	2.4
Mean course grade	3.6	3.7	3.5	3.6	3.5	3.6
Standard deviation	0.7	0.5	0.5	0.5	0.5	0.5
Total Science						
Mean number of semesters	7.0	6.8	7.0	6.0	8.4	7.6
Standard deviation	2.4	2.0	2.4	2.4	2.8	2.4
Mean course grade	3.6	3.7	3.5	3.6	3.6	3.6
Standard deviation	0.3	0.4	0.5	0.5	0.5	0.4
Percentage taking biology	83	97	89	93	89	94
Percentage taking chemistry	89	93	91	86	89	88
Percentage taking physics	78	68	77	58	76	57
Percentage of total taking a science course	98	100	98	97	98	99
Calculus						
Percentage taking calculus	62	42	69	34	66	43

more boys than girls took two courses in calculus. The differences were significant beyond the .001 level, with a medium effect size (h = .53). No significant sex difference was found in grades earned in calculus, which were mostly As and Bs. For further discussion of the sex difference in mathematical ability and course-taking see Benbow and Stanley (1980, 1982a), where they conclude that socialization theories (differential course-taking, etc.) probably cannot account for all of the sex difference in mathematical ability.

SMPY students studied mathematics much longer than 1979–80 college-bound twelfth-graders in the middle states region of the United States (New York, Pennsylvania, New Jersey, Delaware, Maryland, and the District of Columbia).[5] Those college-bound twelfth-graders took 7.4 semesters of mathematics during high school if male and 6.8 semesters if female (ATP 1980). The difference between the two groups was significant by a t-test beyond the $p < .001$ level. The effect size, d, varied between .50 and 1.22, which is in the medium to large range. Furthermore, in the National Longitudinal Study of the High School Class of 1972, eight semesters of mathematics were taken by only 8.8 percent of the males and 3.4 percent of the females (Wise, Steel, & MacDonald 1979). This was a decline in mathematics course-taking of almost ¾ for the men and about ⅔ for the women from the 1960 Project Talent data (ibid.). Calculus had been taken by only 4.7 percent of male and 3.1 percent of female 17-year-olds in 1977–78 (NAEP 1979). At least ten times that percentage (for each sex respectively) of the SMPY students took calculus. The difference in proportions between the two groups was significant beyond the $p < .01$ level for both sexes. The effect size equalled 1.45 for the boys and 1.02 for the girls, both of which are considered large. It can thus be concluded that SMPY students take much more mathematics than students in general.

SCIENCE COURSE-TAKING

Essentially all SMPY students took science in grades eight through twelve (see table 2.2). Biology and chemistry courses were most frequently taken. Fewer students — more boys than girls — took physics, whereas more girls took biology. This agrees with Kelly's (1979) findings. The mean number of semesters of science taken by the students was 7.6; the grades received in those classes were mostly *A*s and *B*s.

The participation in science of this group compares favorably with the participation in science of the 1978–79 college-bound seniors in the middle states. The mean number of semesters of studying biological science was 2.8 for such boys and girls (ATP 1980). For the physical sciences the mean was 4.2 for boys and 3.4 for girls (ibid.). Although the total number of semesters spent studying science was somewhat lower for college-bound seniors than for SMPY's students, the difference was not significant.

Benbow (1981) found that a comparison between the number of semesters of mathematics and science taken in high school revealed that SMPY students were significantly more likely to have taken a mathematics course than a science course. It is possible that this difference reflects a greater access to mathematics courses than to science courses.

ACHIEVEMENT TEST SCORES

The students were asked to report their performance on the College Board's achievement tests. Table 2.3 is a breakdown of the performances by sex for those tests that at least 8 percent of the students indicated they had taken at any time in high school. It can be seen in table 2.3 that for every one of these tests, SMPY students' mean scores were superior to the means of college-bound high-school students. SMPY males scored on the average 107 points better, and the SMPY females, 97. Boys were superior to girls on the science and mathematics tests, while girls were superior on the English composition and French examinations.

To test for significant differences in performance on the achievement tests between the SMPY group and college-bound high-school students, a sign test was utilized. The resulting chi-square equalled 5.2, which was significant beyond the $p < .05$ level. The effect size, *g,* equalled .5, which is

TABLE 2.3. Reported Performance on the College Board's High-School-Level Achievement Tests Taken by at Least 8 Percent of the Students in a Group (by Wave and Sex)

	First Wave ($N = 202$)		Second Wave ($N = 531$)		Third and Fourth Waves ($N = 1,263$)		National Sample of 1978 College-Bound High-School Students[a]
	Males	Females	Males	Females	Males	Females	
Math Level I							
Mean score	692	664	698	656	695	644	541
Standard deviation	81	99	74	70	65	76	99
N	34	19	60	58	149	100	146,426
Math Level II							
Mean score	742	676	751	724	748	705	665
Standard deviation	67	93	60	57	59	71	95
N	46	7	91	29	281	99	32,743
English Composition							
Mean score	653	667	634	656	624	638	512
Standard deviation	85	55	85	66	84	80	109
N	61	25	145	94	363	199	195,173
Biology							
Mean score	689	605	667	644	652	613	544
Standard deviation	86	134	78	68	71	93	111
N	11	2	27	23	58	43	47,291
Chemistry							
Mean score	670	619	675	634	678	651	577
Standard deviation	78	66	66	72	85	78	102
N	25	10	50	16	146	50	35,007
Physics							
Mean score	684	530	683	618	672	607	591
Standard deviation	74	—	71	84	81	86	106
N	23	1	42	8	100	15	15,408
French							
Mean score	595	591	616	642	632	646	552
Standard deviation	121	103	84	93	74	95	109
N	12	8	26	41	45	68	25,673

NOTE: SMPY students scored significantly higher than college-bound high-school seniors on all the achievement tests ($X^2 = 5.2$, $p < .05$, $g = .5$ [large effect size], and the power of the test was greater than .43).

[a] Taken from Admissions Testing Program of the College Board, *National Report: College-Bound Seniors, 1979* (Princeton, N.J.: Educational Testing Service, 1979).

considered large and thus important. Interestingly, SMPY students did not score higher on the mathematics achievement test relative to the other tests.

More males took the more difficult Math Level II than the easier Math Level I test (see table 2.3). In contrast, slightly more females took Math Level I than Math Level II. The SMPY males' mean scores on the Math Level II approximated the maximum reported score, 800. Finally, SMPY males scored better than SMPY females on both mathematics tests. The sex difference was statistically significant except on Math Level I in the first wave of the follow-up.

In science the boys also took significantly more of these achievement tests than girls, especially the ones in chemistry and physics (see table 2.3). Scores were high and above the national mean for both boys and girls. Boys scored better than girls — significantly so, except in biology in the first and second waves of the follow-up and chemistry in the first wave (see Benbow 1981; Benbow & Stanley in press).

FAVORITE COURSES IN HIGH SCHOOL

When asked what their favorite course in high school was, respondents named mathematics most frequently (36 percent of the males and 31 percent of the females). The second favorite was science (34 percent of the males and 25 percent of the females). In a national survey of 17-year-olds, NAEP (1979) also found that the most frequently mentioned favorite course was mathematics (18 percent named it as their favorite). This was followed by English (16 percent), social studies (13 percent), and then science (12 percent). The SMPY group tends to follow this pattern, but mathematics and science are significantly more strongly preferred ($p < .01$). The effect size was medium (.70). Thus the difference between the groups was judged as important.

RATED LIKING FOR MATHEMATICS
AND SCIENCE

These findings were further affirmed when the students were asked to rate their liking for biology, chemistry, mathematics, and physics on a five-point scale ranging from strong dislike to strong like. For all of these subjects the students had, on the average, a moderate liking. Mathematics was most preferred by males and females. Boys appeared to like the sciences about equally well, while for girls the ranking of preference was biology (most), chemistry, and then physics.

PARTICIPATION IN SCIENCE FAIRS AND
MATHEMATICS CONTESTS

Approximately 23 percent of the boys and 12 percent of the girls had participated in at least one mathematics contest. This was significantly different at the $p < .001$ level. With regard to science fairs, 17 percent of boys and girls participated in at least one. Michael (see chapter 3 of this volume) discusses the relationship between science fair and mathematics contest participation and ability on the SAT and family variables. He concludes that "a modest *negative* relationship exists between SAT-M scores and extent of participation in science fairs for girls (but not for boys) and that a modest *positive* relationship occurs between SAT-M scores and amount of involvement in mathematics contests for boys (but not for girls)."

Summarizing, it appears from the preceding three sections that mathematically talented high-school students, boys more so than girls, are interested in mathematics and the related field of science.

ACTIVITIES AND JOBS

The students were asked to list the number of in-school and out-of-school activities engaged in during grades eight through twelve. Activities were grouped into seventeen categories ranging from academic to religious (see Appendix 2.1). The mean of the total number of activities engaged in by participants was twenty-three across all four waves of the follow-up. The total reported numbers ranged from zero to ninety-one activities per student. The three most popular categories of activities for both males and females were, in order of preference, reading and spectator activities, social hobbies, and performing arts.

The number of jobs held by the students were also ascertained. Across all waves of the follow-up approximately 87 percent of the students reported having had at least one job in grades eight through twelve. The mean number of jobs held was 2.2.

We conclude that SMPY students were actively doing many different things throughout high school. There appears to be no evidence that these gifted students have a narrow range of interests.

AWARDS AND HONORS

The students in the follow-up were asked to report any awards or honors won and their degree of participation in the National Merit Scholarship Competition. Performance in the latter is judged on the basis of the students' scores on the Preliminary Scholastic Aptitude Test (PSAT), typically taken in October of the eleventh grade. SMPY students did well on the PSAT. At least 50 percent of them satisfied the criteria for receiving at least a Letter of Commendation (see table 2.4). Any student in the competition who goes further has to satisfy the criterion for the previous level. For example, students who satisfy the criterion for a National Merit Finalist have also satisfied the criterion for Semi-Finalist and Letter of Commendation. Approximately 5 percent of SMPY students received National Merit Scholarships (the highest level of the competition). This finding attests to the fact that SMPY students are extremely able.

With respect to academic awards and honors won in high school, approximately 67 percent reported receiving at least one. The mean number won by the students is 2.5. The mean numbers of other awards won can also be seen in table 2.4. They average 2. These were won by approximately 59 percent of the students. Clearly, the group won a large number of awards and honors.

TABLE 2.4. Reported Performance in the National Merit Scholarship Competition and Number of Awards and Honors Won in High School (by Wave)

	First Wave (N = 202)	Second Wave (N = 531)	Third and Fourth Waves (N = 1,263)
National Merit[a] (%)			
Letter of Commendation only	27	41	38
Semi-Finalist	5	19	17
Finalist	13	15	14
Scholarship winner	4	4	5
Academic awards			
Mean number	2.7	2.4	2.5
Standard deviation	2.4	2.8	3.1
Other Awards			
Mean number	0.7	2.2	2.5
Standard deviation	1.2	3.0	3.2

[a]Except for a Letter of Commendation, every student in successive echelons of the National Merit Competition had satisfied the requirement for the previous level.

USE OF ACCELERATIVE OPTIONS

The various accelerative options available for facilitating a gifted student's education (Stanley 1978; Benbow 1979) and their use by the SMPY students can be seen in table 2.5. The most widely known of these options is grade skipping. Approximately 15 percent of SMPY students skipped at least one grade or entered school early. The most frequently skipped grade was the twelfth. No significant sex difference was found, except for the first wave of the follow-up, in which 30 percent of males vs. 17 percent of females skipped at least one grade ($p < .05$).

AP examinations can secure college credit for advanced course-work completed in high school if the person scores highly enough on them (Benbow 1978; Benbow & Stanley 1978). They are taken mainly by highly able students (Hanson 1980). Approximately 40 percent of SMPY males and 25 percent of SMPY females took at least one AP examination. Since fewer than 5 percent of high-school students take an AP examination (Hanson 1980), this is a high degree of participation by the SMPY group. The mean number of examinations taken was almost 1 for boys and about .5 for girls (see table 2.5). Although there was a significant sex difference in the taking of AP examinations ($p < .001$), there was no difference in the scores received on these examinations except in the first follow-up ($p < .05$, Cohn 1980). The mean was approximately 3.6 on a five-point scale, where a 3, 4, or 5 is considered a good score and makes a student eligible for some college credit at most colleges.

The most popular AP examinations for the boys were the mathematics, which were taken by 29 percent of the boys (12 percent took the Calculus

TABLE 2.5. Reported Use of Accelerative Options by the Beginning of College (by Wave)

	First Wave (N = 202)	
	Males	Females
Grade skipping		
Mean number	0.5	0.2
Standard deviation	0.8	0.5
Percentage skipping at least one grade	30	17
APP exams		
Mean number taken (s.d.)	0.8 (1.2)	0.3 (.6)
Mean score[a] (s.d.)	3.7 (1.0)	3.1 (1.0)
Percentage taking at least one exam	41	19
College courses as high-school student		
Mean number taken	0.8	0.4
Standard deviation	2.0	1.2
Percentage taking at least one course	24	10
Early entrance to college (%)	29	16
Advanced standing in college (%)	48	30
Mean number of credits for those		
students (s.d.)	11.5 (8.8)	8.0 (5.6)

[a] Scores on the APP exams can range from 1 (the lowest possible) to 5 (the highest possible). Many colleges give credit for a two-semester course for 3s. Most give such credit for 4s and 5s, except that only one semester of credit is usually awarded for 3-5s on the less comprehensive of the mathematics examinations (i.e., Level AB).

AB and 17 percent took the more difficult Calculus BC exam). For girls the English examination was most popular (second most popular for boys); 19 percent of the girls took it. For girls, the mathematics examinations were second most popular; 13 percent of the girls (8 percent took Calculus AB and 5 percent took Calculus BC) took them. The students' scores were not better on the mathematics tests than on the other tests.

Another accelerative option available to students who want to move ahead in their educational careers is the taking of college courses on a part-time basis while still in high school (George & Solano 1976a). Although the numbers varied for each wave, approximately 20 percent of the SMPY students took college courses while they were still in high school (see table 2.5). Significant sex differences were not observed.

Early entrance to college is yet another educationally accelerative option (Eisenberg & George 1978; Benbow & George 1979). Of the 1978-79 college freshmen, only 3.4 percent entered college at least one year early (Astin 1978). Among the SMPY students, 14 percent did so (see table 2.5). This difference in proportions was significant beyond the $p < .01$ level. The effect size equalled .42, which is considered to be almost a medium effect.

Entering college with advanced standing earned through AP examinations or through college course-taking in high school, for example, is one of the favorite accelerative options. Approximately 38 percent of the SMPY students did this, with a mean number of credits ranging from eight to twelve (see table 2.5). Males used this option significantly more than females ($p < .005$ for the four waves).

| Second Wave (N = 531) | | Third and Fourth Waves (N = 1,263) | |
Males	Females	Males	Females
0.2	0.2	0.2	0.2
0.5	0.5	0.5	0.4
13	15	12	14
0.8 (1.3)	0.4 (.8)	0.9 (1.4)	0.6 (1.0)
3.6 (.9)	3.7 (.9)	3.6 (.9)	3.6 (1.0)
40	25	43	32
0.3	0.2	0.4	0.4
0.8	0.5	1.3	1.1
19	18	19	19
15	17	11	13
35	24	44	37
12.1 (10.6)	9.6 (8.8)	11.4 (10.0)	8.2 (6.4)

It is clear that a fairly high percentage of SMPY students used at least one of the educationally accelerative options for facilitating their education. Furthermore, the students who did accelerate felt that this had affected their social and/or emotional development somewhat positively. Only 5 out of 1,104 (0.5 percent) students in the second, third, and fourth waves of the follow-up who considered themselves to have been accelerated felt that acceleration had affected their social and/or emotional development much to the worse. In contrast, 203 (18 percent) of the students felt the opposite.

COLLEGE ATTENDANCE

Over 90 percent of the SMPY students were attending college at the time they completed the questionnaire (see table 2.6). The colleges attended by these students were rated using the Astin (1965) scale. Each college was given an intellectualism and status score, T-scores having a mean of 50 and a standard deviation of 10. Astin (1965, p. 54) defines a four-year college with a high intellectualism score as having a student body that "would be expected to be high in academic aptitude (especially mathematical aptitude) and to have a high percentage of students pursuing careers in science and planning to go on for Ph.D. degrees." A four-year college with a high status score is defined as having a student body that "would be expected to have a high percentage of students who come from high socioeconomic backgrounds and who themselves aspire to careers in enterprising fields (lawyers, business executives, politicians)" (ibid.). Among the colleges attended by SMPY students the mean intellectualism score was almost 59 and the mean status score 57 (see table 2.6). Thus the SMPY group attended colleges or universities that were rated on the average almost one standard deviation above the mean for four-year colleges and universities

TABLE 2.6. Talent-Search Students' Attitudes toward College and Ratings on Intellectualism and Status of Their Colleges

	First Wave (N = 202)	Second Wave (N = 531)	Third and Fourth Waves (N = 1,263)
Percentage attending college	95	92	92
College intellectualism score			
Mean (s.d.)[a]		58.4 (11.5)	58.8 (11.8)
Mean for colleges, including community colleges (s.d.)[b]		56.1 (14.5)	55.7 (16.0)
College status score			
Mean (s.d.)[a]		57.1 (9.4)	57.3 (9.4)
Mean for colleges, including community colleges (s.d.)[b]		55.1 (13.0)	54.3 (14.1)
Liking for college			
Mean[c]	4.4	4.4	4.4
Standard deviation	0.8	0.9	0.8

[a] College intellectualism and status scores are T-scores, mean 50 and standard deviation of 10. Ratings are from A. W. Astin, *Who Goes Where to College?* (Chicago: Science Research Associates, 1965).
[b] An arbitrary value of 15 was given to a community college.
[c] Liking for college was coded as follows: 5 = strong like, 4 = moderate like, 3 = neutral or mixed feelings, 2 = moderate dislike, 1 = strong dislike.

in academic difficulty, and almost as high in status. The students had a fairly strong liking for their colleges (see table 2.6).

The intended college majors of the SMPY students as college freshmen can be seen in table 2.7. Approximately 61 percent of the males and 50 percent of the females are planning to major in science, mathematics, or engineering. Except in the engineering area, where more boys are majoring, relatively small differences are seen between males and females. Compared to college-bound high-school seniors of whom 45 percent of males and 33 percent of females intend to major in science, mathematics, or engineering (ATP 1979b), this mathematically talented group shows a strong interest in these fields.

EDUCATIONAL ASPIRATIONS

The educational aspirations of the SMPY group were high. Fewer than 4 percent of the students hoped to obtain less than a bachelor's degree. The most frequently aspired to educational level was a doctorate (39 percent). Compared to educational aspirations of high-school students in general, where only 51 percent aspire to obtain a bachelor's degree or more (Charles Kettering Foundation 1980), the SMPY students are highly motivated. The difference between proportions aspiring to at least a bachelor's degree was significant beyond the $p < .01$ level, and the effect size, h, equalled 1.5, which is considered large. Thus the difference is considered important.

TABLE 2.7. Reported Intended College Majors (in Percentages)

Majors	Males	Females	Total
Mathematical sciences/engineering	36	25	32
Science	26	25	26
Social science	10	13	11
Liberal arts	8	11	9
Other	11	12	11
Undecided	10	14	12

USE OF EDUCATIONAL OPPORTUNITIES

Overall, SMPY students felt that their use of all available educational opportunities was a bit above average. Only 2 percent felt that they had made extremely poor use of their opportunities. In contrast, 58 percent felt that they had used their opportunities either rather or extremely well.

SMPY'S INFLUENCE

Although, subsequent to the talent search itself, SMPY had had little contact with most of the students in its talent searches (only through its bulletin, the *ITYB,* for the most part), the students were asked to rate how SMPY had helped them educationally and how SMPY had affected their social and/or emotional development. The results can be seen in table 2.8. Over 60 percent of the students felt that SMPY had helped them educationally at least some. Less than 2 percent felt that SMPY had hurt them educationally. The majority (almost 80 percent) felt that SMPY had not affected their social and/or emotional development at all. Since most felt that SMPY had helped them educationally — a major purpose of SMPY — and few (less than 3 percent) felt SMPY had negatively affected their social and/or emotional development, the main goal of SMPY can be said to have been fulfilled.

Summary

This chapter is an attempt to trace the progress through high school of the intellectually talented students identified by the Study of Mathematically Precocious Youth in its first three talent searches (Keating 1974, 1976a). The students who were followed up had scored as seventh- or eighth-graders better on the College Board's Scholastic Aptitude Test-Mathematics and/or -Verbal sections than a national sample of eleventh- and twelfth-grade females had. Students were asked to complete an eight-page questionnaire about themselves. Of the 2,188 students selected for this study, over 90 percent (1,996) returned the survey form to us. The

TABLE 2.8. Ratings on Degree of Educational Help Received from SMPY and SMPY's Affect on Students' Social and/or Emotional Development

	First Wave (N = 202)	Second Wave (N = 531)	Third and Fourth Waves (N = 1,263)
Educational help[a]			
At least some (%)	61	63	60
None (%)	39	36	38
Unfavorable influence (%)	0	1	2
Mean[b]	2.9	2.8	2.8
Standard deviation	0.9	0.8	0.8
Social and/or emotional development[c]			
Positively (%)	21	18	21
No influence (%)	79	80	77
Negatively (%)	—	2	3
Mean	—	3.2	3.2
Standard deviation	—	0.5	0.5

[a] The perceived degree of educational help received from SMPY was coded as follows: 1 = hurt me; 2 = none; 3 = a little; 4 = considerably; 5 = much.
[b] The distribution of responses was significantly skewed and had a significant amount of kurtosis.
[c] The rated influence of SMPY on students' social and/or emotional development was coded as follows: 1 = much for the worse; 2 = negatively; 3 = no influence; 4 = positively; 5 = much for the better.

general conclusion is that these students did fulfill their potential during high school.

These students maintained their initial superior ability throughout high school. Compared to a national sample of college-bound seniors, SMPY students' mean scores on the SAT-M and SAT-V in high school were approximately 200 and 170 points superior, respectively. The mean scores on the SAT were close to the top possible score on that test, which is designed for above-average students. SMPY boys and girls showed a mean score gain on SAT-M of 155 points and 145 points, respectively, from the time of the talent search until they took the tests again in high school. On the SAT-V males improved by 159 points and females by 144. Thus males improved significantly more than females during high school in both their verbal and mathematical abilities (see Benbow & Stanley 1982a). Furthermore, SAT-V scores were lower than SAT-M scores on the 200- to 800-point scale and in percentile ranks by sex both at the time of talent-search participation and in high school, as would be expected on the basis of regression toward the mean.

To assess the SMPY students' level of achievement, performance on the College Board's achievement tests was studied. Over all tests taken during the high school years by at least 8 percent of the SMPY group, SMPY students' mean score was approximately 100 points above the mean for 1978–79 college-bound seniors (107 points for boys and 97 for girls). The highest scores were not necessarily found for the mathematics achievement tests. On not one of the tests studied was the SMPY group mean lower than the college-bound seniors' mean. Thus these students are superior not only in ability but also in achievement.

Benbow (1981) showed that SMPY students took significantly more of the college-level AP examinations taken in high school than students in general do. Furthermore, on every single test taken by at least ten persons, SMPY students scored above the mean, as they had done on the achievement tests. Again, scores on the mathematics examinations were not necessarily the highest.

A major purpose of this study was to determine the degree to which mathematical talent of students in grades seven and eight relates to subsequent course-taking, achievements, interests, and attitudes in high school. The results suggest strong relationships.

The degree of participation in high-school mathematics by the mathematically talented students was outstanding. As a group the SMPY students took one year more of mathematics than college-bound seniors and received mainly *A*s and *B*s for their course-work. With respect to calculus, almost 66 percent of the boys took at least one calculus course, compared to 40 percent of the girls. This is ten times the rate (for each sex separately) at which high-school students in general take calculus. Thus for both boys and girls, respectively, it was concluded that students identified as mathematically gifted in grade seven or eight did have a high level of participation in high-school mathematics courses. Participation and achievement in high-school science courses were almost as high as for mathematics and compared favorably to the 1978–79 college-bound seniors' performance.

A high degree of interest was also shown in mathematics and science. Mathematics and science were the favorite courses in high school, with mathematics being the most preferred course. When the students rated their liking for mathematics, biology, chemistry, and physics on a five-point scale, their responses were equated to a moderately strong liking. Again, mathematics was rated most highly. The strong interest in mathematics and science was exhibited not only in the number of courses taken in these fields in high school but also in the high degree of participation in science fairs and mathematics contests.

The use of accelerative options (Stanley 1978; Benbow 1979) was at a level much higher than that of the general population. The students who considered themselves at least somewhat accelerated felt that this acceleration had benefited their social and/or emotional development.

Although these students were highly successful academically and were interested in academics, they pursued a wide variety of extracurricular interests in high school. The mean number of activities was twenty-three; reading, social activities, and performing arts were the most popular. Most of the students also won some type of award or honor. Although a high percentage of them were academic awards, many other types of honors were also won. It can thus be concluded that SMPY students did not have a narrow range of interests and were not one-sided in their activities.

Over 90 percent of the students were attending college, typically at academically and socially elite universities, and were enjoying it. Over 50 percent of the students were intending to major in mathematics, science, or engineering. This is a high percentage compared to college-bound seniors. Furthermore, the educational aspirations of the whole group were extremely high. Over 96 percent of the students wanted to receive at least a bachelor's degree. A doctorate was the most popular choice.

Sex differences were found throughout this study in participation in mathematics and science, performance on the SAT-M, and the taking of and performance on the mathematics and science achievement tests. No statistically significant differences were found, however, in attitudes toward mathematics and science. For further discussion of sex differences found in this group see Benbow (1981) and Benbow and Stanley (1982a). Some other studies in sex differences are Benbow and Stanley (1980), Fox, Brody, and Tobin (1980), and Fox, Benbow, and Perkins in chapter 7 of this volume.

It is clear that this group of intellectually able students identified by SMPY were in general quite successful in high school. But how much had SMPY to do with that? In many cases a great deal, it appears. It is difficult, however, to reach and help personally 2,000 students. Yet this group of SMPY students did feel that SMPY had given them some help educationally while not detracting from their social and/or emotional development. This was as much as SMPY had aspired to influence the whole group, since the members of its small staff concentrated their efforts on the ablest, best-motivated students among the group.

In conclusion, SMPY has shown that its identification measure is effective in selecting students in the seventh grade who achieve at a superior level in high school, especially in science and mathematics. The SAT-M score of an intellectually talented seventh- or eighth-grader does have predictive validity.

Notes

1. For more complete coverage of this topic see Benbow (1981).
2. Some *accelerated* ninth- and tenth-graders were also eligible.
3. The responsibility for conducting the first wave of the follow-up with 214 students who had met the science criterion and/or had scored at least 420 on

SAT-M was Cohn's. The data collection for the remaining three waves ($N = 1,974$) was my responsibility.

4. The first wave of the follow-up consisted only of students who had been at least eighth-graders in the talent search, the second wave consisted mainly of ex-eighth-graders but of some ex-seventh-graders in the talent searches, and the combined third and fourth waves consisted mainly of ex-seventh-graders and also of some ex-eighth-graders. The talent-search mean score difference on SAT-M and SAT-V for the waves is probably accounted for by this difference in composition of the groups.

5. They were considered to be the appropriate comparison group, since SMPY students resided in that area.

References

Admissions Testing Program of the College Board. 1979a. *ATP guide for high schools and colleges, 1979–81.* Princeton, N.J.: Educational Testing Service.

_____. 1979b. *National report: college-bound seniors, 1979.* Princeton, N.J.: Educational Testing Service.

_____. 1980. *Middle states report: College-bound seniors, 1980.* Princeton, N.J.: College Entrance Examination Board.

Angoff, W., ed. 1971. *The College Board Admissions Testing Program.* Princeton, N.J.: College Entrance Examination Board.

Astin, A. W. 1965. *Who goes where to college?* Chicago: Science Research Associates.

_____. 1978. *The American freshmen: National norms for fall, 1978.* Los Angeles: American Council of Education and University of California.

Benbow, C. P. 1978. Prepare now for APP examinations. *Gifted Child Quarterly* 22 (3, Fall): 415.

_____. 1979. The components of SMPY's smorgasbord of accelerative options. *Intellectually Talented Youth Bulletin* 5(10): 21–23.

_____. 1981. Development of superior mathematical ability during adolescence. Ph.D. diss., The Johns Hopkins University.

Benbow, C. P., and George, W. C. 1979. Creating bridges between high school and college. *Intellectually Talented Youth Bulletin* 5(5): 2–3.

Benbow, C. P., and Stanley, J. C. 1978. It is never too early to start thinking about AP. *Intellectually Talented Youth Bulletin* 4(10): 4–6.

_____. 1980. Sex differences in mathematical ability: Fact or artifact? *Science* 210: 1262–64.

_____. 1981. Mathematical ability: Is sex a factor? *Science* 212: 118–21.

_____. 1982a. Consequences in high school and college of sex differences in mathematical reasoning ability: A longitudinal perspective. *American Educational Research Journal* 19 (4): 598–622.

_____. 1982b. Intellectually talented boys and girls: Educational profiles. *Gifted Child Quarterly* 26 (2, Spring): 82–88.

_____. In press. Majoring in science: Predictable for either sex? In *Women in science,* ed. M. W. Steinkamp and M. L. Maehr. Greenwich, Conn.: JAI Press.

Charles Kettering Foundation. 1980. *New Ways.* Spring-Summer, p. 8.

Cohn, S. J. 1980. Two components of the Study of Mathematically Precocious Youth's intervention studies of educational facilitation and longitudinal follow-up. Ph.D. diss., The Johns Hopkins University.

Eisenberg, A., and George, W. C. 1978. Early entrance to college: The Johns Hopkins experience. *College and University* 54(2, Winter): 109–18.

Fox, L. H.; Brody, L.; and Tobin, D. 1980. *Women and the mathematical mystique.* Baltimore: Johns Hopkins University Press.

George, W. C., and Solano, C. H. 1976a. College courses and educational facilitation of the gifted. *Gifted Child Quarterly* 20(3, Fall): 274–85.

_____. 1976b. Identifying mathematical talent on a statewide basis. In *Intellectual talent: Research and development,* ed. D. P. Keating, 55–89. Baltimore: Johns Hopkins University Press.

Hanson, H. P. 1980. Twenty-five years of the Advanced Placement Program: Encouraging able students. *College Board Review,* no. 115(Spring), pp. 8–12, 35.

Keating, D. P. 1974. The study of mathematically precocious youth. In *Mathematical talent: Discovery, description, and development,* ed. J. C. Stanley, D. P. Keating, and L. H. Fox, 23–47. Baltimore: Johns Hopkins University Press.

_____. 1976a. Discovering quantitative precocity. In *Intellectual talent: Research and development,* ed. D. P. Keating, 23–31. Baltimore: Johns Hopkins University Press.

_____, ed. 1976b. *Intellectual talent: Research and development.* Baltimore: Johns Hopkins University Press.

Keating, D. P., and Stanley, J. C. 1972. Extreme measures for the exceptionally gifted in mathematics and science. *Educational Researcher* 1(9): 3–7.

Kelly, A. 1979. *Girls and science: An international study of sex differences in school science achievement.* Stockholm, Sweden: Almqvist and Wiksell International.

National Assessment of Educational Progress. 1979. *Attitudes toward science: A summary of results from the 1976-77 national assessment of science.* Report no. 08-5-02. Denver: National Institute of Education.

Nie, N. H.; Hull, C. H.; Jenkins, J. G.; Steinbrenner, K.; and Bent, D. H. 1975. *SPSS: Statistical package for the social sciences.* 2nd ed. New York: McGraw-Hill.

Shaycoft, M. F. 1967. *The high school years: Growth in cognitive skills (Project Talent).* Palo Alto, Calif.: American Institutes for Research.

Shesko, M. M. 1975. *Harvard Business School Dec System-1070: SOS user's guide.* Cambridge: The Presidents and Fellows of Harvard College.

Stanley, J. C. 1973. Accelerating the educational progress of intellectually gifted youths. *Educational Psychologist* 10(3): 133–46.

_____. 1977. Rationale of the Study of Mathematically Precocious Youth (SMPY) during its first five years of promoting educational acceleration. In *The gifted and the creative: A fifty-year perspective,* ed. J. C. Stanley, W. C. George, and C. H. Solano, 75–112. Baltimore: Johns Hopkins University Press.

———. 1978. Educational non-acceleration: An international tragedy. *G/C/T,* no. 3, pp. 2–5, 53–57, 60–64.

Stanley, J. C.; George, W. C.; and Solano, C. H., eds. 1977. *The gifted and the creative: A fifty-year perspective.* Baltimore: Johns Hopkins University Press.

Stanley, J. C.; Keating, D. P.; and Fox, L. H., eds. 1974. *Mathematical talent: Discovery, description, and development.* Baltimore: Johns Hopkins University Press.

Wise, L. L.; Steel, L.; and MacDonald, C. 1979. *Origins and career consequences of sex differences in mathematics achievement. Palo Alto, Calif.: American Institute for Research.*

APPENDIX 2.1: Questionnaire used to Follow Up SMPY Students after High-School Graduation

The Johns Hopkins University - Baltimore, MD 21218   **1979/1980**
Study of Mathematically Precocious Youth (SMPY)
**Follow-up survey of SMPY students who are
of High School graduate age**

Please fill out **ALL** of this questionnaire carefully and completely. Please print or type all answers. For any questions that do not apply, write N/A; if your answer is "None" write None. Please send it as soon as possible in the enclosed envelope to **SMPY**, The Johns Hopkins University, Baltimore, Maryland 21218. All information will be kept **STRICTLY CONFIDENTIAL**; you will not be publicly identified with the information herein in any way. If you have any questions, please feel free to call (301) 338-7086.

I. GENERAL INFORMATION

A. PRINT your full name: _____
Last   First   Middle   Maiden (if applicable)

Print your parents' names: Father: _____
Last   First   Middle

Mother: _____
Last   First   Middle   Maiden

Your home address: _____
Street No.   Street

_____ County: _____
City   State   Zip Code

Your telephone no: _____( )_____
Area Code   7-digit number

B. Your mailing address, if different from your home address:

_____

C. Please print the name and address of a relatively young but stably located adult, not living in your home, who would know your address in case you move. We need this information in order to keep in touch with you in the coming years if you move.

( )
Name: _____
Last   First   Middle   Relationship

Address: _____
Street No.   Street

( )
_____
City   State   Zip Code   Tel. No. with Area Code

D. Your sex (circle):   F   M
Your marital status: ☐ Single
☐ Married
☐ Divorced

Your birthdate: _____
Month/day/year
Today's date: _____
Month/day/year
Spouse's name: _____
Given name   Former Surname

E. Social Security No.: ☐☐☐ ☐☐ ☐☐☐☐

F. Driver's license number: _____ State: _____

G. Which, if any, grade(s) have you skipped? _____

H. When did you enter kindergarten? _____
Month/Year

I. When did you enter the first grade? _____
Month/Year

Go to the next page.

II. GRADES 8 THROUGH 12

A. List all the schools below the college level that you have attended from September of 1974 onward, in order of attendance, with dates of attendance. Indicate with a checkmark (✔) each of the schools from which you were graduated and the dates of your graduation.

School	City, State	Years during which you attended	Gradu- ated?	Year of Graduation

B. Indicate all of the math courses you took in grades 8 through 12. When possible, list the final (overall) grade (e.g., A,B,C,D, or F) you received for the subject, as well as the school grade you were in when you took the course. Also list how long you were in the course (e.g., half year, whole year) and any special comments about the course (such as, no grade received). If you took a college course in lieu of a high school course, list it under "D. College courses while in high school," which is on the next page. (If more room is needed, continue on separate sheet.)

Subject	Final course grade	School grade	Length of course	Special comments
1. Algebra I				
2. Algebra II				
3. Plane geometry				
4. College algebra				
5. Trigonometry				
6. Analytic geometry				
7. Calculus I (Differential)				
8. Calculus II (Integral)				
9. Probability				
10. Statistics				
11. Computer Science				
12. Other (specify)				

13. Unified Math Curriculum (please describe under "Comments" on last page of questionnaire) ☐ yes

C. Indicate all of the science courses you took in grades 8 through 12. When possible, list the final (overall) grade (e.g., A,B,C,D, or F) you received for the subject, as well as the school grade you were in when you took the course. Also list how long you were in the course (e.g., half year, whole year) and any special comments about the course (such as, no grade received). If you took a college course in lieu of a high school course, list it under "D. College courses while in high school," which is on the next page. (If more space is needed, continue on separate sheet.)

Subject	Final course grade	School grade	Length of course	Special comments
1. General science				
2. Biology				
3. Chemistry				
4. Physics				
5. Advanced biology				
6. Advanced chemistry				
7. Advanced physics				
8. Other (specify)				

Go to the next page.

D. List all the courses you took **for credit** at a college **before** becoming a **full-time** college student, as well as the name of the institution, the year you took the course, the grade you were in at the time, the final (overall) grade you received in the course, and the number of credits.

Title of college course	College	Year	School grade	Course grade	Number of credits

E. List in the appropriate spaces below the exact name **and level** (such as, Calculus AB or BC, or Physics C Mechanics) of all Advanced Placement Program (APP) **examinations** you have taken. (Omit those subjects for which you took APP courses but did not take the APP exams.) Show the year(s) you took the exam(s) and the school grade(s) you were in at the time.

Name of APP exam	Score on APP exam	Year exam taken	School grade at the time

F. List your scores on the following standardized examinations, as well as the month and year you took the exam and the grade you were in at that time. If you took the exam more than once, list each score in order of when taken. If you took the exam but cannot locate the scores, so indicate.

Exam	Math	Verbal	TSWE*	Date (Mo./year)	School grade
Scholastic Aptitude Test (SAT)					
Preliminary Scholastic Aptitude Test (PSAT)					

*Test of Standard Written English

College Board Achievement Tests	Subject and level	Score	Date (Mo./year)	School grade

College-level Examination Program (CLEP) Test	Subject and level	Score	Date (Mo./year)	School grade

	Mathematics	Verbal	Natural Science	Social Science	Total	Date (Mo./year)	School grade
American College Testing Program (ACT)							

Go to the next page.

G. What were your favorite subjects in grades 9 through 12? (Let 1 mean "most preferred.")

1. _____ 2. _____ 3. _____

H. Check the **one** of the five rating-scale categories below that most appropriately describes your attitude toward **each** subject listed. Then in the column entitled "Ranking" rank your preference (1=most preferred, 2=next, 3=next, and 4=least. Please rank all 4 and use **no** ties in ranking.)

Subject	Strong liking	Moderate liking	Neutral or mixed feelings	Slight dislike	Strong dislike	**Ranking**
Biology						
Chemistry						
Mathematics						
Physics						

I. Have you considered a career in any of the areas listed in item H?   ☐ Yes   ☐ No

If yes, which one(s)? _____

Why? _____

J. List all of the science fair projects you submitted to science fairs in your school, state, region, or nation. Please indicate the title of the project, science area (e.g., biology, chemistry, physics), year, the school grade you were in at the time, and any prizes you received.

Science fair project title	Level	Area in science	Year	School grade	Prize

K. List all of the national, regional, or state mathematics contests in which you have competed. Please indicate which contest, your score, and awards you received.

Contest	Year	Score	Award(s)

L. Did you take the PSAT?   ☐ Yes   ☐ No

Did you receive a National Merit Letter of Commendation?   ☐ Yes   ☐ No

Were you a National Merit Scholarship semi-finalist?   ☐ Yes   ☐ No

Were you a National Merit Scholarship finalist?   ☐ Yes   ☐ No

Did you receive a National Merit Scholarship?   ☐ Yes   ☐ No

M. List (next to the appropriate categories) all honors or awards you won while in grades 8 through 12. Under the column entitled "Total number" indicate the total number of awards and/or honors you won for each category.

Type of Award	Total number	Name(s) of award(s)	How won	Year	School grade
National scholastic					
Regional scholastic					
School scholastic					
Artistic (music, theatre, art)					
Athletic					
Community, service, religious or political					

Go to the next page.

33

N. List (next to the appropriate categories) the fairly important in-school activities in which you participated during grades 8 through 12. Under the column entitled "Total number of years" indicate in the appropriate box the total number of school years you participated in each type of activity in this time period. Then name the activities and next to each one list each school grade during which you participated in it.

Type of activity	Total number of years	Activities	School grades
Academic			
Leadership			
Membership (non-academic clubs, committees)			
Performing arts			
Sports			
Technical (stage crew, photography, etc.)			
Writing			

O. List (next to the appropriate categories) your hobbies and out-of-school activities (including summer activities) in which you participated from the summer following your seventh grade through the summer following your twelfth grade. Under the column entitled "Total number of years" indicate in the appropriate box the total number of calendar years you participated in each type of activity. Then name the activities and next to each one list the years during which you participated in it.

Type of activity	Total number of years	Activities	Year(s)
Academic			
Arts & crafts			
Collections (coins, stamps, etc.)			
Community service/ volunteer			
Performing arts			
Political			
Reading & spectator activities (watching sports, listening to music, etc.)			
Religious			
Social hobbies (cards, dating, etc.)			
Technological hobbies			

P. How many different types of summer or part-time jobs did you have during grades 8 through 12? List your three most recent jobs, along with the employer(s) and dates of employment.

Type of job	Employer (firm)	Dates (from/till)

Go to the next page.

III. HIGHER EDUCATION

A. When did you become a **full-time** student or trainee beyond high school?_____
Month/year

At which school or program?_____
Name of school or program

_____
City   State

B. Did you enter any college, university, or other school or training program **full-time** earlier than your agemates?   ☐ Yes   ☐ No

If yes, after which grade? ☐

C. Did you enter with advanced standing? That is, had you earned any applicable credits before entering the post-secondary institution?   ☐ Yes   ☐ No

If yes, what was the total number of semester, or quarter, hours of advanced-standing credits of all sorts you received?

Semester hour ☐   Quarter hour ☐

D. What college, university, or other school or training program are you now attending? (If none, so state.)

_____
Name of school or program

What is your mailing address at this school or program? _____
Street no. & street

_____
City   State   Zip Code   Tel. no. (including area code)
(   )   -

E. List **all** of the colleges and universities and/or other schools or programs to which you submitted a complete application for admission.

College, school or program	accepted	waiting list	rejected

F. List **all** scholarships or fellowships you were awarded, and for each one list the amount and the sponsor of the award.

Description	Amount	Sponsor

G. As far as you know now, what is your major field of study likely to be? _____

H. List the **titles** of the courses you have taken thus far at college as a full-time student. (If you prefer, enclose a xeroxed copy of the transcript of your college credits.)

_____

_____

_____

_____

Go to the next page.

I. List (next to the appropriate categories) the program activities in which you are participating now either in school or outside of school, or which you plan to join this school year. Under the column entitled "Total number of activities," indicate in the appropriate box the total number of activities within each category shown.

Type of activity	Total number of activities	Name of activities
Academic		_____
Leadership		_____
Membership (non-academic clubs or committees)		_____
Performing		_____
Sports		_____
Technical (e.g., stagecrew)		_____
Writing		_____
Religion		_____

J. How well do you like college? (Check **one.**)

☐ Strong liking

☐ Moderate liking

☐ Neutral/mixed feelings

☐ Moderate dislike

☐ Strong dislike

K. What is the highest level of education you hope to obtain? (Check **one.**)

☐ Less than high school

☐ High school diploma

☐ Less than two years of college

☐ Two or more years of college, but not a bachelor's degree

☐ R.N. (Registered Nurse, but not a bachelor's degree)

☐ Bachelor's degree

☐ Master's degree

☐ Doctorate (e.g., Ph.D., Ed.D., M.D., D.D.S., LL.B., J.D., D.V.M.)

☐ Post-doctoral study

In what field(s) of study? _____

IV. ATTITUDES

A. How well, to date, do you feel that you have used all available educational opportunities? (Check **one.**)

☐ Extremely well

☐ Rather well

☐ About average

☐ Rather poorly

☐ Extremely poorly

Go to the next page.

B. To what extent do you feel that your association with the Study of Mathematically Precocious Youth (SMPY) has helped you educationally via its talent searches, various mailouts, letters, personal contacts, articles, local and national publicity, and special opportunities? (Check **one**.)

☐ Much

☐ Considerably

☐ A little

☐ None

☐ It has hurt me educationally.

Please explain your answer: _____

_____

C. How does your social and/or emotional development seem to have been influenced by your association with SMPY? (Check **one**.)

☐ Much for the better

☐ Positively

☐ No influence

☐ Negatively

☐ Much for the worse

Comments:_____

_____

D. Have you been accelerated in subject matter placement?   ☐ Yes   ☐ No

Have you been accelerated in grade placement?   ☐ Yes   ☐ No

If yes to either of the above, how do you feel your social and/or emotional development has been affected by this acceleration? (Check **one**.)

☐ Much for the better

☐ Positively

☐ No influence

☐ Negatively

☐ Much for the worse

Comments: _____

_____

E. How might SMPY have been of more value to you, especially if its resources had been greater?

_____

_____

_____

_____

F. Any other comments you care to make:

G. I hereby certify that I have read over my responses carefully and thoroughly. They are as complete and accurate as I can make them.

_____
Signature

37

3

Manifestation of Creative Behaviors by Maturing Participants in the Study of Mathematically Precocious Youth

WILLIAM B. MICHAEL

Abstract

The creative performance of mathematically apt adolescents was investigated. In order to provide a framework for the identification and evaluation of the predictors of creative behavior reported by SMPY students, two empirical studies based on SMPY data were reviewed briefly. A summary of the statistical results of the first three talent searches and of the follow-up showed that SAT-M score is negatively related to participation in science fairs for girls and positively related to participation in mathematics contests for boys. Major attention was given to the problems encountered in analyzing these studies. The ambiguity and inconclusiveness of the results were attributed to substantive limitations associated with the conceptualization of creativity, the operationalization of the construct, and the nature of the learning environment. Methodological difficulties occurring in relation to the unreliability of the measures, the restricted ability range, and the violation of assumptions central to the statistical procedures used were identified. In conclusion, several recommendations for future investigations were offered.

38

How creatively have the boys and girls identified as being highly talented mathematically by the Study of Mathematically Precocious Youth been performing as they have been maturing? In an effort to answer this important question, the writer examined four volumes that have evolved from SMPY (George, Cohn, & Stanley 1979; Keating 1976b; Stanley, George, & Solano 1977; Stanley, Keating, & Fox 1974), studied a master's thesis (Kusnitz 1978) and a journal article (Albert 1980), and explored for the first three talent searches the statistical relationships between selected antecedent variables (responses to items) in questionnaires employed in the talent searches and those criterion variables (item responses) in follow-up survey forms completed after high-school graduation (Benbow, chapter 2 of this volume) that were thought possibly to reflect creative behaviors. Recent professional literature concerned with the relationship of creativity to giftedness also was consulted to provide additional insights. As had been expected, it became apparent that answering the question would not be easy and that both substantive and methodological difficulties encountered in answering the question would indeed be disconcerting.

In view of the many difficulties encountered, it was decided that following a brief review of two significant empirical studies based on SMPY data and a summary of relevant statistical results from a survey of members of the first three talent searches (approximately four to five years after their selection for participation in SMPY) major attention would be focused upon delineating several major substantive and methodological limitations and then upon suggesting recommendations for future studies that could furnish the kinds of evidence needed to answer the question posed. This approach appeared to provide some promise for facilitating future research efforts that could demonstrate possible relevant relationships between later creative behaviors in mathematics and in science-related activities to antecedent variables such as scholastic aptitude, family background factors, personality characteristics at time of selection, and initial indicators of creative potential.

Two Empirical Studies

In the SMPY endeavor two empirical studies (Keating 1976a; Kusnitz 1978) have afforded some evidence regarding not only the standing of groups of mathematically talented youth on measures of creative behaviors in comparison to that of normative samples but also the extent of the relationship of measures intended to reflect creativity to those indicative of general intelligence, selected abilities, value orientation, vocational interests, artistic preferences, and life-history factors. A brief review of each of these investigations provides a pertinent framework within which statistical results of post-high-school graduation follow-up studies of individuals in SMPY from the first three talent searches can be reported and evaluated.

In his empirical study Keating (1976a) administered to a sample of seventy-two male junior-high-school students who had scored highly in the 1972 and 1973 talent searches several cognitive and affective measures that had been hypothesized as potential predictors of later creativity. These measures were concerned with values, life-history characteristics, preferences for various geometric figures, personality traits, and general reasoning capabilities. Although the findings were somewhat contradictory from one measure to another, Keating demonstrated a strong theoretical-investigative orientation for the group. He concluded that his results supported the feasibility of a multifactor theory of creative behavior that would permit the manifestation of creativity in different ways by different individuals. It was anticipated that longitudinal follow-up studies would resolve questions concerning the long-term predictive validity of several of the measures.

By far the more comprehensive of the two empirical studies regarding the relationship of creative behaviors of mathematically talented students to selected cognitive abilities and affective characteristics was the one completed by Kusnitz (1978). Employing a highly homogeneous (in terms of cognitive ability) subsample of sixty boys between 12 and 14 years of age who had scored at a high but not at the highest level in the fourth annual talent search conducted by SMPY, Kusnitz typically found low and statistically nonsignificant correlations between measures of ability and those measures hypothesized as indicative of creative behaviors. Ability was defined by scores on (a) the College Board's Scholastic Aptitude Test-Mathematics (Educational Testing Service 1948–80), (b) the Mathematics and Natural Sciences Reading subtests of the American College Testing (ACT) Assessment (American College Testing Program 1959–80), (c) the Abstract Reasoning, Mechanical Reasoning, and Spatial Relations parts of the Differential Aptitude Tests (DAT) (Bennett, Seashore, & Wesman 1947–80), and (d) an achievement test – the Cooperative Mathematics Tests: Algebra I and II (Educational Testing Service 1962) – of first-year high-school algebra before it was studied formally. Creative behaviors were revealed by three scores in Fluency, Flexibility, and Originality in the Verbal Test and by four scores in Fluency, Flexibility, Originality, and Elaboration in the Figural Test of the Torrance Tests of Creative Thinking (TTCT), Form A (Torrance 1966, 1974),[1] by standing on each of two scales – Art-Writing and Mathematics-Science – of the Biographical Inventory–Creativity (BIC) (Schaefer 1970), by performance on the Barron-Welsh Art Scale (BWAS) (Barron & Welsh 1952; Welsh 1959;

Welsh & Barron 1963), and by placement on the Watson-Glaser Critical Thinking Appraisal Form (WGCT), Form YM (Watson & Glaser 1964). In addition, Kusnitz explored the relationship between scores on each of these measures representing creativity and those reflecting essentially non-cognitive (affective) components on each of six scales — Theoretical, Economic, Aesthetic, Social, Political, and Religious — of the Study of Values (SOV) (Allport, Vernon, & Lindzey 1970) and on each of the six categories — Intellectual (Investigative), Artistic, Realistic, Conventional, Social, and Enterprising — of the sixth edition of the Vocational Preference Inventory (VPI) (Holland 1965). Somewhat consistent with MacKinnon's (1962) observation that high scores on both the Theoretical and the Aesthetic scales of the SOV were present for a sample of creative mathematicians and scientists was the finding that the scores on the Theoretical scale were significantly correlated with those on the Mathematics-Science subtest of the BIC and that the scores on the Aesthetic scale were reliably correlated with those on the Art-Writing subtest of the BIC.

After relating his findings to those of several investigators whose work he had carefully reviewed, Kusnitz formulated conclusions indicating that (a) students of high mathematical ability within a sample having an extremely narrow range of high (but not the highest) cognitive ability did not constitute a particularly distinguished group in their standing on measures of creativity, (b) measurement of creativity was complex and ambiguous, and (c) the most helpful way to view creativity is through centering attention upon an individual rather than a group. Furthermore, he suggested that use of a comparison group of highly talented students in mathematics in conjunction with one of students with so-called normal ability in mathematics would furnish data that would clarify the nature of the relationship between mathematical ability and creativity. He also urged that tests of creativity be employed as predictors of academic achievement across groups representing different ability levels.

Follow-Up Studies of Students in the First Three Talent Searches

For the follow-up studies involving both boys and girls in the first three talent searches, correlation coefficients were calculated between the ordered (quantifiable) responses to several questions (antecedent variables) in talent-search questionnaires and similarly quantifiable responses to items (criterion variables) on the follow-up survey forms (of which more than 90 percent were returned) (Benbow, chapter 2 of this volume). Items in the talent-search questionnaire dealt with (a) number of siblings of the respondent, (b) his or her birth order, (c) occupational status of the father and the mother, (d) educational level of the father and the mother, (e) degree of liking for school and for mathematics, (f) amount of involvement with others in learning mathematics, and (g) other life-history factors. Questions in the follow-up survey form were concerned with (a) amount of participation in science fair projects, (b) amount of participation in mathematics contests, (c) number of honors or awards received, (d) number of years of involvement in various academically oriented school-related activities, and (e) number of years of association in a host of out-of-school activities (see Appendix 2.1, p. 5 of follow-up survey). Although initially correlations were found only for the whole group, subsequently separate correlations for males and females were determined for selected pairs of variables of greatest interest.

In chapter 2 of this volume Benbow presents comprehensive findings of the interrelationships among several items within the questionnaire and follow-up survey forms and describes how the follow-up study was conducted and analyzed. Only those criterion variables that were thought to be especially relevant to creativity have been included in the data reported for this study. The not entirely unexpected result was this: only 1 of the 655 correlation coefficients calculated between antecedent and criterion variables from the questionnaires reached a value as large as .19. Approximately 18 percent of the coefficients were statistically significant at or beyond the .05 level.

In view of the somewhat disappointing results, it was decided that for each sex a small number of what appeared to be the most nearly relevant and promising criterion variables (number of projects submitted to science fairs and number of mathematics contests in which participation occurred) would be related to each of four antecedent (predictor) variables (level of father's education, level of mother's education, occupational status of father, and occupational status of mother). In addition, the two criterion measures reflecting creativity in science and in mathematics were correlated with SAT-M scores earned by the participants while they were in the seventh or eighth grade (at the time of the talent search) and again while they were typically in the eleventh or twelfth grade, that is, four or five years later in their academic program.

Except for the coefficient of $-.22$ ($p < .001$) between father's level of education and number of projects submitted to science fairs for the sample of girls in the second wave of the follow-up survey [2] and that of $-.16$ ($p < .05$) between father's level of education and number of mathematics contests entered for the sample of boys in the first wave of the follow-up, all other coefficients (excluding SAT variables as predictors) were less than .15. In the instance of the SAT-M measure as a predictor of number of projects submitted to science fairs, coefficients with absolute values in excess of .20 were found for samples of girls (only) in the first wave of the follow-up ($r = -.37$, $p < .001$) when they were in the seventh or eighth grade, in the second wave of the follow-up ($r = -.22$, $p < .001$) when they were in the seventh or eighth grade, and in the second wave of the follow-up ($r = -.22$, $p < .001$) when they were in the twelfth grade. Relative to the prediction of number of mathematics contests in which students participated from SAT-M scores, correlations in excess of .20 were obtained only for boys: .33 ($p < .001$) and .28 ($p < .001$), respectively, for seventh-and eighth-graders in the second and in the combined third and fourth waves of the follow-up, and .28 ($p < .001$) for twelfth-graders in the second wave of the follow-up. Thus the data suggest that a modest *negative* relationship exists between SAT-M scores and extent of participation in science fairs for girls (but not for boys) and that a modest *positive* relationship occurs between SAT-M scores and amount of involvement in mathematics contests for boys (but not for girls). One could hypothesize that the science fairs may be social occasions for the less able girls and that the mathematics contests are competitive affairs for the more able boys. In any event, attention should be called to the fact that within each of the three talent-search samples at least 80 percent of the students had not submitted a project to a science fair and that in two of the three talent-search samples more than 80 percent of the students had not competed in a mathematics contest. (Obviously, the resulting distribution of responses to the criterion item would be anticipated to contribute to an attenuation in the magnitude of any resulting correlation coefficient with SAT-M scores.)

Substantive and Methodological Limitations

That the findings in the two empirical studies were somewhat conflicting and ambiguous and that the outcomes of the follow-up survey studies were not definitive or conclusive could be attributed to a number of substantive limitations associated with the conceptualization of creativity, to the operational definition of this construct, and to the nature of the learning environment. There were also identifiable methodological difficulties occurring in relation to the unreliability of measures, the restricted range in the ability levels of the subjects within the samples employed, and the violation of assumptions central to the statistical procedures used.

SUBSTANTIVE LIMITATIONS

Among the principal substantive limitations that could have accounted for the somewhat ambiguous and inconsistent outcomes were: (a) inability to conceptualize (to identify or to define psychologically) subconstructs of creativity relevant to problem-solving activities involved in mathematics and science-related tasks, (b) corresponding inappropriateness of the measure (test or scale) chosen to provide a meaningful operational definition or duplication of psychological processes central to creative problem-solving endeavors in mathematics or science, (c) absence of questions in follow-up surveys that were indicative of actual creative behaviors during later years of schooling or during time spent in part-time work or recreation, and (d) failure to provide in the school or home learning environment opportunities as well as reinforcement (rewards) for creative production on the part of the SMPY students. Although one could argue quite convincingly that limitations (b) and (c) were methodological rather than substantive, the conceptualization of creative behavior is so dependent upon and interwoven with its measurement that these two limitations were categorized as substantive.

Need to conceptualize subconstructs underlying creativity in problem-solving in mathematics and the sciences. Although the two empirical studies reported provided interesting information, they appeared to lack a preliminary theoretical framework to afford a direction for research. Somewhat fragmented in nature (as evidenced by the introduction of numerous measures without the presence of a unified rationale for their selection), the rather theoretically barren studies were able to permit only a limited basis for meaningful generalization. Similar comments would also apply to the selection of items incorporated within the questionnaires and follow-up survey forms that were employed. In short, there seemed to be no definition of creative behaviors or products within the context of problem-solving endeavors central to success in mathematics and scientific thinking.

One possible theoretical orientation would be that of the structure-of-intellect (SOI) model (Guilford 1967, pp. 60–66; Guilford & Hoepfner 1971; Guilford & Tenopyr 1968, pp. 26–29) or, preferably, that of the information-processing structure-of-intellect problem-solving (SIPS) model (Guilford & Tenopyr 1968, pp. 30–34). In a recent paper Michael (1977, pp. 156–65) has combined the constructs of the SOI and SIPS models and has related them in a systematic way to Rossman's (1931) seven-step paradigm for invention to furnish what could be at least a partial description of the sequence of steps required for creative production and for problem-solving endeavors in mathematics, science, engineering, and technological invention. This formulation could provide some guidelines for (a) the selection of research questions in future studies that are concerned with the manifestation of creative behavior appropriate to mathematics, science, and engineering curricula, (b) the development of testing instruments and the design of items to be included in follow-up surveys, and (c) the planning of curricular orientations and instructional strategies of relevance to SMPY students.

An alternative theoretical orientation appropriate to study of creative problem solving in mathematics has been developed during the past few years by Sternberg (1977a, 1977b, 1978, 1979, 1980; see also Carroll 1980), who has presented an information-processing methodology involving a componential analysis of tasks leading to use of analogical reasoning. The model is particularly applicable to many kinds of inferential thinking and to syllogistic reasoning. Sternberg's theory of intelligence should have important implications for the understanding of creative production.

Inappropriateness of measures intended to reflect creative behaviors. As so often has occurred in a number of published works about creativity, testing instruments have been chosen, it would seem, by their titles or superficial properties rather than in terms of carefully hypothesized constructs or psychological operations relevant to the problem situation at hand. Such a circumstance may have taken place in the instance of some of the measures used in the two empirical studies that have been reviewed. For example, Kusnitz (1978) made use of Torrance's (1966, 1974) TTCT measures that emphasize divergent thinking primarily in a verbal and figural context of content — abilities that for the most part are not very relevant to creative production in mathematics, but possibly are quite important to tasks in language arts and visual arts. Thus in terms of the formulations of Guilford about problem solving as summarized by Michael (1977, pp. 154–56, 162–65), the creative abilities required in problem solving in mathematics and in the sciences are quite different from those needed by writers and artists.

For instance, whereas creative writers and public speakers are relatively more dependent upon verbal fluency and elaboration (divergent production abilities) than are mathematicians and scientists, mathematicians and scientists often rely quite heavily upon use of convergent production abilities reflecting a flexibility of closure or redefinition of a problem situation or upon cognition, as in being sensitive to new problems or to the implications of their solutions. Evaluation would also be an important component in problem solving in providing a critical judgment concerning the appropriateness of a solution.

Although divergent production may be important to the mathematician in the generation of hypotheses and although memory plays an important part in the retrieval of needed information to cognize a problem situation, *adaptive flexibility* may come closest to reflecting the originality or cleverness of the mathematician or inventor in finding a new solution or a unique solution to a problem encountered in a new context. Thus adaptive flexibility often requires finding new uses of familiar objects or of existing knowledge in ambiguous or foreign contexts to attain a specific goal or unique solution (convergent response), and the *sensitivity to problems* frequently demands an awareness (cognition) of implications, difficulties, and risks that one is likely to encounter in undertaking a new assignment or in solving a problem — risks that need to be evaluated along with the promise and correctness of any solution proposed. In short, it would appear that most measures of creative production employed in the context of problem-solving endeavors by gifted students in the areas of mathematics and science have not been addressed to these complex components of the problem-solving process.

Absence of relevant questions in follow-up surveys.   One of the most likely reasons for lack of realization of correlation between antecedent variables in a talent-search questionnaire and the criterion items in the follow-up survey forms is the failure to ask the appropriate or relevant question indicative of creative behaviors in mathematics and in science-related activities in the school setting. Of course it is possible that the inclusion of relevant questions in the survey form still would have resulted in a lack of significant correlations with the antecedent variables because of the actual lack of relationship of background variables to subsequent creative behaviors.

Failure to provide in the learning environment opportunities and rewards for creative endeavor.   It is not known precisely the extent to which opportunities were present for students to take part in science fairs and in competitive contests in mathematics. Hence, some degree of attenuation in correlation coefficients might have occurred for lack of availability of experiences challenging the students' creative potentialities. Even if relevant questions about creative endeavors had been posed in follow-up surveys, significant correlations with antecedent variables might not have been attained because many a teacher — even one of gifted children — fails to offer a learning environment in which students can be given unique, unusual, or challenging problems within the classroom setting or can be rewarded for creative problem solving that can be initiated either within or outside of school. Many a teacher is likely to be threatened or inconvenienced by any change in the status quo of the classroom setting or of the curriculum. Clearly, unless a teacher is prepared to individualize instruction, the mathematically gifted child may become frustrated and hence lost to society as a potentially creative contributor. Information regarding how teaching for creative endeavor may be achieved was set forth in detail by Michael (1968, pp. 237–60; 1977, pp. 165–68).

METHODOLOGICAL LIMITATIONS

Several procedural and methodological shortcomings undoubtedly contributed to the realization of only a small degree of relationship between pairs of variables studied. Unfortunately, the extent to which practical remedial steps can be taken is often far short of what would be desired.

Unreliability of measures.   Partly because of the restriction in range of talent, the potential reliability of measures employed in the two empirical studies was probably quite attentuated. Furthermore, reliability of scoring the TTCT was questioned. Responses to single items in the questionnaire and survey forms employed by SMPY could be expected to be comparatively unreliable. Combining items into clusters to enhance the reliability of resulting composites did not seem to be appropriate in most instances because of the lack of homogeneity in the items.

The extent to which lack of uniformity in conditions underlying administration of tests, questionnaires, and survey forms or lack of accuracy in the scoring and recording of data might have contributed to unreliability cannot be determined. Another interesting concern would rest upon the possible facilitating or inhibiting effect of the use of the word *creativity* in a number of measures employed.

Restriction of range.   In addition to its effect upon the reliability of the criterion and antecedent measures obtained, restriction of range would contribute concomitantly to a reduction to the coefficient of correlation between any two measures. No attempt was made to correct coefficients for restriction of range, as it was difficult to specify any rules of explicit or implicit selection. Thus one should realize that the marked reduction in range of talent probably militated substantially against obtaining higher indexes of relationship between variables.

Violation of statistical assumptions in data analyses.   That several of the distributions of responses to items with ordered alternatives were truncated or skewed probably resulted in the inappropriate use of the Pearson product-moment correlation coefficient relative to the analysis of data in the follow-up studies of students. As curvilinearity was probably often present in many pairs of variables, the correlation estimates were very possibly lower than would have been the corresponding eta values. It must be noted, however, that if two variables being correlated have quite different distribution shapes, they cannot correlate even close to the usual -1.00 and 1.00 limits. Not unless every examinee has the same z-score on the X variable as he or she has on the Y variable can Pearson r's have the unit limits. Obviously, in the instance of the two empirical studies reviewed, no immediate determination of possible curvilinearity could be made.

Recommendations

On the basis of this critique, several recommendations are offered in carrying out future investigations that might contribute to the realization of an improved or more nearly accurate answer to the question posed at the beginning of the paper:

1.   At the time of selection of future SMPY students, supplementary measures reflecting the creative abilities required in successful problem solving in mathematics and in the sciences (as determined from theoretical considerations and the results of empirical studies) should accompany use of the SAT-M to provide evidence of the nature and the degree of the relationship between creativity and general intelligence. In addition, these

measures could be used as a basis for selection, placement, and counseling of students.

2.   Alternate forms of these same measures could be administered to students just prior to their college entrance to examine gains in scores on each of the measures and to ascertain whether a change in degree of relationship between creativity and intelligence has occurred. (It is of interest to note that in the current study mean SAT-M scores for samples of boys in the first, second, and the combined third and fourth waves of the follow-up surveys while they were in the seventh or eighth grade were 567, 549, and 526, respectively; four to five years later the respective means were 691, 693, and 695. In the instance of girls the corresponding mean scores while they were in the seventh or eighth grade were 505, 510, and 498; four to five years later, 652, 643, and 650.)

3.   It is urged that affective measures such as those pertaining to locus of control and field independence (constructs based upon extensive theoretical conceptualization and empirical research) also be administered to determine whether any moderating effects could be identified and whether subsequent prediction of college success could be enhanced.

4.   In a manner somewhat parallel to that followed by Terman and Oden (1959) and Oden (1968) long-term longitudinal studies should be initiated for all participants in recent and in future SMPY groups to obtain evidence of tangible creative contributions to mathematics, science, engineering, business, industry, and health professions in terms of products such as published papers, books, awards, honors, patents, and other original or innovative works. If possible, the use of comparison or control groups of individuals with somewhat modest levels of mathematical ability should be employed to obtain evidence of differential rates of productivity, both in quality and in quantity.

5.   In future studies parallel to those just described efforts should be made to follow males and females as separate groups to learn whether women with requisite qualifications comparable to those of men achieve at an essentially equivalent level, or are possibly inhibited by societal restraints.

Concluding Statement

The Study of Mathematically Precocious Youth has made significant contributions to the identification of highly talented youth in mathematics and has substantially facilitated their progress in the educational system. It is incumbent upon the professional members of SMPY to monitor the attainments of this truly exceptional group to ensure to the maximum degree possible the fruition of their creative potentialities. From the information gained through frequent communication with these gifted individuals during the next several years modifications can be made in educational programs that will probably lead to increasingly significant creative attainments on the part of members of newly selected groups.

Notes

1. Because the TTCT was not scored by the staff of SMPY, Kusnitz had no control over the reliability and quality of scoring of this test.
2. The follow-up of the students in the first three talent searches was conducted in four waves so as to have the questionnaire reach the student in the fall after high-school graduation (see Benbow, chapter 2 of this volume).

References

Albert, R. S. 1980. Exceptionally gifted boys and their parents. *Gifted Child Quarterly* 24(4, Fall): 174–78.

Allport, G. W.; Vernon, P. E.; and Lindzey, G. 1970. *Manual for the Study of Values: A scale for measuring the dominant interests in personality.* 3d ed. Boston: Houghton Mifflin.

American College Testing Program. 1959–80. *ACT Assessment.* Iowa City, Iowa.

Barron, F., and Welsh, G. S. 1952. Artistic perception as a possible factor in personality style: Its measurement by a figure preference test. *Journal of Psychology* 33:199–203.

Bennett, G. K.; Seashore, H. G.; and Wesman, A. G. 1947–80. *Differential Aptitude Tests.* New York: Psychological Corporation.

Carroll, J. B. 1980. Remarks on Sternberg's "Factor theories of intelligence are all right almost." *Educational Researcher* 9(8): 14–18.

Educational Testing Service. 1948–80. *College Board Scholastic Aptitude Test.* Princeton, N.J.

————. 1962. *Cooperative Mathematics Tests: Algebra I and II.* Princeton, N.J.

George, W. C.; Cohn, S. J.; and Stanley, J. C., eds. 1979. *Educating the gifted: Acceleration and enrichment.* Baltimore: Johns Hopkins University Press.

Guilford, J. P. 1967. *The nature of human intelligence.* New York: McGraw-Hill.

Guilford, J. P., and Hoepfner, R. 1971. *The analysis of intelligence.* New York: McGraw-Hill.

Guilford, J. P., and Tenopyr, M. L. 1968. Implications of the structure-of-intellect model for high school and college students. In *Teaching for creative endeavor,* ed. W. B. Michael, 25–45. Bloomington: Indiana University Press.

Holland, J. L. 1965. *Vocational Preference Inventory.* 6th ed. Palo Alto, Calif.: Consulting Psychologists Press.

Keating, D. P. 1976a. Creative potential of mathematically precocious boys. In *Intellectual talent: Research and development,* ed. D. P. Keating, 262–72. Baltimore: Johns Hopkins University Press.

―――, ed. 1976b. *Intellectual talent: Research and development.* Baltimore: Johns Hopkins University Press.

Kusnitz, L. A. 1978. Creativity in mathematically gifted children. Master's thesis, Johns Hopkins University.

MacKinnon, D. W. 1962. The nature and nurture of creative talent. *American Psychologist* 17(7): 484–95.

Michael, W. B. 1968. The college and university. In *Teaching for creative endeavor,* ed. W. B. Michael, 237–60. Bloomington: Indiana University Press.

―――. 1977. Cognitive and affective components of creativity in mathematics and the physical sciences. In *The gifted and the creative: A fifty-year perspective,* ed. J. C. Stanley, W. C. George, and C. H. Solano, 141–72. Baltimore: Johns Hopkins University Press.

Oden, M. H. 1968. The fulfillment of promise: Forty-year follow-up of the Terman gifted group. *Genetic Psychology Monographs* 77:3–93.

Rossman, J. 1931. *The psychology of the inventor: A study of the patentee.* Washington, D.C.: Inventors Publishing.

Schaefer, C. E. 1970. *Biographical Inventory: Creativity.* Princeton, N.J.: Educational Testing Service.

Stanley, J. C.; George W. C.; and Solano, C. H., eds. 1977. *The gifted and the creative: A fifty-year perspective.* Baltimore: Johns Hopkins University Press.

Stanley, J. C.; Keating, D. P.; and Fox, L. H., eds. 1974. *Mathematical talent: Discovery, description, and development.* Baltimore: Johns Hopkins University Press.

Sternberg, R. J. 1977a. Component processes in analogical reasoning. *Psychological Review* 84(4): 353–78.

―――. 1977b. *Intelligence, information processing, and analogical reasoning: The componential analysis of human abilities.* Hillside, N.J.: Lawrence Erlbaum Associates.

―――. 1978. Isolating the components of intelligence. *Intelligence* 2:117–28.

―――. 1979. The nature of mental abilities. *American Psychologist* 34(3): 214–30.

―――. 1980. Factor theories of intelligence are all right almost. *Educational Researcher* 9(8): 6–13, 18.

Terman, L. M., and Oden, M. H. 1959. *The gifted group at mid-life: Thirty-five years' follow-up of the superior child.* Vol. 5 of *Genetic studies of genius.* Stanford, Calif.: Stanford University Press.

Torrance, E. P. 1966, 1974. *Torrance Tests of Creative Thinking, Form A.* Princeton, N.J.: Personnel Press.

Watson, G., and Glaser, E. H. 1964. *Watson-Glaser Critical Thinking Appraisal.* New York: Harcourt Brace Jovanovich.

Welsh, G. S. 1959. *Preliminary manual for the Welsh Figure Preference Test.* Palo Alto, Calif.: Consulting Psychologists Press.

Welsh, G. S., and Barron, F. 1963. *Barron-Welsh Art Scale: A portion of the Welsh Figure Preference Test.* Palo Alto, Calif.: Consulting Psychologists Press.

Mathematics Taught at a Fast Pace: A Longitudinal Evaluation of SMPY's First Class

CAMILLA PERSSON BENBOW,
SUSAN PERKINS, and
JULIAN C. STANLEY

Abstract

Fast-paced classes have been advocated in SMPY's proposals for curricular flexibility. To evaluate the long-term effects of such a class, the responses to two questionnaires completed nine years later by both the participants and the nonparticipants of SMPY's first two mathematics classes were analyzed. The participants scored significantly higher in high school on the SAT-M, expressed greater interest in mathematics and science, and accelerated their education much more than the nonparticipants. Gaps in knowledge of mathematics by the participants were not found. All groups attended selective colleges, but the students who completed the fast-paced class chose the most academically difficult. It is concluded that when highly able youths are presented the opportunity, many of them will accumulate educational advantage.

In chapter 11 of this volume Feldhusen argues that "eclectic" educational programming is necessary to meet the needs of gifted students. To meet the special needs of the highly gifted, Feldhusen advocates acceleration. To meet the special needs of highly mathematically precocious students, the Study of Mathematically Precocious Youth devised a "fast-paced" mathematics class (Fox 1974; George & Denham 1976; Stanley 1976; Bartkovich & George 1980). As the name indicates,

51

mathematics in it was taught at a rapid pace geared to the ablest members of the class. The content was the regular precalculus curriculum taught in junior high and senior high school (algebra I and II, geometry, college algebra, trigonometry, and analytic geometry). The first class, designated Wolfson I in honor of its splendid teacher, Joseph R. Wolfson, met from June 24, 1972, until August 11, 1973.

The program was designed primarily for students in Baltimore County public schools who had finished the sixth grade. In order to be eligible, the students had to have scored on the Academic Promise Test (APT) (Psychological Corporation 1959) at the ninety-ninth percentile of sixth-grade norms on the number (arithmetic) subtest and at the ninety-ninth percentile of sixth-grade norms on either the abstract reasoning or the verbal subtest. In addition to the twenty-five students so identified there were six highly recommended, able students known by SMPY. Thus thirty-one students (nineteen boys and twelve girls) were invited to attend the class; fourteen boys and seven girls accepted. One boy [1] dropped out of the class during the first week and a second one did so within the first few weeks. One boy and two girls were added to the class in September. As a result, thirty-four students had the opportunity to attend SMPY's first fast-paced mathematics class; twenty-two stayed long enough to reap some benefits from it.

The initial success and progress of this class have been discussed previously (Fox 1974; Stanley 1976, pp. 156–59). Thus only a brief summary is supplied here. As noted, nineteen students stayed in the program and studied algebra I for nine weeks on Saturday mornings, two hours each week during the summer of 1972. Of those nineteen, fourteen scored high enough on the Educational Testing Service's (ETS) Cooperative Mathematics Tests: Algebra I (ETS 1962) to be able to continue in the program and study algebra II. The other five students were advised to take algebra I as seventh-graders the next year in school. At this time one other student chose to drop the class because her girlfriend did, but three others (two ex-seventh-graders and one ex-sixth-grader) were added. Thus in the fall of 1972 sixteen students (nine boys and seven girls) began the study of algebra II for two hours on Saturday mornings. This group was later split into a "fast" class or group and a "slow" class or group. The members of the slow group (two boys and four girls) had had trouble keeping up with the pace of the class or had scored low on the standardized Algebra II test. The goal of the slow group was to finish algebra II by June, 1973, when most of them would be completing the seventh grade. The goal of the fast group was to complete algebra II, college algebra, geometry, trigonometry, and analytic geometry by August, 1973. Of the ten persons in the fast group, two girls decided not to study plane geometry with the class during the summer of 1973.

Although the goals for this pioneering group were impressive, they were met successfully (see Fox 1974). The original Wolfson I class surpassed SMPY's expectations. In twelve to fourteen months, eight students completed 4½ years of mathematics, two completed 3½ years, and six completed 2 years.

More than nine years had passed since the inception of this class when this evaluation of its fairly long-term effects took place.

Longitudinal Follow-Up Procedure

In May 1980 two questionnaires were mailed to each of the thirty-four students who had been given the opportunity to attend the Wolfson I class. One of the questionnaires was an eight-page follow-up survey that had been sent to SMPY students in the fall when the students would have been graduated from high school (see Appendix 2.1). Most of the students had been mailed this questionnaire as part of the general follow-up conducted by SMPY. For information on how the follow-up was carried out and the general results for the whole SMPY group, see Benbow, chapter 2 of this volume. The students who were not in this follow-up or who had not responded were sent another follow-up questionnaire with a $5 inducement for completion, along with the second questionnaire, in May, 1980 (see Appendix 4.1). The additional three-page questionnaire brought each student's educational progress up to date as of the summer of 1980. An autographed copy of one of SMPY's volumes in the Studies in Intellectual Precocity series was offered as a compensation for completing that questionnaire. The response rates for the two questionnaires were 100 percent for the follow-up questionnaire and 94 percent for the additional Wolfson I questionnaire.

ANALYSIS

The resulting data were coded and keypunched onto the computer by use of the Filgen and Qgen systems (The Johns Hopkins University Computing Center). The students in the study were classified into four groups upon which the data analysis was performed using the SPSS program (Nie et al. 1975). The composition of the four groups can be seen in table 4.1. The student who had attended only one session of Wolfson I was excluded from all analyses. The following year he had attended the second fast-paced mathematics class conducted by SMPY (Wolfson II). It was felt that his inclusion for Wolfson I would bias the results.

TABLE 4.1. Classification of the Students Included in the Analysis Who Were Given the Opportunity to Attend Wolfson I (by Their Course of Action)

Group A		Group B	
Finished Wolfson I in the Fast Class[a]		Finished Wolfson I in the Slow Class	
	Number		Number
Boys	7	Boys	2
Girls	3	Girls	4
Total	10	Total	6
Group C		Group D	
Dropped Out or Were Asked to Leave Wolfson I		Did Not Attend Wolfson I	
	Number		Number
Boys	5	Boys	5
Girls	2	Girls	5
Total	7	Total	10

NOTE: To reduce bias, one boy was excluded from the analysis because he attended only one meeting of Wolfson I and later completed Wolfson II.
[a] Two girls in this group did not complete the whole sequence, because they did not attend the class meetings during the summer of 1973.

Results

SAT SCORES

Most of the students who were extended the opportunity to join Wolfson I participated in one of SMPY's talent searches, where they took the College Board's Scholastic Aptitude Test-Mathematics and -Verbal in January or February of 1973. Three were in SMPY's March, 1972, search. Their performance on the SAT in the talent search as either seventh- or eighth-graders and then later in high school is contrasted by group in table 4.2. Every group's mean SAT-M score in the talent search surpassed the mean score obtained in any of SMPY's talent searches (Benbow & Stanley 1980). Furthermore, the mean scores on the SAT of the groups in high school were much superior to the mean scores obtained in high school by the participants in the first three talent searches (Benbow, chapter 2 of this volume) and by college-bound seniors.

Although there were certain biases between the groups with respect to taking the SAT in a talent search (e.g., all ten members of Group A took the SAT, whereas only four of six — 67 percent — of Group B did), it seems that at the time of the talent search the members of Group A (the ones who completed Wolfson I in the fast class) received the highest SAT scores, followed by Group B (the ones who completed Wolfson I in the slow class). Groups C (who dropped out of or were asked to leave Wolfson I) and D (who did not attend Wolfson I) scored similarly on SAT-M (scoring

TABLE 4.2. SAT Scores at the Time of Talent-Search Participation and
as Reported in High School (by Group)

Group[a]	N	Mean SAT-M	Standard Deviation	Mean SAT-V	Standard Deviation	Mean of Year Taken[b]
			Talent Search			
A	10	633	64	487	78	73
B	4	563	86	525	76	73
C	5	488	53	382	67	73
D	5	492	85	420	46	73.4
			High School			
A	10	751	47	624	80	75.2
B	6	736	30	645	108	76.3
C	7	708	61	582	56	77.3
D	10	708	39	613	71	77.2

[a] For the meaning of A, B, C, and D here and in tables 4.2–4.8, see table 4.1.
[b] 1973 talent-search SAT scores were used if available.

approximately 140 points lower than Group A or 70 points lower than
Group B). The differences between the groups were significant by an
Analysis of Variance (ANOVA) ($F = 6.9$, $p < .01$). The talent search SAT-
V scores were also significantly different between groups by an ANOVA
($F = 3.8$, $p < .05$). Group B, followed by A, had the highest scores.

In high school there is a complicating factor when comparing performance on the SAT — the groups did not take the SAT at the same time.
Group A took their SATs in high school one year earlier, on the average,
than Group B, who took the SAT one year earlier than Groups C and D.
Yet on SAT-M Groups A and B scored essentially the same and superior to
Groups C and D, who scored similarly. The differences between the
groups were significant by an ANCOVA (analysis of covariance) controlling for year taken ($F = 3.7$, $p < .05$). On the SAT-V, however, Group B
scored better than the other three groups, but the mean difference between
groups was not significant.

MATHEMATICS COURSE-TAKING
IN HIGH SCHOOL

The mathematics course-taking in high school by the students in the
various groups is shown and contrasted in table 4.3. Because of the format
of Wolfson I, 80 percent of the fast group would have finished the 4½
years of precalculus mathematics, while 100 percent of the students in the
slow group should have finished algebra II. Later in high school all but one
(83 percent) of the students in the slow group finished the precalculus
sequence, and everyone in the fast group did. This percentage of students
reporting a completion of precalculus was much higher than for the other
groups.

TABLE 4.3. Reported High-School Mathematics Course-Taking (by Group)

Group	Taking Course/Total	Course Grade[a] Mean	Course Grade[a] Standard Deviation	Number of Years of Precalculus Courses Mean	Number of Years of Precalculus Courses Standard Deviation
A	10/10	–	–	4.5	0
B	6/6	3.4	0.6	4.3	0.3
C	7/7	3.6	0.6	4.0	0.5
D	10/10	3.6	0.6	3.9	0.6

		Course Grade[a] Mean	Course Grade[a] Standard Deviation	School Grade[b] Mean	School Grade[b] Standard Deviation
			Calculus I (Differential)		
A	9/10[c]	3.4	0.5	10.1	1.1
B	4/6	3.8	0.5	11.3	1.0
C	5/7	3.2	1.3	11.8	0.4
D	8/10	3.6	0.5	11.3	0.9
			Calculus II (Integral)		
A	9/10[c]	3.6	0.7	10.4	0.9
B	4/6	3.8	0.5	11.3	1.0
C	2/7	4.0	0	12.0	0
D	5/10	3.8	0.5	11.2	0.8

NOTE: None of the group differences in course grades and school grades was significant by an ANOVA.
[a] $4 = A; 3 = B; 2 = C; 1 = D; 0 = F.$
[b] 8 = eighth grade, etc.
[c] While still in high school the missing person took calculus at a college.

With regard to the next level of mathematics in high school, 100 percent of Group A completed one year of calculus (one person did so at a community college as a high-school student), whereas 67 percent, 29 percent, and 50 percent of Groups B, C, and D, respectively, did so (table 4.3). Not shown in Table 4.3 is that high-school mathematics enrichment courses were taken mostly by Group B.

The grades earned by the students in the mathematics classes were uniformly high. As expected, Group A students took their mathematics at an earlier age than did students in all the other groups. Group B students took precalculus mathematics, but not calculus or enrichment courses, earlier than either Group C or Group D students (table 4.3).

AP MATHEMATICS EXAMINATIONS

Of the mathematics courses taken in high school, the most advanced and difficult are those that have as their goal the taking of the Advanced Placement Program examinations. Students are offered their choice of two AP mathematics examinations, Level AB and the more advanced Level BC. A high score on the Level AB examination can yield credit for a one-

TABLE 4.4. Performance of the Groups on the Advanced Placement Program Mathematics Examinations (by Group)

Group	Taking Exam/ Total	Mean Score[a]	Standard Deviation	Mean of Year Taken
		Calculus AB		
A	3/10	3.7	0.6	75.3
B	2/6	4.0	1.4	76.5
C	2/7	3.5	0.7	78.0
D	1/10	4.0	−	78.0
		Calculus BC		
A	6/10	4.2	0.8	75.6
D	2/10	3.5	0.7	77.0

[a] Grades on the APP exams can range from 1 (the lowest possible) to 5 (the highest possible).

semester college course in calculus, while two semesters of credit in college calculus can be gained from success on the BC examination. Grades on these examinations range from 1 to 5, where 3, 4, or 5 are considered high. Ninety percent of the students in Group A took these exams, which is a higher percentage than for the other groups (see table 4.4). Group A took mostly the BC exam. This was not true for the other three groups. Furthermore, Group A took these exams earlier, on the average, than the other groups.

COLLEGE COURSES AS A HIGH-SCHOOL STUDENT

Some of the students took college courses on a part-time basis for college credit while they were still in high school. With respect to college courses, Group A, with a mean number of 4.8 taken, was much more active than Groups B, C, and D, which took a mean of 0, .14, and .3, respectively. Group A had taken at least sixteen times as many college courses as the other groups. College courses taken by the students in Groups C and D were mainly in the field of mathematics. Especially disappointing, however, is Group B's lack of use of this educational alternative, coupled with the fact that not one member of the group had taken the AP Calculus BC exam. They had been the poorer achievers in SMPY's first fast-paced mathematics class and continued to be so thereafter.

COLLEGE BOARD ACHIEVEMENT TESTS

The performance of the four groups on nine of the fifteen achievement tests of the College Board can be seen in table 4.5. These tests measure the students' achievement in a high-school subject, usually during the eleventh or twelfth grade.

TABLE 4.5. Reported Performance on the College Board's Achievement Tests Taken by at Least One Person (by Group)

Group	N	Mean Score[a]	Standard Deviation	Mean of Year Taken	Mean	Standard Deviation	Percentile Rank of SMPY Students' Scores
					National Sample of 1978 College-Bound Students Taking the Test		
				Math Level I			
A	1	800	—	76.0			99+
B	3	697	95	74.5	541	99	93
C	2	745	49	77.0			97
				Math Level II			
A	7	778	37	75.8			87
B	3	710	28	76.0	665	95	62
C	1	800	—	75.0			91
D	6	760	48	77.5			81
				English Composition			
A	6	683	102	75.8			94
B	4	655	41	76.3			90
C	4	589	169	76.5	512	105	74
D	4	727	17	77.5			98
				Biology			
A	1	710	—	77.0			92
B	2	555	78	75.0	544	111	50
				Chemistry			
A	4	630	99	75.5			67
B	1	540	—	77.0			40
C	2	620	71	76.5	577	102	63
D	3	727	47	77.7			91
				Physics			
A	2	670	85	77.0			72
B	2	545	92	75.5	591	106	35
				French			
C	2	615	35	76.5			72
D	2	640	28	77.5	552	109	75
				Spanish			
C	1	540	—	78.0	544	120	53
				Russian			
A	2	580	99	76.5	587	148	51

[a] The differences between groups were not significant.

Of special interest is the groups' performance on the mathematics achievement tests, Level I and the more difficult Level II. In table 4.5 it can be seen that all the groups scored extremely high. The mean scores are not far from the maximum score of 800, except for Group B's performance on Mathematics Level I, which they took at an early age. The percentile ranks of the mean scores were also high. Furthermore, the groups' mean score on Mathematics Level I was 189 points superior to the mean of a national sample of college-bound seniors, and on Mathematics Level II 96 points, also more than a standard deviation. Thus the performance of all the groups was excellent. Learning mathematics at a rapid pace is seen not to be detrimental to longer-term retention or achievement in mathematics, because if this were the case, we would expect Groups A and B to receive lower scores than the other two groups.

Several interpretations of the data can be made from the performance on the remaining achievement tests (see table 4.5). A high percentage of the students took the English Composition examination in high school. Group D made the best scores, but the members of Group D were also much older than the other groups' members when the test was taken. The mean difference between groups was significant by an ANCOVA controlling for year taken ($F = 3.6$, $p < .05$).

Another trend in the data of table 4.5 is that of the science examinations; Chemistry (with ten takers) was most popular. Performance on all the examinations was excellent and for the most part was above the means for a college-bound sample of high-school students (CEEB 1979).

AWARDS AND HONORS

In the two questionnaires the students were asked to report any awards and honors won, including National Merit Scholarship Corporation and mathematics contest participation. The National Merit competition is judged on the basis of high scores on the Preliminary Scholastic Aptitude Test.[2] All the groups, except perhaps C, did well in this competition (i.e., 100 percent of Group A, 66 percent of Group B, 75 percent of Group D, and 14 percent of Group C received at least a Letter of Commendation). Two members of Groups A and D did not take the PSAT.

With respect to scholastic awards and honors won in high school, 40 percent, 67 percent, 43 percent, and 80 percent of Groups A, B, C, and D, respectively, reported receiving at least one. In college the percentage of the groups' members reporting having received at least one award or honor ranged between 29 and 60 percent.

With regard to participation in mathematics contests (not including SMPY's talent searches), 60 percent of Group A reported having participated in at least one, while no one in Group B did and only 43 percent and 10 percent of Groups C and D, respectively, did.

COLLEGE ENTRANCE AND STATUS

Every student except one in Group C had entered a college or university on a full-time basis (see table 4.6). The students' ages at college entrance varied greatly, however. Group A was on the average two years ahead of Group B and at least three years ahead of Groups C and D in date of college entrance. Furthermore, the difference between groups in percentage of students entering college early is large (see column 10 of table 4.6). Of Group A, 90 percent entered early, while only 33 percent and 10 percent of Groups B and D, respectively, did so, and no one in Group C did. To test for significant differences between groups on date of college entrance, an ANOVA was performed. The difference was significant ($F = 9.7$, $p < .001$).[3] In addition, Group A students had on the average at least six times as many advanced-standing credits as students in the other groups when they began college. Appendix 4.2 updates where in college or graduate school each student in the four groups was as of the summer of 1980; clearly the students in the fast group are much ahead of members of the other groups.

COLLEGE INTELLECTUALISM AND STATUS SCORES

The colleges attended by the students were given, where available, an intellectualism and a status score obtained from the Astin (1965) scale. Astin (1965, p. 54) defines a four-year college with a high intellectualism score as having a student body that "would be expected to be high in academic aptitude (especially mathematical aptitude) and to have a high percentage of students pursuing careers in science and planning to go on for Ph.D. degrees." A four-year college with a high status score is defined as having a student body that "would be expected to have a high percentage of students who come from high socioeconomic backgrounds and who themselves aspire to careers in enterprising fields (lawyers, business executives, politicians)" (ibid.). The scores are T-scores having a mean of 50 and a standard deviation of 10.

The means of the college ratings by group were all above 50, but they were not significantly different from each other by group. The mean intellectualism scores ranged between 57 for Group C and 67 for Group A. Group A attended the most academically difficult colleges or universities,[4] followed by B, D, and C, in that order. In terms of the status scores, Group D came out highest, with a mean of 59, followed by A, B, and C, all with mean scores of 55. Clearly, the four groups attended intellectually and socially elite schools. Appendix 4.2 lists the colleges attended by the students.

TABLE 4.6. Year of Reported College Entrance and Comparison of Reported College Status at Time of Entrance and Degree of Educational Acceleration (by Group)

Group	Year of College Entrance						Mean of Entrance Year[b]	Standard Deviation	Percentage Entering Early	Mean Number of Advanced Standing Credits[c]	Standard Deviation
	1974	1975	1976	1977	1978[a]	1979					
A	2	1	4	1	2	0	75	1.4	90	24.7	11.9
B	0	0	2	0	4	0	77.3	1.0	33	2.0	3.1
C	0	0	0	0	6	0	78	0	0	3.4	3.8
D	0	0	0	1	6	3	78.2	0.5	10	4.1	7.7

Degree of Acceleration
(Percentage of Group)

Group	N	None	Some, But Less than One Year	At Least One Year, But Fewer than Three Years	Three Years or More	Mean[d, e]	Standard Deviation
A	10	0	10	20	70	2.6	0.7
B	6	50	17	33	0	0.8	1.0
C	7	29	43	29	0	1.0	0.8
D	10	30	50	20	0	0.9	0.7

[a] Expected year for most of these students.
[b] The difference between group means was significant (F = 9.7, p < .01).
[c] The difference between group means was significant (F = 5.0, p < .01).
[d] Acceleration was coded as follows:
0 = None
1 = Less than 1 year
2 = One year or more but fewer than 3
3 = Three years or more
[e] The difference between group means was significant (F = 13.7, p < .001).

TABLE 4.7. Reported Use of Accelerative Options

Group	N	Mean Number of Grades Skipped	Standard Deviation	Mean Number of College Credits Received from APP Exams
A	10	2.0	1.2	8.0
B	6	0.7	1.0	2.0
C	7	0.4	0.8	3.4
D	10	0.1	0.3	3.3

ACCELERATION

Each student was rated on the degree to which his or her educational progress had become accelerated eight years after the beginning of the Wolfson I class (see table 4.6). Members of Group A were much more accelerated than members of the other groups. In Group A 70 percent were accelerated by three or more years, while not one person in the other groups was. Members of all the other groups were, however, somewhat accelerated on the average, but no big differences can be seen between Groups B, C, and D. The differences between groups in acceleration were statistically significant ($F = 13.7$, $p < .001$).

The way the students' acceleration was achieved is shown and contrasted by group in table 4.7. Group A made use of all the options and to a much greater extent that did the other groups, which used the accelerative options to about the same degree. Not included in table 4.7 is the fact that Groups A and B had been initially accelerated in mathematics as part of the Wolfson I class. Appendix 4.2, where the status of each student's educational progress as of June, 1980, is shown, highlights the results of tables 4.6 and 4.7.

ACCELERANTS' VIEW OF ACCELERATION

The accelerated students in all groups were asked to rate how they felt their educational acceleration had affected their social and/or emotional development. They were also asked to reconsider their decision to accelerate. Overall, the students felt positive about their acceleration.

With regard to social and/or emotional development, only one (in Group C) of the twenty-two accelerants felt that acceleration had affected him much to the worse. This same person, however, would accelerate his educational progress again if he had a chance to reconsider the decision. In contrast, 18 percent of the accelerants felt acceleration had affected him/her much for the better. On the average, all the groups felt that acceleration had slightly benefited their social and/or emotional development and certainly had not hindered it. There were group differences, but they

Standard Deviation	Mean Number of Credits Received for College Work Completed in High School	Standard Deviation	Percentage Completing College in Fewer Than Four Years	Percentage Receiving Master's Degree Concurrently with Bachelor's
6.0	11.0	8.9	50	10
3.1	0	0	0	0
3.8	3.8	3.8	0	0
7.8	3.2	0	10	0

were not found to be significant by an ANOVA. It must be noted that Group A was much more accelerated than the other groups and still held overall positive feelings.

How did the accelerants reconsider their decision to accelerate? Most students would accelerate at least as much as they had already done. Only one student, who had skipped three grades and received a high number of college credits for AP work, would in retrospect accelerate somewhat less. Thus in conclusion it can be said that accelerated students tend to view acceleration as being beneficial.

COLLEGE MAJORS: SCIENCE
VERSUS MATHEMATICAL SCIENCES

At least 50 percent of students are majoring in either science (including engineering) or mathematical sciences in college (ranging from 50 percent for Group B to 80 percent for Group A). Mathematical sciences are most popular for Group A, with 50 percent majoring in them, while science is at least equally as popular for the other groups (ranging between 30 and 40 percent majoring in science for all four groups). For Group A, computer science is by far the most popular field. Each student's major is shown in Appendix 4.2.

COLLEGE COURSE-TAKING

The number of undergraduate courses taken in mathematics, science, and engineering by the summer of 1980 and the mean grades received by group can be seen in table 4.8. Even though they had the most advanced standing in mathematics, members of Group A had taken the greatest number (6.9) of mathematics courses by summer, 1980. This was also true for science and engineering. But of course Group A had been in college much longer. The differences between the groups in grades received were not significant, but the differences in number of courses taken in mathematics and engineering were (F = 5.1, $p < .01$ for mathematics and F = 4.6, $p < .01$ for engineering). Their mean grades were for the most part

TABLE 4.8. Reported Mathematics, Science, and Engineering Course-Taking in College (Full-Time Students, by Group)

Group	N	Mean Number of Mathematics Courses[a]	Standard Deviation	Mean Grade in Mathematics	Standard Deviation	Mean Number of Science Courses	Standard Deviation	Mean Grade in Science	Standard Deviation
A	9	6.9	4.1	3.0 (N = 8)	0.7	6.6	3.7	3.3 (N = 8)	0.4
B	6	4.0	2.9	3.0 (N = 5)	0.6	4.3	1.6	3.1 (N = 6)	0.7
C	6	3.2	1.2	3.3 (N = 6)	0.5	3.8	3.9	3.4 (N = 5)	0.5
D	9	1.9	1.5	3.1 (N = 7)	1.3	4.1	3.2	3.2 (N = 9)	0.6

	Mean Number of Engineering Courses[b]	Standard Deviation	Mean Grade in Engineering	Standard Deviation
A	5.7	5.5	3.2 (N = 7)	0.7
B	1.3	2.4	3.8 (N = 2)	0.2
C	1.0	2.5	2.5 (N = 1)	0
D	0.1	0.3	2.0 (N = 1)	0

[a] The differences between the groups were significant by an ANOVA (F = 5.1, $p < .01$).
[b] The differences between the groups were significant by an ANOVA (F = 4.6, $p < .01$).

64

above a *B,* and many courses were taken, except for in engineering for Groups B through D.

USE OF EDUCATIONAL OPPORTUNITIES

The students were asked to rate how well they had made use of all their available educational opportunities. For the students in all groups, the mean response was "above average." No significant differences emerged between the groups, although it would objectively seem that Group A had made the best use of all available educational opportunities.

EDUCATIONAL AND OCCUPATIONAL ASPIRATIONS

The educational aspirations for all students were for the most part high. The means for all groups were to obtain more than a master's degree. Not one student aspired to obtain less than a bachelor's degree. Only 51 percent of students in the general population aspire to obtain a bachelor's degree or more (Charles Kettering Foundation 1980).

The occupational status of each student's career goal was rated by the Reiss (1961) scale. The average status occupation for the norm group on this scale was 70, which is a score assigned to a nurse. On this scale the highest score given to an occupation was a dentist, with 93 points, and the lowest was to a tobacco laborer, with 20 points. For the students in the four groups the means of the occupational status of their career goal ranged from 81.5 (Group B) to 84.2 (Group C). Occupations falling into that range on the scale include engineers and college professors. Thus the students in all groups have high educational and occupational aspirations, with no significant group differences.

SMPY'S INFLUENCE

The final item of interest is how the students felt their association with SMPY had helped them educationally. Not unexpectedly, the students who had remained in Wolfson I felt that SMPY had helped them educationally more than did the students in the other groups ($t = 2.9, p < .01$). The students in Groups A and B felt that SMPY had helped them considerably, while Groups C and D felt that SMPY had helped them slightly more than not at all.

Summary

Participation in a fast-paced mathematics class for highly mathematically precocious junior-high-school students appears to have many long-term benefits, not only in time needed to complete the study of mathematics but also in time needed to complete a student's education. This has been demonstrated by this study and by the evaluation of the second fast-paced mathematics class, called Wolfson II (see Appendix 4.3). Because of the small number of students, however, most differences between the students participating at various levels were not found to be significant.

Most of the students who were extended the invitation to join the Wolfson I class participated in at least one of SMPY's talent searches. At the time of the talent search the students completing Wolfson I in the fast group received the highest SAT-M scores, followed by the students finishing in the slow group. The difference between groups was significant ($p < .01$). On SAT-V at talent-search participation the slow group, followed by the fast group, had the highest scores. Again, the difference between groups was significant ($p < .05$). In high school, when the SAT was taken again, no significant difference was found between the groups on SAT-V, but a significant difference was found on SAT-M ($p < .05$). Groups A and B received the higher scores. We do not know whether the students in the Wolfson I class earned significantly higher SAT-M scores in the talent search and in high school than the students who dropped out or did not participate because of their participation in the class or because they were initially abler. Most likely it is a combination of the two, since the students in Wolfson I also earned higher SAT-V scores,[5] but their superiority on SAT-V was not as great as that on SAT-M. Furthermore, all the students had met the same ability criteria before the class was begun. Therefore, the fast-math class itself may serve to boost the students' aptitudes for mathematics.

The mathematics course-taking in high school was obviously affected by Wolfson I. Many more of the students who stayed in the program finished calculus in high school. Furthermore, many more of the students who finished in the fast group took the AP mathematics examinations, especially Level BC, and took many more college mathematics courses (and other college courses) while still in high school. When the College Board's mathematics achievement tests were taken in high school, the students in all groups who took them tended to make quite high scores. Because Groups A and B did not score less well than Groups C and D (whose members did not participate in the fast-paced mathematics program), we conclude that having covered the content of the high-school mathematics curriculum in an accelerated manner did not hinder long-term retention or achievement or leave holes and gaps in students' knowledge. The scores on the other, nonmathematics, achievement tests were mostly above the mean score for college-bound high-school students.

The students who completed Wolfson I in the fast group became much more accelerated in their educational progress than the other students. The amount was more than could be accounted for by just the fact that the students were in Wolfson I. The difference between groups was significant

($p < .001$). On the average the accelerated students had positive feelings toward their acceleration. Most would do it over again, perhaps to an even greater extent.

All the students except one are attending or have attended college full time at, on the average, academically and socially elite schools. Most of the students majored in science or mathematically related fields. More of the students in the fast group majored in mathematically related fields than did those in the other groups. Furthermore, so far in college they had also taken more courses in science, mathematics, and engineering than students in the other groups. No significant differences were found between the groups in terms of educational aspirations and status of their career goals.

The most successful students in Wolfson I (i.e., the ten finishing in the fast group) had achieved much more by summer, 1980, than the six students who finished in the slow group. Since the slow group was comprised mostly of girls (4:2) and the fast group mostly of boys (7:3), this difference in achievement could perhaps be due partly to the unwillingness of girls to accelerate their educational progress, especially in mathematics (Fox 1976; Daggett, chapter 9 of this volume).

Thus a fast-paced mathematics class offered to mathematically precocious students does have educational benefits eight years after the class was conducted. The especially successful students in that class have achieved much more in high school and college than the students who did not participate but who had been essentially equally able (see Appendix 4.2).

Conclusions

How much did the actual procedures and content of the Wolfson I class help the members of Group A, who obviously have done extremely well academically thus far? As is inevitable in a study involving highly meaningful, demanding activities with human beings, one cannot fully disentangle the influences of general and special abilities, motivation, and facilitation by the student's family and teachers. Comparisons of the four Wolfson I groups help, especially because (as shown in table 4.2) ability differences in high school were not large.

The five boys and five girls who chose not to attend Wolfson I (Group D) seem to have done so mainly because they had competing activities in the summer of 1972. Not much time elapsed between the invitation to enroll and the June 24 starting date, so some youths — likely, those from the most affluent families — had made other plans. This inference receives some support from inspection in Appendix 4.2 of the colleges they later attended. As already noted, Group D students attended higher-status colleges than did students in Groups A, B, or C. As of the 1980–81 academic year not a single member of Group D was accelerated in college placement by age, and three of the ten were less than age-in-grade. In contrast, only one of the Group A students was not accelerated. All but one of the seven males were more than one year ahead of their age-mates. One earned his master's degree at age 19, another at age 20, and a third at age 21. One is the fourth youngest person to receive a bachelor's degree from Johns Hopkins in its 105-year history; until 1981 he was the youngest graduate since 1887 (Stanley & Benbow 1982).

Therefore, even though it is possible that superior motivation alone accounts for the splendid showing of Group A, we consider such an interpretation most implausible. What has been demonstrated clearly is that when highly able youths are offered the opportunity to forge ahead far faster and more rigorously in precalculus, many will accept the offer, and a considerable percentage of those will make mighty educational and professional strides, probably for the rest of their lives. This observation, based on the Wolfson I class, is amply supported by SMPY's many replications of and extensions of the fast-paced mathematics model in a wide variety of curricular situations (e.g., Keating, Wiegand, & Fox 1974; George & Denham 1976; Stanley 1976; Mezynski & Stanley 1980; Bartkovich & George 1980; Bartkovich & Mezynski 1981; Mezynski, McCoart, & Stanley, chapter 6 of this volume). It demonstrates the multiplicative effect of the accumulative advantage (here, participation in the special mathematics class) that Zuckerman (1977) describes as characterizing Nobel Laureates.

Of the three girls in Group A, two are accelerated one year each, both by finishing high school one year early. One girl in Group B finished college two years younger than average, as did one boy. One boy in Group C is accelerated one year in college – actually, by high-school entering rules in his state, by just two days, because he was born on January 2. As noted earlier, no one in Group D was accelerated. In agreement with these results, SMPY's researchers have usually found only a few girls accelerated even a single year by the time the baccalaureate is awarded; an appreciable percentage of the boys proceed far faster (see Daggett, chapter 9 of this volume).

There are some signs that this gender differential is changing, however. Twenty-five of the Johns Hopkins 632 fall of 1980 entrants were at least two years accelerated in grade placement relative to chronological age; 9 of them (36 percent) were female. This is slightly greater than the percentage of Johns Hopkins students who are female. One of these girls entered at age 13 with sophomore standing, having already completed one year each of college inorganic and organic chemistry, calculus, and biology, and one semester of physics.

Paradoxically, however, whereas seven of the twenty males in Groups

A through D attended Johns Hopkins, not a single one of the thirteen females did. The chi-square for this difference was 3.87, $p < .05$. That unintentional, unexpected side (or main?) effect of the Wolfson I recruitment and instruction suggests that ingratiating effects for an institution of having youngsters study at it may be related to gender. It will be interesting to compare the mathematics course results with those found for fast-paced verbal courses conducted by Johns Hopkins to see whether a similar pattern holds for them.

Notes

1. He later joined SMPY's second fast-paced mathematics class, Wolfson II (see Appendix 4.3).
2. The formula for qualifying as a semi-finalist is 2(PSAT-V score) + 1(PSAT-M score). The minimum composite score varies from state to state and is greatest in those states where the highest-scoring students reside.
3. Acceleration by the groups is discussed further later in this chapter.
4. Six of the ten students in Group A attended Johns Hopkins.
5. High verbal ability was found to be important for success in a fast-paced mathematics class (Fox 1974; George & Denham 1976).

References

Admissions Testing Program of the College Board. 1979. *ATP guide for high schools and colleges (1979–81)*. Princeton, N.J.: Educational Testing Service.

Astin, A. W. 1965. *Who goes where to college?* Chicago: Science Research Associates.

Bartkovich, K. G., and George, W. C. 1980. *Teaching the gifted and talented in the mathematics classroom*. Washington, D.C.: National Education Association.

Bartkovich, K. G., and Mezynski, K. 1981. Fast-paced precalculus mathematics for talented junior-high students: Two recent SMPY programs. *Gifted Child Quarterly* 25 (2, Spring): 73–80.

Benbow, C. P., and Stanley, J. C. 1980. Sex differences in mathematical ability: Fact or artifact? *Science* 210:1262–64.

Charles Kettering Foundation. 1980. *New Ways*. Spring-Summer, p. 8.

Educational Testing Service. 1962. *Cooperative Mathematics Tests: Algebra I*. Princeton, N.J.

Fox, L. H. 1974. Facilitating educational development of mathematically precocious youth. In *Mathematical talent: Discovery, description, and development,* ed. J. C. Stanley, D. P. Keating, and L. H. Fox, 47–69. Baltimore: Johns Hopkins University Press.

———. 1976. Sex differences in mathematical precocity: Bridging the gap. In *Intellectual talent: Research and development,* ed. D. P. Keating, 183–214. Baltimore: Johns Hopkins University Press.

George, W. C., and Denham, S. A. 1976. Curriculum experimentation for the mathematically talented. In *Intellectual talent: Research and development,* ed. D. P. Keating, 103–31. Baltimore: Johns Hopkins University Press.

Keating, D. P.; Wiegand, S. J.; and Fox, L. H. 1974. Behavior of mathematically precocious boys in a college classroom. In *Mathematical talent: Discovery, description, and development,* ed. J. C. Stanley, D. P. Keating, and L. H. Fox, 176–85. Baltimore: Johns Hopkins University Press.

Mezynski, K., and Stanley, J. C. 1980. Advanced placement oriented calculus for high school students. *Journal for Research in Mathematics Education* 11(5): 347–55.

Nie, N. H.; Hull, C. H.; Jenkins, J. G.; Steinbrenner, K.; and Bent, D. H. 1975. *SPSS: Statistical package for the social sciences.* 2d ed. New York: McGraw-Hill.

Psychological Corporation. 1959. *Academic Promise Test.* New York.

Reiss, A. J. 1961. *Occupations and social status.* New York: Free Press.

Stanley, J. C. 1976. Special fast-mathematics classes taught by college professors to fourth- through twelfth-graders. In *Intellectual talent: Research and development,* ed. D. P. Keating, 132–59. Baltimore: Johns Hopkins University Press.

Stanley, J. C., and Benbow, C. P. 1982. Using the SAT to find intellectually talented seventh graders. *College Board Review* 122:2–7, 26–27.

Zuckerman, H. 1977. *Scientific elite: Nobel laureates in the United States.* New York: Free Press.

APPENDIX 4.1: Supplementary Questionnaire Used to Update the Educational Progress of All the Students Eligible for the Wolfson I Class

THE JOHNS HOPKINS UNIVERSITY • BALTIMORE, MARYLAND 21218

STUDY OF MATHEMATICALLY PRECOCIOUS YOUTH (SMPY)

Please reply care of: DEPARTMENT OF PSYCHOLOGY

PROFESSOR JULIAN C. STANLEY, Director of SMPY

Ms. LOIS S. SANDHOFER, B.A., Administrative Assistant

127 Ames Hall, (301) 338-7087

Mr. WILLIAM C. GEORGE, Ed. M., Associate Director

125 Ames Hall, (301) 338-8144

Ms. CAMILLA P. BENBOW, M.A., Assistant Director

126 Ames Hall, (301) 338-7086

QUESTIONNAIRE FOR EVALUATING SMPY'S FAST-PACED MATHEMATICS PROGRAM

Please fill out carefully and completely all of the questionnaire below that applies to you. Please print or type all answers and send the fully completed questionnaire as soon as possible to the address on the letterhead. All information will be kept strictly confidential; you will not be publicly identified with the information herein in any way.

NAME: _____
         First   Middle   Last   (Maiden if applicable)

Permanent Address: _____ Telephone: (___) _____
                    Street   City   State   Zip   (Area Code)

Temporary Address if different from above: _____
                                                        Street

_____ Telephone (___) _____
    City   State   Zip   (Area Code)

1. Are you currently employed full-time? (Circle one.)   Yes   No

   If yes, please supply the following information about your present and past post-high school occupations in chronological order.

	Type of Occupation	Duties Involved	Employer	Dates of Employment
1)				
2)				
3)				

   If you need more space, please continue on a separate sheet.

2. Please check the box that applies to you with regard to your attendance at an institution of higher education (including technical school).

   ___ I am currently a full-time undergraduate student.

   ___ I have graduated from college and am not furthering my education at the present time.

   ___ I have graduated from college and am furthering my education on a part-time basis.

   ___ I have graduated from college and am (or will be this fall) furthering my education on a full-time basis.

71

____ I am currently a part-time undergraduate student after having attended full-time.

____ I am a part-time undergraduate student.

____ I am not currently enrolled as a student but was previously.

____ I am not and have not been enrolled as a student in an institution of higher education. (Go to question 3.)

a. Which school are you currently, will you, or were you attending? (Do not list schools from which you have transferred.) _____

b. Dates of attendance:_____

c. If you have graduated, please indicate the date of graduation: _____

From which school if different from above? _____ Month/Year

d. What is or was your undergraduate major? _____

e. If you have switched majors in college, please list the previous one(s) in chronological order. _____

f. If you are furthering your education beyond college, please name the planned field. _____

g. Please list the titles of the mathematics course(s) you have already taken as an undergraduate (including your grade in this course(s) and the semester(s) of attendance.) If you prefer, send us a copy of your transcript.

Mathematics Course	Final Course Grade	Semester(s) of Attendance (Include semester and date)
1.		
2.		
3.		
4.		
5.		
6.		

If you have taken more mathematics, please continue on a separate sheet.

h. Please list the title(s) of the science course(s) (including engineering and computer science) you have already taken as an undergraduate in college, your final grade in these courses, and the semester(s) of attendance. If you prefer, send us a copy of your transcript

Science Course	Final Course Grade	Semester(s) of Attendance (Include Semester and Date)
1.		
2.		
3.		
4.		
5.		
6.		

If you have taken more science, please continue on a separate sheet.

i. Please list any awards, honors, or scholarships you may have won as an undergraduate or graduate of college (Phi Beta Kappa, etc.). _____

3. Please list the college-level mathematics courses (if any) that you are planning to take in the future. _____

4. Please describe your career goal (i.e., professor of mathematics or a practicing pediatrician). _____

5. Have you been accelerated in your educational progress (circle one)? Yes No

    a. If no, do you wish you would have been? Yes No (Circle one.)

    b. If yes to Question 5, please circle the letter of the sentences that are applicable to you and then complete them.

        1) I skipped the following grades: _____

        2) I took _____ Advanced Placement Program (APP) examinations for which I
           (Number)
           received _____ credits of advanced placement in college.
           (Number)

        3) I was accelerated in subject matter placement in _____ different subjects.
           (Number)

        4) I took college courses on a part-time basis as a secondary school student, for which I received _____ credits of advanced standing in college.

        5) I finished college in ___ years, rather than 4.

        6) I received my master's degree concurrently with my bachelor's.
           (Circle one.) Yes No

        7) Other (Departmental examination, etc. Please specify.): _____
           _____

    c. If you were to reconsider your decision to accelerate, which one of the following would best describe your thoughts (check the most appropriate box)?

        ☐ I would not accelerate my education at all.

        ☐ I would accelerate my education somewhat but not as much as I have done.

        ☐ I would accelerate my education to the degree which I have already done.

        ☐ I would accelerate my education somewhat more than what I have already done.

        ☐ I would accelerate my education much more.

6. How important do you feel mathematics will be or is in your career? (Circle one.)
                    Very   Fairly   Slightly   Not very   Not at all

7. If you have taken the Graduate Record Examinations (GRE), please supply the following: GRE Quantitative Score___ GRE Verbal Score ___
                    Advanced test score _____ in _____ area.

I hereby certify that I have read over my responses carefully and thoroughly. They are as complete and accurate as I can make them.

Please return this questionnaire to: _____
Ms. Camilla Benbow   Signature
SMPY, Dept. of Psychology
The Johns Hopkins University
Baltimore, Maryland 21218

73

APPENDIX 4.2: Educational and Occupational Status of the Students Eligible for the Wolfson I Class as of June, 1980

Student (Sex) (Date of Birth)	Undergraduate Institution	Year Graduated	Major	Graduate Institution	Field or Degree	Employer
Fast Group (N = 10)						
M 4/10/63	Johns Hopkins University	Senior	Mathematical Sciences			
M 8/9/60	Johns Hopkins University	B.Engr.S., 79	Mechanics and Material Sciences	Part-time, Carnegie-Mellon	Master's in Mech. Eng.	Electrical/Mechanical Engineer, Westinghouse
F 8/6/60	Princeton University	Junior	Architecture			
M 5/5/60	Johns Hopkins University	B.A., 79	Electrical Engineering, Biomedical Engineering	Drexel Institute	Master's, Elec. Engr., 12/81	Electrical Engineer, AAI Corporation
F 5/2/60	University of Virginia	Senior	Russian			
M 4/12/60	Johns Hopkins University	B.A., 78	Mathematical Sciences	University of California, Santa Barbara	Computer Science, Master's, 81	Westinghouse
M 12/4/59	Johns Hopkins University	B.A., 1/77	Quantitative Studies	University of Chicago, Business	M.B.A., 1979 Ph.D. in Finance, 12/81	
M 10/29/59	Johns Hopkins University	B.A., 80	Mathematical Sciences	Carnegie-Mellon	Computer Science	Assoc. Engineer, JHU Applied Physics Lab.
F 2/1/59	University of Michigan	M.S.Engr., 80 B.S.Engr., 80	Computer Engineering			
M 9/18/58	University of Steubenville	B.A., 79	Mathematics			Computer Programmer, Mellon Bank NA

Student (Sex) (Date of Birth)	Undergraduate Institution	Year Graduated	Major	Graduate Institution	Field or Degree	Employer
			Slow Group (N = 6)			
F 11/12/60	Virginia Polytechnic Institute	Withdrew, 5/79[a]	Forestry			Paid by CETA to take accounting and office skill courses
M 9/20/60	Johns Hopkins University	B.A., 80	Economics	University of Pennsylvania	Law	
F 5/30/60	College of Wooster	B.A., 80	Religion	Yale University	Social Work	
F 5/20/60	University of Pennsylvania	Junior	Computer Science, Engineering			
M 5/6/60	University of Delaware	Junior	Civil Engineering			
F 1/5/60	Virginia Polytechnic Institute	Junior	Civil Engineering			

[a] Later entered The Bryant Institute, Tulsa, Oklahoma; graduated in data processing, 9/82.

Student (Sex) (Date of Birth)	Undergraduate Institution	Year Graduated	Major	Graduate Institution	Field or Degree	Employer
			Group That Dropped Wolfson I (N = 7)			
M 10/5/61	Did not attend[a]					
M 1/2/61	University of Maryland, College Park	Junior	Electrical Engineering			
M 10/12/60	University of Delaware	Junior	Chemistry			
M 9/20/60	University of Virginia	Junior	Economics			
F 4/11/60	University of Delaware	Junior	Accounting			
F 2/29/60	James Madison University	Junior	English			
F 1/30/60	University of Richmond	Junior	Political Science, Sociology			

[a] Later entered and then withdrew from the University of Tampa, Florida.

Student (Sex) (Date of Birth)	Undergraduate Institution	Year Graduated	Major	Graduate Institution	Field or Degree	Employer
Group That Never Enrolled in Wolfson I ($N = 10$)						
M 12/28/60	Wharton School, University of Pennsylvania	Junior	Accounting and Finance			
M 10/8/60	Youngstown State	Withdrew				
F 8/8/60	University of Denver	Junior	Biology			
M 6/9/58	Harvard	Sophomore	Biochemistry			
F 5/9/60	University of Chicago	Sophomore	Mathematics			
F 4/2/60	Yale University	Junior	Biology			
M 2/26/60	Towson State University	Junior	Accounting, Computer Science			
M 2/21/60	Maryland Institute College of Art	Junior	Graphic Design			
M 2/6/60	Georgia Institute of Technology	Junior	Mechanical Engineering			
F 1/6/60	Western Maryland College	Junior	English and German			

APPENDIX 4.3: Evaluation of the Wolfson II Class

In evaluating the long-term effects of SMPY's fast-paced mathematics classes, we followed up the students who were eligible for and participated in Wolfson I, the results of which were discussed in this chapter, and also the students eligible for and participating in the second class of this kind conducted by SMPY (Wolfson II). The initial selection procedures and results for this class can be found in George and Denham (1976). The students in the Wolfson II class were somewhat older (mainly end-of-year eighth-graders) than those in Wolfson I. Furthermore, to be eligible for the class the students had to have scored at least 500 on SAT-M, 400 on SAT-V, and above a combined score criterion on two standardized tests of knowledge of algebra I. Of the ninety-two students eligible for the class, thirty-three participated. All but two students began to study algebra II in June, 1973.

George and Denham (1976) discussed the success of this class. In summary, twenty-three students of the thirty-three (the fast group) mastered algebra II and III and plane geometry. Among the twenty-three, fifteen students also mastered trigonometry, and fourteen analytic geometry. As a result, twelve students were able to enter a calculus class in the fall of 1974, 120 class hours after the start of algebra II. An additional five students in Wolfson II (but in its slow group) successfully mastered algebra II and plane geometry. One person among them also completed algebra III. Five youths dropped the class before completing the study of algebra II.

The longitudinal evaluation of Wolfson I and II resulted in quite similar findings. The most successful students in both classes (i.e., the fast groups) achieved much more in high school and became more accelerated than the other students eligible for or participating in the classes. Furthermore, the students completing the program in the slow groups were more successful than the students who dropped the classes or never enrolled.

It was found that the students in the fast group were somewhat abler than the other students on the SAT in high school but not on the College Board's achievement tests. It was of special interest to take note of the students' performance on the College Board's Math Level I and the more difficult Math Level II achievement tests. On both tests most of the students earned nearly the top score possible. Thus we can conclude with confidence that learning mathematics at a rapid and accelerative pace is not detrimental to long-term achievement or learning. The opposite seems to be true, because many more of the successful students in the Wolfson classes than students not in the classes took calculus in high school, took the AP examinations in calculus, and in college took more courses in mathematics. In addition, those students showed more interest in mathematics.

There was one major difference between the Wolfson I and II classes. This was in terms of acceleration. The successful students in Wolfson I were much further ahead educationally (course-work and acceleration) than the successful students in Wolfson II, although both fast groups were much further ahead of the other groups. This difference might be related to the age difference between the two classes. Members of Wolfson II were older than members of Wolfson I when they began the class. Perhaps by the time a bright student reaches the end of the eighth grade he or she has lost some motivation because of the extra time spent in a classroom not geared to his or her intellectual level. Thus it seems more beneficial or necessary to find and educationally stimulate students earlier than the eighth grade.

Finally, members of both classes felt that their association with SMPY had been of considerable help to them, and they viewed their acceleration as benefiting them positively.

The fast-paced mathematics classes did have long-term educational benefits. Since the students involved also had positive feelings toward their experiences in class and with SMPY, we conclude that this is one excellent way of catering to the differential needs of the intellectually talented.

5 Fast-Paced Mathematics Classes for a Rural County

JOHN F. LUNNY

Abstract

A fast-paced mathematics program adapted from the SMPY model was developed to meet the needs of mathematically talented students in a rural county. After meeting screening requirements, eighth-grade students are selected on the basis of PSAT scores. Combining enrichment and acceleration, the program offers weekly two-hour evening classes in mathematics to students who take related classes during the day. The entire precalculus sequence as well as computer science can be completed at the end of three years in this program. Calculus can then be pursued for college credit, free of charge, at the local community college. The use of pre- and post-tests with appropriate review sessions enables the students' progress to be monitored closely. Approximately 25 percent of each year's initial program enrollment completes the three-year program, through computer science. Thus SMPY's model works fairly effectively even when the number of students is small.

Charles County is a rural county located on the Southern Maryland peninsula approximately thirty-five miles southeast of the District of Columbia. In 1968 the student population was 11,692; according to the 1980 census it was then 17,641. The average county student's intelligence quotient (I.Q.) on the Cognitive Ability Test is 102.5. Only about 8 percent of the county's senior-high-school population is college bound.

Development of a Fast-Paced Mathematics Program

Because a target group of 24 Charles County students were identified as mathematically talented in SMPY's 1974 talent search (Keating 1976), a "Fast-Math Program" was developed to meet their needs. This program was modeled after the SMPY fast-paced accelerative mathematics classes (Fox 1974; George & Denham 1976). The goal was to prepare these mathematics students for college.

STUDENT SELECTION

The first class consisted of students from the SMPY 1974 talent search. These students had initially scored in the top 2 percent nationwide on the mathematics subtest of a standardized achievement test (Keating 1976). Then, in the talent search, as seventh- or eighth-graders, the students took the College Board's Scholastic Aptitude Test-Mathematics. Charles County students scoring at least 400 on SAT-M, a score that is 10 points above the mean for a national high-school sample of eleventh- and twelfth-graders (CEEB 1978), were invited to join the class.

During the subsequent years it was decided that any eighth-grade student meeting these requirements would be an eligible participant: (1) scored in the upper 4 percent (using national norms) on a standardized mathematics achievement test; (2) received As on classroom tests; (3) had an intelligence quotient of 130 or better; and (4) was recommended by the classroom teacher and school guidance counselor on the basis of maturity. Parental permission was also required. Participants satisfying these requirements are given the Preliminary Scholastic Aptitude Test. Any eager and willing student who scores at least forty on the mathematics portion and thirty-six on the verbal section of the PSAT and has a combined mathematics and verbal score of eighty or greater is invited. There is, however, some leeway in these requirements.

THE PROGRAM

The program is a combination of enrichment and acceleration. Students are offered a special two-hour-per-week course beginning with algebra I. This is followed by algebra II, college algebra, and computer science. Simultaneously, during their regular school day, the students are offered geometry, trigonometry, and analytic geometry. Hence at the end of three years the students have satisfied all the prerequisites for calculus. A flow chart of the sequence of classes is shown in figure 5.1.

The weekly two-hour class is held outside the regular school session, and no limit is placed on the duration of the course. A pre-test is given in

FIGURE 5.1. Flow Chart for Sequence of Courses in the
Charles County Fast-Math Program

	Year 1	Year 2	Year 3	Year 4
Day Class	Algebra I	Geometry	Trigonometry, Analytic Geometry	Free
Evening Class, First Semester		Algebra II	Computer Science	Calculus
Evening Class, Second Semester	Algebra I	College Algebra	Computer Science	Calculus

which content weaknesses are noted. The teacher then covers the content
for the course, giving special emphasis to the students' weak areas. When
the teacher decides that sufficient time has elapsed for mastery of the
course content, a post-test is administered. Usually between ten and twelve
weeks is sufficient time to master the material. This model also recognizes
that a student may drop out of the Fast-Math Program. If that occurs at
any level, the student just continues with his or her daytime class schedule
without embarrassment or loss of sequentiality.

At this point the fast-math student who has completed the Fast-Math
Program has also completed the mathematics course offerings at the high-
school level. Calculus is not a part of the high-school mathematics curriculum in Charles County. So, at the conclusion of their three-year program, as high-school juniors, fast-math students take calculus, free of
charge, for college credit at the Charles County Community College.

Currently five classes are following this model with teachers who have
competency in the content area, who are flexible in presenting the subject,
and who can creatively motivate the minds of the students in an atmosphere of productivity without being repetitive.

THE TESTING PROGRAM AND
FOLLOW-UP PROCESS

The importance of pre-tests and post-tests has been mentioned. The
Cooperative Mathematics Tests (CMT) series developed by the Educational Testing Service in Princeton, New Jersey, are used in the pre-testing
and post-testing program. Pre-test results serve as a guide in the selection
and development of the mathematics content for the class, and post-test
results are used for evaluation. The mathematics specialist assumes the
responsibility for post-testing. Thus objective decisions can be made
regarding whether certain students should continue in the program. For
grading purposes, achievement at the ninety-third percentile or better on
the forty-item CMT series is equivalent to an *A* grade; eighty-seventh
percentile or better is equivalent to a *B*; and a seventy-fifth percentile or

better is equivalent to a *C*. This performance puts the students in the seventy-fifth through ninety-ninth percentiles on national norms of students who have taken the course for an entire year.

Following each test students attend a review session conducted by the specialist in which all test items that were missed by four or more students are explained in detail. The grades are then sent to parents and to home-based schools to be placed on students' permanent records. A Carnegie unit of credit is received by students upon successful completion of each course.

Standards for the course are determined using the raw score and the national norm. If these standards are not met by 80 percent of the class a follow-up reteaching session is immediately initiated. The specialist enters as teacher and reviews with the group the total content area for that course. This review takes four to eight weeks. At the end of this session CMT Form B is administered. The scoring and standards for this second test are identical to those for the first. Those students who fail to meet the expected achievement level are advised to leave the Fast-Math Program.

EVALUATION

A review of the successive fast-math groups of Charles County indicates that the goals of the program have been reached. Flow charts of the progress made by the first three groups (which began classes in 1974, 1975, and 1976) can be seen in tables 5.1, 5.2, and 5.3. The most successful class was the first; approximately 40 percent of its initial enrollment completed the program (see table 5.1). Most of the drop-outs left at the first semester of the calculus level of the program. The remainder of the drop-outs from the class occurred because, unlike the first year, when the students are self-motivated and highly motivated by their parents, the second year finds many parents considering it a chore to transport their children on a weekly

TABLE 5.1. Progress of the First Fast-Math Class in Charles County

Step in Selection	Criteria	Total Students	Mean	Standard Deviation	Percentage Proceeding to Next Step
Entered algebra I	SAT-M $\geq$ 500	23	520.00	54.51	100.0
Algebra I: post-test	CMT $\geq$ 28/40	23	33.34	4.10	100.0
Geometry: post-test	CMT $\geq$ 58/80	22	47.65	10.13	95.6
Algebra II: post-test	Grade *A, B*	22			95.0
Trigonometry: post-test	Grade *A, B, C*	21			91.3
Analytic geometry: post-test	Grade *A, B*	20			84.7
College algebra: post-test	Grade 28/40	20	24.2	5.96	84.7
Computer science: post-test	Grade *A, B*	20			84.7
Entered calculus	Grade *A, B*	14			60.8
Calculus: post-test	Grade *A, B*	9			39.1

TABLE 5.2. Progress of the Second Fast-Math Class in Charles County

Step in Selection	Criteria	Total Students	Mean	Standard Deviation	Percentage Proceeding to Next Step
Entered algebra I	PSAT-M ≥ 40	20	45.86	4.64	100.0
	PSAT-V ≥ 36		40.71	3.73	
Algebra I: post-test	CMT ≥ 28/40	20	30.76	4.88	65.0
Algebra II: post-test	CMT ≥ 26/40	13	29.92	4.94	65.0
Geometry: post-test	CMT ≥ A, B, C	13			45.0
Trigonometry: post-test	Grade A, B, C	9			35.0
Analytic geometry: post-test	Grade A, B	7			35.0
College algebra: post-test	Grade 28/40	7	20.91	3.82	35.0
Computer science: post-test	Grade A, B	5			

TABLE 5.3. Progress of the Third Fast-Math Class in Charles County

Step in Selection	Criteria	Total Students	Mean	Standard Deviation	Percentage Proceeding to Next Step
Entered algebra I	PSAT-M ≥ 40	16	28.76	4.73	100.0
	PSAT-V ≥ 36				
Algebra I: post-test	CMT ≥ 28/40	16	33.07	3.64	87.5
Algebra II: post-test	CMT ≥ 26/40	14	25.75	6.13	56.2
Geometry: post-test	CMT ≥ A, B, C	9			25.0
Trigonometry: post-test	Grade A, B, C	4			25.0
College algebra: post-test	Grade 28/40	4	24.0	5.93	25.0
Computer science: post-test	Grade A, B	4			

basis to the class site, which is in excess of twenty miles from their homes. While some of the students in the first class were college bound, their academic goals did not include a high level of mathematics. The preferred course was to enter the community college prior to setting fixed goals for future careers. Of the nine students who completed the calculus course, six students (one girl and five boys) attended a four-year college. Of the remaining three students, one girl attended community college, one girl married, and one boy entered the family business.

Originally seventh- and eighth-grade students were permitted to enter the program. Early in the development of the program, however, we found that many of the seventh-grade students dropped out while taking algebra II. Therefore at present only eighth-grade students are screened for this program. This accounts for the drop-out rate of the second class between algebra I and algebra II. There is also a significant rate of dropping-out between algebra II and college algebra (see figure 5.1). Both are evening courses. These students are also taking geometry in their day-time mathematics classes. The main cause of dropping the program for the second class is peer pressure. Recognizing the opposite sex for the first time, not wanting to appear smarter than the boyfriend, and participation in sports are some of the other reasons given for dropping out. Approximately 5 percent of the student drop-outs are due to the individual's inability to cope with the content area or his or her unwillingness to work alone. The remaining classes follow the same pattern. In the second and third classes no students pursued calculus as part of this program. However, several students were college bound.

Each year this county has an average of eight students who complete the program through computer science, which is approximately 25 percent of the initial enrollment for that particular group. Charles County feels that this is a sufficient return for the investment in the program.

Summary

"In retrospect the following five items seem needed for a successful class: (1) the identification of qualified, mathematically oriented, and highly apt students through appropriately difficult tests of mathematical and verbal reasoning ability and prerequisite achievement; (2) the selection of a bright, dynamic, assertive teacher who can create an atmosphere of fun and productivity while introducing the mathematical reasoner to challenging materials at a rapid-fire pace; (3) compatible learning styles between student and teacher; (4) the development of good study habits, learning new materials by doing homework well; and (5) voluntary participation and self-motivation by the students" (George 1976). All five of these ingredients can be found in the Fast-Math Program in Charles County. We are giving the students a better foundation in the knowledge of mathematics than they previously received. Our county is raising its standards so that we are reasonably equal to our peers in other counties in the state of Maryland and even in the nation. As a result, we have broadened our own educational system.

References

College Entrance Examination Board. 1978. *Guide to the admissions testing program, 1978–1979.* Princeton, N.J.: Educational Testing Service.

Educational Testing Service. 1962. *Cooperative Mathematics Tests.* Princeton, N.J.

Fox, L. H. 1974. A mathematics program for fostering precocious achievement. In *Mathematical talent: Discovery, description, and development,* ed. J. C.

Stanley, D. P. Keating, and L. H. Fox, 101–25. Baltimore: Johns Hopkins University Press.

George, W. C. 1976. Accelerating mathematics instruction for the mathematically talented. *Gifted Child Quarterly* 20 (3, Fall): 246–61.

George, W. C., and Denham, S. A. 1976. Curriculum experimentation for the mathematically talented. In *Intellectual talent: Research and development,* ed. D. P. Keating, 103–31. Baltimore: Johns Hopkins University Press.

Keating, D. P. 1976. Discovering quantitative precocity. In *Intellectual talent: Research and development,* ed. D. P. Keating, 23–31. Baltimore: Johns Hopkins University Press.

6

Helping Youths Score Well on AP Examinations in Physics, Chemistry, and Calculus

KAREN MEZYNSKI,
JULIAN C. STANLEY, and
RICHARD F. McCOART

Abstract

Special supplementary courses in physics, chemistry, and calculus were developed to prepare mathematically apt high-school students for the AP examinations in those areas. The courses, texts, and instructional approaches are described. Overall, SMPY students who remained in the classes throughout the year scored as high as or higher than the average highly able student taking the examination; most scored well enough to qualify for college credit. The students for whom the AP-level classes proved most beneficial were young, oriented toward careers in science or mathematics, academically motivated, and highly able mathematically. Several specific recommendations for improving future courses of this type are offered.

Many intellectually talented students find that the level and speed of instruction offered in the typical secondary school do not challenge them. Fast-paced instruction is one potential solution (see Fox 1974; George 1976; George & Denham 1976; Stanley 1976; Bartkovich & George 1980; Mezynski & Stanley 1980; Bartkovich & Mezynski 1981), and there are many others (e.g., early graduation from high school, taking college courses part time while still in high school). A particularly feasible option for many is the Advanced Placement Program (AP), which was begun by the College Board in 1955 (Benbow & Stanley 1978; Hanson 1980). Through the AP, high-school students are able to do college-level course-work and receive college credit by examination in a wide range of subjects.

In this chapter we discuss three experimental AP classes that were conducted by the Study of Mathematically Precocious Youth during the 1979–80 academic year. These were physics (Level C, both parts: mechanics, and electricity and magnetism), chemistry, and mathematics Level BC (the more comprehensive of two calculus programs offered by AP).

Earlier AP Classes

The 1979–80 classes were not the first AP courses sponsored by SMPY. Supplementary AP calculus classes were held during the 1974–75 and 1975–76 school years. The details and results of those classes are discussed in Stanley (1976, pp. 146–50) and Mezynski and Stanley (1980). In general, the students became well prepared for the AP examination in Level BC mathematics: the vast majority of them scored well enough to qualify for two semesters of college credit. Students in both classes received higher scores than high-school students who had not received the supplemental instruction.

A third AP calculus class was conducted during the 1978–79 school year. Results from this class have not been formally reported elsewhere and are therefore summarized herein and in table 6.1.

Although the previous two classes had been taught by a college professor, this one was taught by two college undergraduates (both of whom had prior "fast-paced" teaching experience from SMPY-sponsored precalculus classes). The students were all quite young, even by the stan-

TABLE 6.1. 1978–79 AP Calculus Students

Student	Age[a]	Grade in School	Score[b]	May, 1979, AP Calculus BC Grade
1	12, 10	8	129	5
2	13, 7	9	189	5
3	13, 11	10	150	5
4	11, 8	9	124	4
5	13, 5	9	114	4
6	14, 7	9	85	3
7	14, 8	10	100	3
8	15, 11	10	101	3

[a] As of September 1, 1978, in years and nearest month.
[b] Possible score ranges: 5: 127–210; 4: 103–26; and 3: 79–102.

dards of SMPY's first calculus class. In September of 1978 the youngest student (who was also the only female) was 11 years, 8 months old; only one student in the class had reached the age of 15. The participants had received most of their precalculus instruction during SMPY's 1978 summer mathematics institute (see Bartkovich & Mezynski 1981).

All eight students who enrolled in the course took the Level BC mathematics examination in May of 1979. Three students received the highest possible score of 5 (see table 6.1). A 14-year-old boy earned one of the highest point scores in the country (189 points on a 210-point scale, where only 127 points were needed for a 5). No student scored lower than 3 on the 1-to-5 scale, which is high enough to earn credit for two semesters of calculus at most colleges.

RATIONALE FOR THE 1979–80 CLASSES

The results of the three previous AP calculus classes indicated that talented young students could indeed benefit from college-level instruction in mathematics. Not surprisingly, many of the students identified by SMPY as being mathematically able also showed a strong interest in the sciences. It seemed reasonable to offer courses that would give such students a solid foundation in core science subjects (chemistry and physics). AP-level courses in these subjects are less likely to be offered in high schools than are AP calculus or biology. When AP science courses are available, typically the high-school level course is a prerequisite, so a student must spend two school years on that subject. The performance of students in earlier calculus classes indicated that, with appropriately paced instruction, highly able students might successfully consolidate those two years of instruction into one year.

Students were expected at least to be enrolled in their high-school-level course, or, preferably, to have completed it. The students in chemistry and physics had to obtain laboratory experience outside of SMPY's course, since no laboratory work was included. The purpose of all three courses was to provide introductory college honors-level instruction in order to give all students excellent preparation for the AP examination.

Overview of the AP Courses

SMPY's ideal target population was junior- and senior-high-school students who were eager to meet the challenge of college-level course-work and who had shown they were capable of such work. SMPY notified more than 400 high-scoring students from its 1976–77, 1977–78, and 1978–79 talent searches about the AP course offerings. Unfortunately, no talent searches had been conducted by SMPY during the 1974–75 and 1975–76 school years. Those students would have been in the eleventh or twelfth grade and the most likely ones to take advantage of these courses. SMPY found a low response from the younger students (eighth-, ninth-, and tenth-graders). Since so few students enrolled, SMPY extended the opportunity to enroll to older students from Baltimore area high schools. For the high-school students, the following Scholastic Aptitude Test (SAT) scores were suggested as minimal qualifications for enrollment: a mathematics (SAT-M) score of at least 600, and a combined SAT-M and verbal (SAT-V) score of at least 1,000. Consequently, roughly one-half of each class was composed of students of the regular age for the course-work, some of whom were only marginally qualified to participate. The ages and grade levels of the students who enrolled were quite diverse. Ages ranged from a 12-year-old female in physics to an 18-year-old male in calculus. With respect to grade placement, the range was eighth through twelfth.

The tuition charged in all three courses was the same: a total of $100 for the two semesters. In addition, students paid for their own textbooks and were responsible for the AP examination fee ($32). Tuition was low because most of the costs were absorbed by National Science Foundation funding.[1]

The classes were scheduled at nonoverlapping times to allow highly motivated students to enroll in more than one of them. Prior to the first instructional meeting, students in all classes attended a two- to three-hour testing session in which several aptitude and achievement measures were administered.

All three courses were taught by college teachers; the professor who had conducted SMPY's first two calculus classes taught that course again. Having taught the same material in college introductory classes, each instructor had clearly defined criteria by which to monitor students' progress. In many cases the lectures were the same ones the instructors used in their college classes, and the in-class examinations often contained many of the same test items. The instructors covered the topics listed in the AP syllabus and in some cases taught additional topics not listed in the AP syllabus. For example, optics and most of modern physics are not included in AP physics Level C, but the professor believed those topics were essential for a sound first-year college physics course.

Each instructor was assigned a college student as a teaching assistant (t.a.). All three t.a.s were young men attending The Johns Hopkins University, and all had been associated with SMPY for several years. They were all accelerated in their high-school and college work. SMPY selected them as role models for the AP students as well as for their competence in their respective subject areas.

Each class met once each week, for a two-and-a-half to three-hour session. Every session compressed the equivalent of an entire week of high-school or college instruction into that one session. For this reason, regular weekly attendance was essential — skipping one class was like missing one full week of school. In all three courses, weekly homework sets were assigned. The students were expected to spend five to ten hours solving problems and studying the textbooks. The relatively heavy assignments were given to help the students assimilate and supplement the lectures.

The Physics Class

The professor teaching the physics class designed the instruction to be similar to the regular introductory physics course given at Johns Hopkins. The textbook and workbook were by Bueche (1975a,b). During the fall semester the first seventeen chapters of the book were covered, which completed the study of mechanics. The last thirteen chapters, covering electricity and magnetism (E & M), were taught in the spring.

Of the thirteen students initially enrolled, ten persisted through May. The ages, sex, and school grades of the physics students are given in table 6.2. Note that nine of the thirteen students were younger than 16 years when the class started in September. One student was only 12 years and 8 months old. Only four students were high-school seniors.

Since calculus was used in both the textbook and lectures, all students were strongly encouraged to have studied that course previously or to take it concurrently. The two students (numbers 11 and 12 in table 6.2) who dropped out of physics during the fall were the only ones who had no calculus background. Of the three students who were taking calculus during the year, one (number 13) dropped out, in February. The other two (numbers 9 and 10) received the lowest AP scores in the class on the May physics examination.

ASSESSMENT

Before instruction began, students in the physics class were given two preinstructional measures, the College Board's achievement test in physics and the Owens-Bennett Mechanical Comprehension Test, Form CC (Owens & Bennett 1949). The latter, the most difficult of several forms of that test, was designed as a screening measure for college freshman engineering students. The physics achievement test measures physics knowledge at the high-school level. The results of both tests are given in table 6.3. In most cases scores on the achievement test were above the mean of students who had taken one year of physics, which indicated that almost all of the students were familiar with basic physics content; the average score was the 65th percentile of students who take the test after completing at least one year of high-school physics. Two of the lowest scores were earned by the students who dropped out; the third drop-out

TABLE 6.2. AP Physics Class Students

Student[a]	Age[b]	Grade in School	Calculus Background (AP Calculus grade)
1[c]	13, 10	10	AP BC (5)
2	15, 0	11	AP BC (5)
3	15, 9	10	AP BC (5)
4[c, d]	15, 3	12	AP AB (4)
5[c]	15, 10	11	College course
6[c]	16, 7	11	College course
7[d]	12, 8	10	AP BC (4)
8[c]	15, 8	10	AP BC (3)
9[c]	17, 4	12	Concurrent
10[c]	17, 6	12	Concurrent
11[e]	14, 0	10	No calculus
12[e]	14, 9	10	No calculus
13[f]	17, 8	12	Concurrent

[a] Listed in order of grades (highest to lowest) on the May, 1980, AP Level C physics examination, and within AP grade by age (youngest to oldest).
[b] As of September 1, 1979, in years and nearest month.
[c] Enrolled in chemistry and physics.
[d] Female.
[e] Enrolled in chemistry and physics but dropped out of physics.
[f] Dropped out.

received a score that tied for fourth lowest of the group. Only one of the seven persons whose AP physics grade was 3 or more scored lower on the physics achievement test than did the highest scoring of the other six students.

The mechanical reasoning test results bore little relationship to scores on the physics achievement test or the AP examination. In addition, they did not help differentiate the three drop-outs from those who finished the course. (It is suggestive, however, that the lowest score on CC [29] was earned by a top student whose 5 on AP physics mechanics was the lowest of the four, but who did much better on E & M.)

Two in-class tests were given during each semester. These were constructed in large part by the instructor and t.a., but they also included some problems taken from past AP examinations. One month before the AP test students were given a full practice AP test, the 1974 examination (Pfeiffenberger 1976).

In May of 1980 all ten of the students who completed the course took both parts of the AP physics examination, Level C. This three-hour test is divided into four forty-five-minute sections: mechanics multiple-choice items, mechanics free-response questions, electricity and magnetism multiple-choice items, and electricity and magnetism free-response questions. Separate scores are given for mechanics and E & M, using the 1-to-5-point grading scale, where 3, 4, and 5 are considered excellent grades.

Results on the test ranged widely, with three students receiving 5s on both sections, three making 2s on both sections, three earning 4 on one sec-

TABLE 6.3. Preinstructional Physics Testing Results

Student	CEEB Physics Achievement		Ownes-Bennett Mechanical Comprehension, Form CC		May, 1980, AP Physics C Grade (and Score)	
	Score	Percentile[a]	Score	Percentile[b]	Mechanics	E & M
1	680	76	29	5	5 (47)[c]	5 (63)[d]
2	740	90	41	45	5 (59)[c]	5 (73)[d]
3	800	98	31	7	5 (64)[c]	5 (59)[d]
4	570	41	38	30	5 (57)[c]	4
5	690	78	46	70	4	5 (52)[d]
6	680	76	40	40	4	5 (66)[d]
7	730	87	34	13	3	4
8	680	76	33	10	2	2
9	580	45	36	20	2	2
10	620	58	37	25	2	2
11	460	9	25	3		
12	580	45	34	13		
13	550	34	37	25		

[a] Interpolated from 1976–77 norms.
[b] Based on scores of first-term Princeton University engineering students.
[c] Number of points earned out of possible 90, where at least 45 were needed for a grade of 5.
[d] Number of points earned out of possible 90, where at least 52 were needed for a grade of 5.

tion and 5 on the other, and one student getting 3 on one section and 4 on the other (see table 6.3). The average grade on the test was 3.9 on mechanics and 3.7 on E & M. These were well above the nationwide average of 3.4 on both parts.

The Chemistry Class

Like the physics course instructor, the chemistry instructor designed her lectures to be similar to the ones used in the introductory chemistry course at Johns Hopkins. The textbook used was Dickerson, Gray, and Haight (1974). This was supplemented with two workbooks, Hutton (1974) and Butler and Grosser (1974). Throughout the course problems from previous AP examinations were used occasionally for homework or test questions.

All chapters of the textbook were covered with the exception of chapter 12 (Special Role of Carbon), which was an introduction to organic chemistry. Organic chemistry is not covered in the introductory course at Johns Hopkins. Moreover, the instructor felt that time did not permit its treatment in the AP course, despite its limited inclusion in the AP syllabus. Students were encouraged to study chapter 12 on their own.

Twenty-two students (six female and sixteen male) enrolled in the course. Sixteen of them attended class regularly and two attended

TABLE 6.4. AP Chemistry Class Students

Student[a]	Sex	Age[b]	Grade in School
1[c]	F	15, 4	12
2	M	15, 3	10
3	M	15, 5	9
4[c]	M	15, 10	11
5[c]	M	16, 7	11
6	M	13, 0	8
7[c]	M	13, 11	10
8[d]	M	14, 0	10
9[d]	M	14, 9	10
10	F	15, 8	10
11[c]	M	15, 8	10
12	F	16, 5	12
13[c]	M	17, 4	12
14[c]	M	17, 6	12
15	M	14, 7	10
16	M	16, 5	12
17	F	17, 7	12
18	M	17, 7	12
19[e]	F	15, 10	11
20[e]	M	16, 11	12
21[e]	M	16, 11	12
22[f]	F	17, 11	12

[a] Listed in order of grades (highest to lowest) on the May, 1980, AP chemistry examination, and within AP grade by age (youngest to oldest).
[b] As of September 1, 1979, in years and nearest month.
[c] Enrolled in chemistry and physics.
[d] Enrolled in chemistry and physics but dropped out of physics.
[e] Dropped out.
[f] Enrolled in chemistry and calculus but dropped out of both.

sporadically throughout the year. Two students dropped out of the class after the first semester. In January another two dropped out.

The ages, sex, and school grades of the twenty-two chemistry students are given in table 6.4. Note that a five-year age difference existed between the youngest and the oldest student. The four students who dropped out of the course were the older students: three were seniors in high school and one was a junior. The two students who attended sporadically throughout the year were seniors. This higher level of attrition among older students is consistent with the pattern found in the calculus class, and is discussed later in detail.

ASSESSMENT

The preinstructional measures used for the chemistry class were the College Board's chemistry achievement test, the American College Testing Mathematics Usage Test, and the ACT Natural Science Reading Test. The results are given in table 6.5. Scores on the ACT Mathematics Usage Test ranged from a low of 20 out of 40 (sixty-third percentile) to three perfect

TABLE 6.5. Preinstructional Chemistry Testing Results

	ACT Mathematics Usage		ACT Natural Science Reading		CEEB Chemistry Achievement		May, 1980, AP Chemistry
Student	Score	Percentile	Score	Percentile	Score	Percentile[a]	Grade
1	39	99	44	99	630	67	5[b]
2	33	89	34	85	460	14	4
3	23	69	34	85	600	57	4
4	37	96	41	96	670	80	4
5	40	99	42	96	770	97	4
6	29	80	43	98	560	44	3
7	38	98	38	93	660	77	3
8	35	92	42	96	530	34	3
9	36	95	42	96	610	60	3
10	31	84	41	96	410	5	3
11	36	95	38	93	580	50	3
12	40	99	39	93	590	53	3
13	28	76	45	99	570	47	2
14	34	89	46	99	550	41	2
15	40	99	38	93	410	5	
16	39	99	42	96	600	57	
17	34	89	37	89	500	25	
18	28	76	27	65	520	31	
19	20	63	30	72	450	11	
20	36	95	38	93	580	50	
21	26	73	38	93	510	28	
22	34	89	47	99	650	74	

[a] Interpolated from 1976–77 norms.
[b] She earned 121 points out of the possible 160 used for scoring the AP examination, where at least 113 were required for a grade of 5.

scores (ninety-ninth percentile). The average score was 34, roughly at the eighty-eighth percentile of college-bound twelfth-graders. Of the five students whose scores placed them lower than the eightieth percentile, two dropped out of the class, one attended class inconsistently throughout the year and did not take the AP chemistry examination, one performed poorly in class throughout the year as well as on the AP test (earning a 2), and one received tutoring in mathematics and performed well in class and on the AP examination (getting a 4).

The results of the ACT Natural Science Reading Test indicated that most students in the class had a good general science background. Seventeen of the twenty-two students scored higher than the ninetieth percentile. The median score was at the ninety-fifth percentile. Only two students scored lower than the eightieth percentile; those students also scored lower than the eightieth percentile on Mathematics Usage. One of them dropped out of the class and the other did not take the AP test.

The College Board's chemistry achievement test scores ranged considerably, from a low of 410 to a high of 770 (on a scale of 200 to 800). The mean score was 564, which was approximately at the forty-fifth percentile for high-school students who had completed one year of chemistry.

Overall, in the chemistry class the amount of high-school chemistry knowledge was less than the knowledge of high-school physics in the physics class prior to the beginning of instruction (forty-fifth compared to sixty-fifth percentile). Chemistry achievement test scores for the fourteen students who later took the AP test averaged 585, while for the eight who did not the average was 528. This difference, however, was not statistically significant.

Five in-class examinations (each lasting about one hour) and one take-home test were given during the course. In addition, the free-response section of a previous AP examination was administered under timed conditions approximately three weeks before the May AP examination. During the last six weeks of class, free-response sections from past AP tests were also assigned as homework. The emphasis on AP free-response questions during the end of the course was desirable for the following two reasons: the questions provided a review (and overview) of all topics covered during the year, and students became familiar with the types of questions they would encounter on the May AP examination. Unfortunately, the College Board does not make public the objective (multiple choice) questions from previous tests, except when previously administered examinations are published (e.g., Jones, Kenelly, & Kreider 1975; Pfeiffenberger 1976). None had been published for chemistry. Therefore students had little practice with multiple-choice items. In lieu of official AP multiple-choice items, the students were given a timed, in-class test using Part I of Raymond's (1979) multiple-choice examination. This examination was designed as part of an annual competition for high-school seniors who studied Dickerson, Gray, and Haight (1979).

Students in the AP chemistry class were quite heterogeneous in terms of ability, chemistry background, and motivation to do class work. As a group these students were the least able compared with those in physics and with those who completed the calculus course. Not surprisingly, the AP results for this class reflected the differences between the students. Of the eighteen students who completed the course, four failed to take the AP examination (two of them were students whose attendance had been inconsistent throughout the year). Of the fourteen students taking the three-hour AP test (half-objective, half-essay), one scored a 5, four made 4s, seven scored 3s, and two scored 2s. Thus, the average for those in the class who took the AP test was 3.3, while the national average is 3.0.

The Calculus Class

The text used in the AP calculus course was Leithold (1976). Fourteen of the sixteen chapters were covered; excepted were chapter 12 (on hyperbolic functions) and chapter 14 (on conic sections). Differential equations were not included in the textbook, but some aspects of them were covered in class. All topics on the syllabus recommended by the College Board for Level BC mathematics were covered during the year.

Seventeen students enrolled in the course (seven females and ten males). The ages ranged from 13 years, 1 month, to 17 years, 11 months. Ten of the students were older than 16 years. Nine of them were twelfth-graders, and one was already a high-school graduate (see table 6.6).

One student withdrew from the course after four weeks. By early November it was clear from homework and in-class performance that many students were not doing well in the course. A letter was sent to all members of the class reminding them of the importance of regular class attendance and the necessity of spending several hours each week completing assignments. Finally, students were warned that SMPY would ask any person whose work was not satisfactory or showed no improvement to withdraw from the course. At the end of November six students were asked to leave and four others were placed on probation. Of the latter, two dropped out immediately and the other two were asked to withdraw in the latter part of December. Six of the initial seventeen students completed the course. This high rate of attrition is atypical of two of the three previous fast-paced calculus classes conducted by SMPY.

ASSESSMENT

Prior to their instructional meeting, the calculus students were administered the Quantitative Evaluative Device (QED; see Stake 1962) and the College Board's achievement test, Mathematics Level II. The scores are presented in table 6.7. The average score on the QED was 35 out of 60 possible points. The six students who finished the course averaged 38 on QED, while the eleven who did not finish averaged 34. This difference is not statistically significant.

The College Board's Mathematics Level II achievement test clearly differentiated between those who completed the class and those who did not. For the whole group the average was 675 (out of 800). The six students who finished averaged 773 (three of these were 800s). The eleven who did not finish averaged 622. This is a 151-point difference. It was especially interesting that on this test score distributions between the two groups did not overlap. Every student finishing the course scored higher than any student not finishing the course.

By the end of the course, six teacher-designed in-class tests had been given, each taking half of a class period (roughly eighty minutes). In March an eighty-minute standardized calculus test, Cooperative Mathematics Tests series, Calculus, Form B, was given. This test was administered to see how the class's performance compared with performance on the national level. One student scored at the ninety-fourth percentile, and the other five scored at or above the ninety-ninth percentile based on

TABLE 6.6. AP Calculus Class Students

Student	Sex	Age[a]	Grade in School
Completed course			
1	M	13, 1	9
2	F	14, 8	11
3	M	14, 11	10
4	M	16, 9	12
5	F	17, 5	12
6	M	17, 10	High-school graduate
Did not complete course			
7	M	14, 6	10
8	M	14, 7	9
9	M	14, 10	10
10	M	15, 2	10
11	F	16, 8	12
12	M	16, 9	12
13	M	16, 10	12
14	F	17, 5	12
15	F	17, 5	12
16	F	17, 5	12
17[b]	F	17, 11	12

[a] As of September 1, 1979, in years and nearest month.
[b] Enrolled in chemistry and calculus, but dropped out of both.

national high-school norms. Scores ranged from 49 to 58 points out of a possible 60. In April, several weeks prior to the May AP calculus test, students were given a full practice AP test under standard three-hour testing conditions. The May 1973 test was used (Jones, Kenelly, & Kreider 1975).

The grades of the class on the official May, 1980, AP examination were exceptional: all six students made the highest possible, 5. The national mean grade on that test was 3.2. Even more strikingly, on the 210-point scoring scale, where at least 144 points were needed for a grade of 5, the lowest scoring of the six exceeded that minimum by 13 points; the other five students were at least 33 points above it, and one — with 190 points — was 46 points ahead (table 6.7, last column). The grade of 5 is equivalent to $A+$ in two semesters of calculus at a college or university such as Johns Hopkins.

Discussion of AP Results

There are many potential reasons for the differentiation in preparation for the AP between the physics, chemistry, and calculus classes. Clearly, high ability and a great deal of intrinsic motivation are required of the students. It also seems that a teacher's firm, steady insistence on maintain-

TABLE 6.7. Preinstructional Calculus Testing Results

	QED[a]		CEEB Mathematics Achievement, Level II		May, 1980, AP Calculus BC
Student	Score	Percentile[b]	Score	Percentile[c]	Grade (and Score)[d]
1	34	89	800	91	5 (181)
2	49	99.5	800	91	5 (178)
3	38	96	740	74	5 (177)
4	35	91	730	71	5 (190)
5	29	74	770	83	5 (157)
6	44	99.5	800	91	5 (187)
7	38	96	670	46	
8	35	91	580	17	
9	33	87	620	27	
10	36	93	640	34	
11	40	98	720	65	
12	31	82	580	17	
13	32	85	610	24	
14	25	58	600	21	
15	32	85	570	15	
16	34	89	620	27	
17	33	87	630	31	

[a] Quantitative Evaluative Device (R. E. Stake, "A Non-Mathematical Quantitative Aptitude Test for the Graduate Level: The QED," *Journal of Experimental Education* 31 [1, Sept., 1962]: 81–83).
[b] Based on 925 postbaccalaureate persons desiring to qualify as graduate students in education at the University of Nebraska.
[c] Interpolated from 1976–77 norms.
[d] Of the possible 210 points, 144 or more were required for a grade of 5.

ing high standards for student performance is an important factor for successful AP preparation.

In comparison with that in the courses in calculus and physics, less emphasis was placed in the chemistry class on diligent completion of homework assignments or on regular class attendance. Early in the school year a fundamental philosophical difference was apparent between the instructors in calculus and physics versus the chemistry instructor. The chemistry instructor's philosophy was that the AP course was an enriching experience for the students. In addition, she believed that even if the students did not get college credit for their efforts, they would receive a good background to build on later. The emphasis was on gaining exposure to concepts. The students could do as much or as little work as they wished.

In sharp contrast, the calculus and physics instructors insisted on regular class attendance and thorough completion of weekly assignments. Students in both of these classes were aware that failure to make consistent efforts would result in their dismissal from the course. In fact, a large number of students in calculus (eleven out of seventeen) either dropped out on their own or were asked to leave. The calculus and physics instructors were strongly oriented toward teaching a year of college-level course-work, with the expectation that their students would subsequently be well prepared for more advanced study in their respective subjects. Explicit attrition from the chemistry class (eighteen percent) was lower than that in either of the other two classes (65 percent for calculus and 23 percent for physics), perhaps because less effort was required from the students in terms of homework and attendance. In supplementary courses such as these, attrition is likely to occur among the less motivated or less able students. This is especially true if the course requires considerable effort. The greater the attrition, the more select the final group becomes. Thus one would expect the test scores for these remaining students to be excellent.

In the calculus class, all students scored a 5 on the AP exam. Only six of the original seventeen completed the course, however. Physics students averaged 3.8 on the AP test, with all ten of the students who remained (of the thirteen who began the class) taking the test. Four students dropped out of chemistry. Of the eighteen who completed chemistry, four did not take the test. The scores of the fourteen who did averaged 3.3.

Attrition

It was suggested earlier that attrition from the AP classes was at least partially a function of the degree of effort required of the students by the instructor. If this was true, what types of students were most likely to persist? Several comparisons were made between students who completed a class and those who dropped out.

An analysis was made of attrition from the three calculus classes (1974–75, 1975–76, and 1979–80), which were all taught by the same instructor. In the 1974–75 class fifteen students enrolled and thirteen completed the class. The majority of students in this first class were young (tenth grade) and had learned much of their precalculus mathematics in SMPY-sponsored fast-paced courses. The 1975–76 calculus class initially enrolled twenty-three students, most of whom were juniors and seniors in high school. Eleven students dropped out. In the 1979–80 class only six of the original seventeen students completed the course. Thus of a total of fifty-five students enrolled in these three classes, thirty-one finished the course and twenty-four did not. The average SAT-M and SAT-V scores of the students who finished as well as those who dropped out can be seen in table 6.8. The average SAT-M score for those finishing was 689; for those who dropped out it was 647. A *t*-test of the difference was significant past the .05 level. The average SAT-V score for those dropping out (536), however, was higher than that for those who finished (516). Although this 20-point difference was not statistically significant, fifteen of the thirty-

TABLE 6.8. SAT Scores for Three AP Calculus Classes

	Students	
	Completed Course (N = 31)	Dropped Out (N = 24)
Average SAT-M	689	647
Average SAT-V	516	536
Average SAT-M plus SAT-V	1,205	1,183
Average difference:		
SAT-M minus SAT-V	172	111

TABLE 6.9. SAT-M Scores for Three AP Calculus Courses (by Age)

	Students			
	Younger than 16 Years Old		16 Years Old or Older	
	Completed Course (N = 16)	Dropped Out (N = 7)	Completed Course (N = 15)	Dropped Out (N = 17)
Average SAT-M	653	624	727	656

one students who completed the course had SAT-M scores *at least* 200 points higher than their SAT-V scores, while only three of the twenty-four students who dropped out had scores that differed so greatly. These comparisons suggest that students whose aptitude for mathematics far exceeds their verbal aptitudes have more interest and motivation to be successful in a fast-paced mathematics class. In contrast, when verbal scores are quite high compared with mathematics scores, the students may tend to have stronger interests in subjects other than mathematics.

The relationship of age, SAT scores, and attrition was also examined for the three calculus classes. The results can be seen in table 6.9. Students were divided into two categories: those who, when the course began, were younger than 16 years (N = 23) and those who were 16 years or older (N = 32). Only 30 percent of the younger students dropped the course (seven of twenty-three), while 53 percent of the older students dropped out (seventeen of thirty-two).

The SAT scores given in table 6.9 cannot be compared directly across age groups. Undoubtedly, the SAT-M scores of the younger students would increase with age. It seems, however, that SAT-M is a better predictor of attrition for older students than for younger ones. A within-age-group comparison showed that there was only a twenty-nine-point difference in SAT-M scores between the drop-outs and non-drop-outs in the young group. The difference of seventy-one points found for the older group was significant at the .01 level. These findings are consistent with a general hypothesis that (possibly because of previous exposure) the younger students were better prepared for a fast-paced class than the older ones were. The older students coming from regular-paced instructional backgrounds were less likely to remain in the class unless they had high mathematical reasoning ability.

In addition to examining attrition from the calculus classes, a comparison was made among students in the three 1979–80 courses. A comparison of twelfth-graders with students in all lower grades combined indicated that a twelfth-grade student was more likely to drop out than a non-twelfth-grader was. This information is presented in table 6.10. Fifty-two students were enrolled in calculus, chemistry, and physics (any student enrolled in two of the classes was counted twice). Thirty-four students finished the course in which they were enrolled; eighteen did not. Forty-four percent of the twelfth-graders dropped out, while only 25 percent of students in lower grades did. The higher percentage of twelfth-grade students dropping out might be explained by less motivation to succeed. The class was not as "accelerative" for the twelfth-graders as it was for the younger students. It is also possible that the older students had acquired poor study habits in slower-moving high-school classes. Older students were also more likely to have other commitments, such as a part-time job. Finally, many of the younger students had had previous exposure to fast-paced instruction, while few of the twelfth-graders had. Experience with the demands of fast-paced course-work may provide important preparation for classes such as these and serve as an excellent screening method.

Homework and Tests as Predictors of AP Performance

Based on experience with previous fast-paced courses, it was expected that diligent completion of homework assignments would relate positively to in-class test scores and subsequent AP examination performance. These relationships were examined separately for calculus, chemistry, and physics.

TABLE 6.10. Attrition in 1979–80 AP Classes (by School Grade)

| | Students: All Three Courses | | | | | |
| | Before Twelfth Grade | | Twelfth Grade | | Total | |
	Number	Percentage	Number	Percentage	Number	Percentage
Completed course	21	72	13	56.5	34	65
Dropped out	8	28	10	43.5	18	35
Total	29		23		52	

Differences in homework and in-class performance between the calculus students who completed that course versus those who did not were large. Perhaps some of the students who performed poorly were in fact working hard but were not ready for the high level of course content. Others clearly were making little effort. The six students who finished the calculus course probably had the strongest mathematics backgrounds of all seventeen students. In addition, they were willing to spend time completing the assignments. Although there was a fairly consistent rank-ordering of the students on homework and test scores, even the weakest student in this group scored extremely well (thirteen points above the minimum score for a 5) on the AP examination.

In both the chemistry and the physics classes, performance on the AP test was heterogeneous enough to warrant investigation of the relationship between homework and in-class test scores and AP test results. In each class some support was found for the conclusion that good in-class performance was required for success on the AP examination. Table 6.11 gives for the chemistry students the intercorrelations of homework, in-class tests, the practice AP test (essay section only), and the May AP examination. Although all the correlation coefficients were positive and moderately large, because of the small number few were statistically significant. In-class tests correlated .70 with the practice AP test scores and .60 with the May AP test results. It is unfortunate that only the essay section of the chemistry AP test was available for practice. Had the class been able to take a full practice test the correlation between it and in-class tests, as well as the May AP test, probably would have been increased. (The essay section contains far fewer items than the objective section and is scored somewhat subjectively. Hence, scores on it tend to be considerably less reliable than for the full AP test, which includes multiple-choice items.) The correlation of homework scores with AP test scores was a surprisingly low .39.

A similarly low correlation was found for the physics students between their homework scores and May AP test scores. These and other correlation coefficients are given in table 6.12. Mechanics and E & M data are

TABLE 6.11. Intercorrelation of Chemistry Student Performances in Four Areas ($N = 14$)

	Homework	In-Class Tests	Practice AP Chemistry Test
Homework			
In-class tests	.53*		
Practice AP chemistry test	.42	.70**	
May, 1980, AP chemistry test	.39	.60*	.50

*$p < .05$.
**$p < .01$.

TABLE 6.12. Intercorrelation of Physics Student Performances in Four Areas ($N = 10$)

		Homework		In-Class Tests		Practice AP Physics Test	
		M	E & M	M	E & M	M	E & M
Homework	M						
	E & M	.59					
In-class tests	M	.68*					
	E & M		.71*				
Practice AP	M	.42		.88***			
physics test	E & M		.52		.82**		
May, 1980, AP	M	.36		.85**		.84**	
physics test	E & M		.36		.68**		.59

*$p < .05$.
**$p < .01$.
***$p < .001$.

treated separately. Many of the *r*s fail to reach the .05 level of significance, again because of the small sample size. Homework performance correlated best with in-class test scores, which were highly related to May AP test scores. In general, in-class and practice AP test scores predicted May AP scores better for mechanics than for E & M.

Despite the relatively weak *direct* relationship between homework and May AP test scores, homework performance showed a clear relationship with in-class test scores. This indicates that over shorter periods of time the effect of homework is quite strong.

Evaluation of the 1979–80 AP Classes

In evaluating the success of the AP classes, two criteria were considered. First, how many students scored well enough to receive college credit? Second, how did SMPY's students score in comparison with the national results and with a representative public school district?

Many colleges and universities grant full course credit for a grade of 3 or higher on the AP examination. Based on this, 100 percent of the six calculus students qualified for two semesters of college credit.

In the physics course, 70 percent of the students who completed the course scored well enough to receive two semesters of college credit. The other 30 percent, with only 2s, would probably receive not even one semester of physics credit.

In chemistry, fourteen of the eighteen students finishing the course took the AP examination. Eleven of them scored 3 or higher, representing 61 percent of those who finished the course.

In summary, most of the students who remained in the classes throughout the year did score well enough to qualify for college credit at institutions accepting 3s for this purpose.

TABLE 6.13. Performance of SMPY's Students, a Public School System's Students, and Students Nationwide

	Score	SMPY's May, 1980, Results (%)	Public School Results (%)[a]	May, 1980, National Results (%)
Physics C,	5	50.0	12.7	24.5
mechanics	4	20.0	13.8	26.8
	3	0	21.8	19.4
	2	30.0	32.2	19.2
	1	0	19.6	10.1
Average		3.90	2.68	3.36
N		10	87	2,121
Physics C,	5	40.0	5.7	26.0
E & M	4	20.0	15.5	26.0
	3	10.0	31.0	19.4
	2	30.0	22.6	15.8
	1	10.0	25.3	12.8
Average		3.70	2.54	3.37
N		10	71	1,690
Chemistry	5	7.1	11.3	12.9
	4	28.6	22.0	19.5
	3	50.0	43.5	36.3
	2	14.3	16.6	19.9
	1	0	6.4	11.4
Average		3.29	3.15	3.03
N		14	282	8,209
Calculus BC	5	100	12.2	21.8
	4	0	18.7	20.7
	3	0	29.9	26.5
	2	0	20.6	16.3
	1	0	18.0	14.7
Average		5	2.87	3.19
N		6	1,599	7,783

[a] Results obtained from reports from the Fairfax County Public Schools of Northern Virginia, 1974–80.

The scores of students in all three courses were equal to or higher than nationwide AP examination performance levels. Table 6.13 is a presentation of the results for the May, 1980, AP examinations for SMPY's students, students in a public school system, and students nationwide in physics, chemistry, and calculus.

The physics students in SMPY's course exceeded the national averages on both the mechanics and the E & M sections. This was due to a relatively high proportion of 5s on each section. The average mechanics grade for SMPY's class was 3.90, with 70 percent earning 3 or higher. The national average, based on 2,121 students, was 3.36, with 71 percent earning 3 or more. On E & M, the average for SMPY's class was 3.70, with 70 percent earning at least a 3. Nationally, the 1,690 students taking E & M averaged 3.37, and 71 percent received grades of 3 or higher.

The grades earned by SMPY's chemistry students were slightly higher than those earned at the national level. A total of 8,209 students took the

AP chemistry examination; their grades averaged 3.03. SMPY's students averaged 3.29; of the fourteen students taking the test, 86 percent earned grades of 3 or higher. Nationally, 69 percent of the students obtained at least a 3.

In calculus, 22 percent of the 7,783 students taking the Level BC examination earned a 5; the average was 3.19. In comparison, 100 percent of SMPY's calculus students received a grade of 5.

For all three courses, then, SMPY's students performed as well as or better than students nationwide.

Information about student AP achievement was obtained from the Fairfax County Public Schools of Northern Virginia for a comparison with SMPY's students' scores.[2] The data from seven years (1974–80) were combined and averaged (see table 6.13). Scores were available only for twelfth-grade students. Over seven years, a total of 1,599 students in Fairfax County took the Level BC mathematics examination (about 228 students per year). Their average grade was 2.87, with 61 percent receiving 3 or higher. In chemistry, 282 students (40 per year, on the average) took the AP test. Their mean grade was 3.15, with 78 percent earning 3 or higher. Not many county students took the physics Level C examinations in mechanics or E & M. The totals for seven years were 87 (12 per year) and 71 students (10 per year), respectively. The average mechanics grade was 2.68; about 48 percent earned at least a 3. On E & M, the average was 2.54; 52 percent received a 3 or higher.

In summary, the performance of SMPY's AP students was equivalent to the levels shown by the Fairfax County school system for chemistry, but exceeded the performance of that county's students on mathematics and physics. This was the case despite the fact that SMPY's students were younger on the average and that each year only a select few of the approximately 10,000 seniors in Fairfax County's twenty-three senior high schools took the examinations.

STUDENTS' EVALUATIONS

In addition to the quantitative comparisons of course success, a valuable source of evaluative information was the students' opinions of the courses. During the summer following receipt of the official AP score, a questionnaire was mailed to all students who had enrolled in the 1979–80 courses. The questionnaire was designed to assess the students' opinions toward the classes, especially regarding AP test preparation. The response rate was 100 percent for all three courses. Tabulations by class of responses to some questionnaire items are given in table 6.14. Note that the percentages given in table 6.14 were calculated based on all students who enrolled, including those who dropped out and/or did not take the AP examination.

TABLE 6.14. Students' Evaluation of 1979–80 AP Courses (in Percentage)

		Calculus (N = 17)	Chemistry (N = 22)	Physics (N = 13)
1. Did you think SMPY's course as a whole prepared you well for the AP exam?	Yes	35	50	54
	No	0	23	23
	Didn't take exam	65	27	23
2. Even if you do nòt get any college credit for the course, do you think it was a worthwhile experience?	Yes	35	73	77
	Somewhat	8	9	15
	Not sure	18	5	8
	No	18	9	0
	No response	12	5	0
3. Would you recommend this course to a qualified friend?	Yes	65	73	92
	Not sure	18	18	8
	No	18	9	0
4. How have your feelings toward the subject changed as a result of your experience with SMPY's course this year?	Like more	12	64	77
	No change	77	23	23
	Like less	12	14	0
	No response	0	0	0
5. Has this course influenced your decision to study the subject further in the future?	Yes	18	41	69
	No	71	41	31
	No response	12	18	0

Responses to the first question (Was SMPY's course good preparation for the AP test?) generally were favorable from students who took the test. All six students who took the calculus test thought SMPY's course provided good preparation. In chemistry, ten (71 percent) of the fourteen students who took the AP exam thought the course was good preparation, as did 80 percent of the ten students who took the physics AP test.

Answers to the second question indicated that all six students who took the AP mathematics test thought the calculus course was a worthwhile experience. Students who had not completed that course showed ambivalent or negative reactions. A more uniformly positive response was found in the chemistry and physics classes. In chemistry, 82 percent felt that the course was at least somewhat worthwhile, as did 92 percent of the physics students.

Another indication of students' opinions about the courses was their willingness to recommend them to a friend. Of the calculus students, 65 percent said they would recommend it, while 73 percent and 92 percent of the chemistry and physics students, respectively, said they would. Therefore, even though some of the students had doubts about how useful the course had been for them, most felt it would benefit other qualified individuals.

Regarding attitude changes as a result of the courses (questions 4 and 5 in table 6.14), a discrepancy was observed between the calculus and science students' responses. Most of the calculus students (77 percent) reported that their liking for mathematics had not changed, while 64 percent of the chemistry students and 77 percent of the physics students said their liking for the subject had increased. A similar pattern of responses was observed regarding whether students would be likely to study the subject again in the future. Possibly this discrepancy reflects the different amounts of prior exposure to the subject students were likely to have had. Chemistry and physics were probably more unfamiliar to the students before they took the courses; they could not know a priori if they would like these subjects. In contrast, students who enrolled in calculus had had considerable prior experiences with mathematics and presumably already had favorable attitudes toward it.

When considering the questionnaire responses as a whole, it was found that reactions were generally less favorable from the students who dropped out. Those who completed the courses and took the AP examination were almost without exception uniformly positive in their reactions to the class.

Conclusions and Recommendations

One of the most salient findings of the 1979–80 AP courses was that the greatest success was obtained with the younger students. For a combination of reasons, the participants who had not yet reached the twelfth grade (or twelfth-graders who were young in grade) were more likely to persist and do well in the courses. Alternately, they may have been abler than their regular-aged twelfth-grade counterparts. These conclusions had been drawn previously from the three AP-level SMPY calculus courses (1974–75, 1975–76, and 1978–79). (See Mezynski & Stanley 1980.) The 1979–80 chemistry and physics courses demonstrated that the younger students do better in the sciences, also.

The courses did help to prepare students for the AP examinations. One criterion was the number of participants who scored high enough to qualify for college credit. All of the calculus students finishing the course did so, as did 61 percent of the chemistry students and 70 percent of the physics students. Relative to national levels, SMPY's calculus and physics students exceeded the average of highly able students taking the examinations. The chemistry class average was about equivalent to the national norms, but a greater percentage of SMPY's students scored 3 or higher. SMPY's students in calculus and physics surpassed the achievement levels of high-school seniors from an excellent county public school system near Washington, D.C., while the chemistry class's performance was about the same as the public school seniors'. Since virtually none of the students in SMPY's courses was receiving AP-level instruction in their high schools, we can conclude that the weekly sessions were largely responsible for the AP results. Thus with about one-half the amount of formal instruction (and, in chemistry and physics, no laboratory experience), SMPY's students performed as well as or better than the highly selected students who study AP courses in their high schools and then take the AP examinations.

Other conclusions drawn from SMPY's courses concern the type of background needed for successful performance in AP-level mathematics, chemistry, and physics. All four calculus courses offered by SMPY indicated that students with previous experience in fast-paced mathematics classes do better than students who have had regular mathematics backgrounds. Successful experience in fast-paced classes is indicative of three prerequisites for success in AP calculus: mathematical reasoning ability, a good foundation in precalculus mathematics, and a high level of motivation. Hence the fast-paced classroom experience itself is not essential if students can be screened well for aptitude and knowledge. The College Board's mathematics achievement test, Level II, is a particularly useful screening device for the latter.

In chemistry and physics there seemed to be no difference between students who had already completed the high-school-level course and those who were taking it concurrently with SMPY's AP-level course. The most important implication of this is that highly able, well-motivated students need not spend two school years studying a course through the AP level (when the high-school course typically is a prerequisite). Consequently, they could take several AP-level science courses during their high-school years. In fact, several students in SMPY's courses completed *both* chemistry and physics at a high level, indicating that well-motivated, exceptionally able students can learn two different AP-level science courses in only one year. In physics, however, it was shown that calculus was a needed prerequisite.

In summary, the population of students for whom SMPY's AP-level courses were most beneficial was young (median school grade, ten), science- or mathematics-career oriented, motivated to move ahead academically, and highly able mathematically. Given a group of students which met those criteria, the courses would probably be satisfactory without major improvements in format or technique. Consequently, the chief recommendation for improving future courses of this type is to improve methods of screening applicants. Several other recommendations can be made on the basis of student questionnaires and informal discussions with the instructors:

1.   A laboratory facility for the chemistry and physics courses, while not essential, would provide valuable "hands-on" experience.

2.   Lectures should incorporate more problem solving and applications of the topics.

3.   The teaching assistant should be accessible before and after class to work with students who need extra help.

4. Short quizzes should be given weekly; longer tests should continue to be administered on a four-to-six-week basis.

5. Individuals who consistently perform below the instructor's standards should be warned, then placed on probation, and, if necessary, dismissed from the class.

AP-level courses of the type conducted by SMPY have shown themselves to be very beneficial to highly motivated, extremely able students. These courses are particularly useful to students who have no access to AP-level instruction in high school, who are ready for it before the twelfth grade, and/or who do not wish to spend two full school years on one subject. The chief difficulty in conducting such courses is attracting a sufficiently large number of qualified individuals to make the program feasible.

RESIDENTIAL SUMMER HIGH-SCHOOL-LEVEL SCIENCE COURSES

The key problems with such recruitment seem to be distance and time. All six of the supplemental AP courses described herein were nonresidential; students had to commute from their homes to the Johns Hopkins campus and back approximately thirty Saturdays or Sundays during the school year. Some came long distances. Others lived too far away to make taking the course feasible. Many potential members of these classes had other activities on weekends that interfered.

In collaboration with SMPY, the Center for the Advancement of Academically Talented Youth at Johns Hopkins has conducted three-week, intensive residential courses for four summers (1980, 1981, 1982, and 1983) in order to permit intellectually talented students from all over the Middle Atlantic Region and, indeed, the entire country to accelerate and enrich their knowledge of several subjects. In 1982, for the first time, the equivalent of one school year of high-school biology was offered in three concentrated weeks to certain highly selected 12- to 15-year-old students. This course, conducted at Franklin and Marshall College in Pennsylvania, included some experience in a college biology laboratory.

During the subsequent three weeks, chemistry was offered in the same way. Thus students could elect to study biology in the first session and chemistry in the second. High-school physics was offered for the first time during the summer of 1983. Biology and chemistry were also available then, both each session, so the ablest students had their choice of any two of the three. They were expected to have completed most of precalculus already (and, for physics, one year of calculus). Precalculus is available at each of the two three-week sessions each year.

It may seem strange for us to recommend high-school-level courses after extolling the virtues of AP-level ones. The main purpose is to save the brilliant student from being incarcerated for 180 to 190 periods in a routine biology, chemistry, and/or physics course when he or she could learn the basic material well among intellectual peers in five or six hours per day for three weeks. In the subsequent school year the student should be able to work on the AP level of the course in whatever fruitful ways can be devised in the local school context. If an excellent AP course is available in the high school, the student will be ready for it. If supplemental AP courses such as those described earlier in this report are available, his or her progress in them is likely to be excellent. The best solution under some circumstances will be to take a college course for credit at as excellent a tertiary institution as the student can reach regularly, and then take the AP exam.

Another sequel to the summer courses that SMPY is exploring for a special subgroup, its extremely special youths who before age 13 have scored at least 700 on the mathematical part of the College Board's Scholastic Aptitude Test, is providing skilled "mentors-by-mail" to help students learn AP-level calculus, biology, chemistry, and/or physics. Initial results with calculus, biology, and chemistry are encouraging, but obviously this method demands great academic maturity from the "mentees," their parents, and their teachers. Other follow-up procedures, where available, will usually be preferable for most students.

Entering college two years early with full sophomore-year standing in calculus, physics, chemistry, biology, and several other subjects is an attainable goal for several hundred youths across the country each year. Most of them will be able to obtain an excellent college education in three, two and one-half, or even two years. Savings of money and time and prevention of boredom will be among the rewards. For other intellectually talented youths who are less accelerable than these several hundred out of more than three million students their age, the pace will be slower. By age 16, however, at least fifty thousand of the age group could benefit greatly from one or more AP-oriented mathematics and science courses. We urge communities, colleges, and universities to help make this possible.

Notes

1. This study was prepared with the support of National Science Foundation Grant SPI 78-27896 for calculus and Grant SED 79-20868 for chemistry and physics. Any opinions, findings, conclusions, or recommendations expressed herein are those of the authors and do not necessarily reflect the views of the National Science Foundation.

2. We are indebted to Joseph Montecalvo for providing us this valuable information.

References

Bartkovich, K. G., and George, W. C. 1980. *Teaching the gifted and talented in the mathematics classroom.* Washington, D.C.: National Education Association.

Bartkovich, K. G., and Mezynski, K. 1981. Fast-paced precalculus mathematics for talented junior-high students: Two recent SMPY programs. *Gifted Child Quarterly* 25(2, Spring): 73–80.

Benbow, C. P., and Stanley, J. C. 1978. It is never too early to start thinking about AP. *Intellectually Talented Youth Bulletin* 4(10): 4–6.

Bueche, F. J. 1975a. *Introduction to physics for scientists and engineers.* 2d ed. New York: McGraw-Hill.

———. 1975b. *Workbook in physics for scientists and engineering students.* New York: McGraw-Hill.

Butler, J. S., and Grosser, A. E. 1974. *Relevant problems for chemical principles.* 2d ed. Menlo Park, Calif.: W. A. Benjamin.

Dickerson, R. E.; Gray, H. B.; and Haight, G. P., Jr. 1974. *Chemical principles.* 2d ed. Menlo Park, Calif.: W. A. Benjamin.

———. 1979. *Chemical principles.* 3d ed. Menlo Park, Calif.: W. A. Benjamin.

Fox, L. H. 1974. A mathematics program for fostering precocious achievement. In *Mathematical talent: Discovery, description, and development,* ed. J. C. Stanley, D. P. Keating, and L. H. Fox, 101–25. Baltimore: Johns Hopkins University Press.

George, W. C. 1976. Accelerating mathematics instruction for the mathematically talented. *Gifted Child Quarterly* 20(3, Fall): 246–61.

George, W. C., and Denham, S. A. 1976. Curriculum experimentation for the mathematically talented. In *Intellectual talent: Research and development,* ed. D. P. Keating, 103–31. Baltimore: Johns Hopkins University Press.

Hanson, H. P. 1980. Twenty-five years of the Advanced Placement Program: Encouraging able students. *College Board Review* 115(Spring): 8–12, 35.

Hutton, W. 1974. *A study guide for chemical principles.* 2d ed. Menlo Park, Calif.: W. A. Benjamin.

Jones, C. O.; Kenelly, J. W.; and Kreider, D. L. 1975. The Advanced Placement Program in mathematics: update 1975. *Mathematics Teacher* 68(Dec.): 654–70.

Leithold, L. 1976. *The calculus with analytic geometry, part 1.* 3d ed. New York: Harper and Row.

Mezynski, K., and Stanley, J. C. 1980. Advanced placement oriented calculus for high school students. *Journal for Research in Mathematics Education* 11(5): 347–55.

Owens, W. A., and Bennett, G. K. 1949. *Mechanical Comprehension Test, Form CC.* New York: The Psychological Corporation.

Pfeiffenberger, W. 1976. Nineteen seventy-four advanced placement examination in physics. *Physics Teacher* 14(6): 344–50.

Raymond, J. 1979. A two-part multiple-choice examination for the Los Angeles section of the American Chemical Society. In *Teacher's guide to chemical principles,* ed. B. Chastain, 72–91. 3d ed. Menlo Park, Calif.: Benjamin Cummings.

Stake, R. E. 1962. A non-mathematical quantitative aptitude test for the graduate level: The QED. *Journal of Experimental Education* 31(1, Sept.): 81–83.

Stanley, J. C. 1976. Special fast-mathematics classes taught by college professors to fourth- through twelfth-graders. In *Intellectual talent: Research and development,* ed. D. P. Keating, 132–59. Baltimore: Johns Hopkins University Press.

7

An Accelerated Mathematics Program for Girls: A Longitudinal Evaluation

LYNN H. FOX, CAMILLA PERSSON
BENBOW, and SUSAN PERKINS

Abstract

Moderately gifted seventh-grade girls were invited to attend a fast-paced summer class in algebra I that provided for the special needs of girls. In addition to emphasizing algebra, the program catered to the social needs of girls, provided interaction with female role models who had careers in the mathematical sciences, and encouraged the girls to study a number of years of mathematics. Two control groups, one of boys and one of girls, similar in ability and parental variables, were chosen. Seven years after the class, its long-term effects were investigated by analyzing the group's responses to two questionnaires. Girls who completed the program successfully (i.e., were placed in algebra II the following fall) were more accelerated and took more mathematics courses in high school and college. Those were, however, the only major differences between the girls who constituted the experimental group and the two control groups. No such effects were found for the girls who attended the class but were not successful in it. There were no major differences in educational experiences, educational aspirations, or career goals. Girls perceived the lack of role models as the greatest barrier women face when contemplating a career in mathematics or science. Boys, however, felt that for women the difficulty of combining career and family responsibilities was the greatest barrier. It is concluded that in order for girls to receive the long-term benefits of an early intervention program, they must complete the program successfully and also be mathematically abler than most of these girls were.

Far fewer women than men pursue careers in mathematical and scientific fields (Dearman & Plisko 1979, pp. 232–33). It has been suggested that many gifted girls limit their opportunities for careers in mathematics and science by not electing to take advanced mathematics courses in high school (Sells 1980). Among college-bound students, more boys than girls take four or more years of high-school mathematics, and far more boys than girls take the College Board's Advancement Placement Program courses and examinations in calculus (CEEB 1975). Therefore, it would seem that efforts to increase the number of women in scientific career areas might begin by developing strategies to encourage high-ability girls to take upper-level mathematics courses in high school.

One way to increase female enrollment in advanced mathematics classes would be to attempt to influence young girls' attitudes about the importance of taking such courses for their future careers. Another more direct strategy would be to have girls who reason well mathematically begin the sequence of advanced mathematics courses at an earlier age.

The Study of Mathematically Precocious Youth is a unique program in which both counseling and accelerated mathematics courses are offered to mathematically highly able boys and girls as early as grade seven. Results of SMPY's first accelerated mathematics class, begun for both boys and girls in the summer of 1972, suggested that attention to the social interests of girls was necessary to attract them to and retain them in an accelerated mathematics program (Fox 1976). Therefore, in the summer of 1973, an experimental mathematics program was conducted for mathematically gifted end-of-the-year seventh-grade girls (Fox 1976). The class met two days each week for approximately two hours from May through July and covered a standard algebra I curriculum. It was hoped that a positive experience in mathematics at the junior-high-school level, when mathematics becomes more abstract, along with the opportunity to accelerate one year in mathematics, would increase the likelihood that the girls would take advanced mathematics courses in high school.

The class was designed to provide social stimulation in several ways. The teacher, a woman, was assisted by two female undergraduate mathematics majors. The structure of the class was informal. Both individualized and small group instruction were utilized. Furthermore, cooperative rather than competitive activities were stressed, and some traditional word problems were rewritten to make them more socially appealing. The classroom work was supplemented by a series of speakers, both male and female, who met with the girls to talk about their careers in mathematics and science (Fox 1976).

Students were selected for the program on the basis of performance on the mathematics subtest of the College Board's Scholastic Aptitude Test-

Mathematics in either the mathematics or the verbal contests conducted by SMPY and the Study of Verbally Gifted Youth (SVGY), respectively, at The Johns Hopkins University in January or February of 1973. Thirty-two seventh-grade girls enrolled in public schools in Baltimore County, Maryland, who had scored at least 370 on the SAT-M as seventh-graders were invited to take part in the class. Two additional girls were invited on the basis of referral and subsequent testing. Twenty-six of these girls (77 percent) enrolled in the course. This was considerably better than the enrollment rates of 58 percent and 26 percent, respectively, for the 1972 and 1973 summer, mixed-sex accelerated classes conducted by SMPY (Fox 1974; George & Denham 1976).[1] Thus the emphasis on social factors was successful in recruiting girls for such an accelerated program.

The mathematics course for the experimental girls was not totally successful. Of the twenty-six girls who enrolled for the course, only eighteen actually attended the classes on a fairly regular basis and completed the course. The completion rate for the course was not significantly higher than the completion rate for girls in the two other accelerated classes, which were coeducational (Fox 1974; George & Denham 1976).

The letters to the experimental girls, their parents, and their schools before the start of the program had explained that girls who were successful in learning first-year algebra during the summer would be allowed to take an algebra II course in the fall. By the end of the summer, eighteen experimental girls were considered to be ready to take the algebra II course in the eighth grade. They had met Baltimore County public school officials' criterion for success — the sixty-fifth percentile on ninth-grade national norms on Form A of the Algebra I Test of the Cooperative Mathematics Series.

During the late summer and early fall, however, nine girls found their principal or guidance counselor reluctant to place them in algebra II. Three of these girls were quickly persuaded by their schools to repeat algebra I, and one girl (in a private school) was placed on one-month probation in algebra II. The remaining fourteen girls were officially enrolled for algebra II by the third week of school.

Negative reactions from the schools appeared to have had a detrimental effect upon the progress of quite a few of the girls in their mathematics classes. Three girls gave in to the wishes of their schools and repeated algebra I. Of the fifteen girls who began algebra II in the fall, two were transferred into algebra I by the end of the first six weeks of school. One girl was put back because she missed two weeks of school and earned a failing grade for the first six weeks. She had been placed in algebra II but because of scheduling problems she could meet with the class for only three of the five class sessions. The second girl who was transferred to algebra I after the first six weeks was the one on probation in the private school.

At the end of the first semester two more girls were put back into algebra I. These girls attended the same school. They were the two girls who had not met the sixty-fifth-percentile criterion on the algebra test at the end of the program but were retested before school began and allowed to enter algebra II. Both of these girls met with unfavorable reactions from their teacher or guidance counselor concerning their acceleration.

Thus, of eighteen girls who completed the program, only eleven (61 percent) were able to accelerate their mathematics progress in school. This is 42 percent of the twenty-six girls initially enrolled for the course. Of the fifteen girls who were initially placed in algebra II, eleven (73 percent) succeeded in staying in algebra II; eight of these girls (53 percent) made excellent progress. Of the eleven girls who completed algebra II, four earned final grades of A, five earned B, one C, and one D. Ten of these girls took geometry the following year (1974–75), and nine of them reported grades of A for the first grading period. The tenth girl did not report her grade.

Two control groups had been formed, one of girls and one of boys (Fox 1976). For each experimental girl enrolled in the course, a control boy and a control girl had been selected from among other seventh-grade participants in the 1973 contests. These students were seventh-graders enrolled in schools in all areas of Maryland except Baltimore County. The control students were matched with the experimental subjects on the basis of scores on the mathematical and verbal subtests of SAT, education and occupation of father, and education of mother.

Although the matching was not perfect, the general pattern was to match within plus or minus twenty points on the SAT-M and the SAT-V while controlling for the educational and occupational levels of parents. The details for the matching variables for the three groups are reported elsewhere (Fox 1976) and are summarized in table 7.1.

The 1980 Follow-Up Study

In the spring of 1980 each student in the experimental and control groups was sent a brief questionnaire to determine his or her educational status and career plans (Appendix 7.1). This was the time at which most of the students were completing their second year of college. Most of these students had also been included in a follow-up survey of 1973 talent-search participants in December, 1978, the fall after which they would normally have become high-school graduates. Students who had not responded to this questionnaire then were requested to complete it in 1980. (Details of the follow-up surveys are contained in Benbow, chapter 2 of this volume.) Short questionnaires were received from all students, and only one experimental girl never completed the follow-up survey. Data from the two

TABLE 7.1. Mean Scores on SAT-M and SAT-V in the 1973 Talent Search and in High School and the Educational Level of Parents (by Group)

Group	N	Mean[a] Talent Search		Mean[a, b] High School		Mean Educational Level[c]	
		SAT-M	SAT-V	SAT-M	SAT-V	Mother	Father
Experimental girls	26	436	399	631	595	2.9	3.3
Control girls	26	433	390	634	594	2.9	3.7
Control boys	26	443	393	658	564	2.7	3.5

[a] The mean scores of college-bound high-school seniors on the SAT-M are 492 (males) and 443 (females); on the SAT-V they are 430 (males) and 418 (females). (Admissions Testing Program of the College Board, *National Report: College-Bound Seniors* [Princeton, N.J.: Educational Testing Service, 1981].)
[b] These scores were reported by the students on their questionnaires. Twenty experimental girls, twenty-three control girls, and twenty-five control boys reported taking the test.
[c] The scale was as follows: 1 = less than high school; 2 = high-school diploma; 3 = some college; 4 = bachelor's degree; 5 = graduate study beyond the bachelor's degree.

surveys include detailed information on course-taking in high school as well as information about the students' attitudes toward acceleration and mathematics. The educational experiences and career goals of the three groups are summarized in the following sections.

SAT Scores in High School. Most of the students in the three groups took the Scholastic Aptitude Test sometime during their junior or senior year of high school. In the 1978 questionnaire they reported their scores on the examination as well as the date they took it. Since the times the examination was taken varied by six months or less, the mean scores for the groups were determined and are shown in table 7.1. An analysis of variance for matched triads was not significant. Thus the groups were very similar in high school on measures of mathematical and verbal aptitude and were superior to a national sample of college-bound seniors, even though the slightly higher SAT-M mean for boys in 1973 had been significant. A table of intercorrelations among the groups is included in Appendix 7.2. It can be seen there that talent-search and high-school SATs correlate highly. Moreover, the *r*s are consistent across the groups. For example, talent-search SAT-M scores of the experimental girls correlate with high-school SAT-M scores of the control girls to the same degree as the talent-search SAT-M scores of the control girls do (i.e., .74 for the experimental girls' talent-search SAT-M with control girls' high-school SAT-M and .73 for control girls' talent-search SAT-M with control girls' high-school SAT-M).

At the time of the talent search the correlation of SAT-M and SAT-V scores of experimental girls and the control boys and girls was much higher (i.e., $r \geqslant .90$). In high school the matching had become less tight, as would be expected, yet it was still significant. The lowering of the *r* can have resulted from different high-school experiences. Also, the date of taking the SAT was not uniform, which would lower the *r*. Nevertheless, in high school the matching was significant.

Acceleration.   As noted earlier, at the end of the 1973–74 school year following the summer of 1973 class, only eleven of the experimental girls were accelerated in their mathematics course-taking. None of the control boys or control girls was accelerated in mathematics at that time. By the end of the ninth and tenth grades the eleven experimental girls were still accelerated, and some of the control girls and boys had begun to accelerate.

An analysis of variance was performed using acceleration in mathematics at the end of the ninth grade as the dependent variable. The independent variables were group belonged to and triad, ranked in order of increasing ability on SAT-M and SAT-V, belonged to. The ANOVA was significant ($F = 4.2$, $p < .05$). By the end of the tenth grade the differences were almost significant ($F = 3.1$, $p = .07$). The control boys, but not girls, had caught up with the experimental girls. The degree of acceleration is shown in table 7.2.

A major reason for attempting the acceleration of the experimental girls was to increase the likelihood of their taking a calculus course in high school. Seven experimental girls did complete the four-year precalculus sequence in the tenth grade but chose another elective instead of calculus the next year. The percentage of students who took calculus in high school within each group is also shown in table 7.2. More boys than girls of either group took a calculus course in high school. As matched pairs, however, the difference was not statistically significant by an ANOVA with two independent variables, membership in group and triad. Triad membership was ranked in order of increasing ability on SAT-M and SAT-V. The *F* equalled 2.6 for the group effect, which was not significant. The effect of triad and the interaction term were also not significant. Essentially equal proportions of experimental and control girls (about 35 percent each) took calculus, compared to 62 percent of the boys. The percentages of boys and girls in this study who took calculus are similar to the percentages of boys and girls, respectively, included in the high-school follow-up of students from the first three talent searches who took calculus (see Benbow, chapter 2 of this volume). Overall, the experimental girls and control boys took more years of high-school mathematics than did the control girls (see table 7.2). Again, the difference in mathematics course-taking between the three groups was not significant by an ANOVA using group and triad membership as independent variables. The *F* for group membership equalled 1.2.

The degree of total acceleration for students in each group can be seen in table 7.3. Although there were no statistically significant differences among the groups, there were more control girls who were accelerated by one or two years. Three of the control girls were accelerated prior to the 1973 talent search, and two skipped eighth grade immediately following

TABLE 7.2. Students Accelerated in Mathematics in Grades 9 and 10, Taking High-School Calculus, and Taking More than 5 Years of High-School Mathematics (by Group, in Percentages)

Group	N	Took Accelerated Mathematics		Took High-School Calculus[a]	Took More than Five Years of Mathematics[a, b]
		Grade 9	Grade 10		
Experimental girls	26	42	42	36	32[c]
Control girls	26	4	8	35	12
Control boys	26	19	31	62	19

[a] The differences between the groups were not significant by an ANOVA.
[b] Data for one experimental girl were incomplete.
[c] This includes the algebra I that some completed during the summer of 1973.

TABLE 7.3. Degree of Educational Acceleration (by Group, in Percentages)

Group	N	Degree of Acceleration[a, b]			
		0	1	2	3
Experimental girls	26	46	31	23	0
Control girls	26	38	27	35	0
Control boys	26	38	38	23	0

[a] Degree of acceleration was coded as follows: 0 = no acceleration; 1 = some acceleration but totalling less than one year; 2 = moderate acceleration totalling 1 year or more but less than 3; 3 = acceleration totalling 3 years or more.
[b] Differences between the groups were not significant by an ANOVA.

the talent search. Only one experimental girl and two control boys had skipped kindergarten or elementary grades prior to the talent search. Acceleration in these two groups had resulted primarily from skipping the senior year of high school.

Students were asked how they viewed their acceleration. The majority of accelerated students within each group now wished they had accelerated more. One experimental girl wished she had not accelerated at all, and two control girls wished they had accelerated less. Of those who had not accelerated, most seemed to feel they had made the right choice.

Students in each group were asked if they felt they had made use of all available educational opportunities. The majority of control girls and control boys felt they had done as well as possible. More experimental girls than control group boys or girls, however, felt that they had not made good use of their opportunities. An analysis of variance on the dependent variable (i.e., rated use of educational opportunities) by matched groups, however, was not significant.

The College Experience.   In the spring of 1980 the majority of students in each group were still enrolled in college as full-time students. One experimental girl and one control girl had never enrolled and were working. A few students in each group were enrolled and were working. Some in each

TABLE 7.4. College Attendance and Intellectualism and Status Scores of
Colleges Attended (by Group)

Group	N	Full-Time Student (%)	Part-Time Student (%)	Not Presently Enrolled (%)
Experimental girls	26	77	4	15
Control girls	26	85	4	8
Control boys	26	77	12	12

[a] Intellectualism and status scores, derived from the scale by A. W. Astin (*Who Goes Where to College?* [Chicago: Science Research Associates, 1965], pp. 57–84), are reported as T-scores for most four-year colleges. Scores reported here were found from twenty,

group were enrolled part time or had dropped out of college. The details of college attendance can be seen in table 7.4. No significant differences were found among the three groups.

The choice of college ranged from local junior colleges to prestigious universities. An analysis of variance of the intellectualism and status ratings of the institutions (Astin 1965), respectively, showed no significant differences among the three groups, as can be seen in table 7.4. The trend, however, was for the males and then the control females to attend the academically more prestigious schools. A more personal analysis of the actual list of institutions suggested that control girls went farther from home to college while the experimental girls and control boys chose more local colleges. Six control boys, one control girl, and one experimental girl attended The Johns Hopkins University. The experimental girl, an evening college student in engineering, left Drexel University for reasons of a family financial crisis. The control girl who enrolled at Hopkins is the daughter of a faculty member. Thus the appeal of Johns Hopkins, due perhaps at least partly to participating in the talent search or experimental class, seems to have been weak for the girls but rather strong for boys. Overall the students seemed happy with their college choices; they did not differ significantly in their rated liking of college. Only two boys and one control girl reported that they disliked college, and no experimental girls did so.

A distribution of students by college major can be seen in table 7.5. For purposes of comparison, five broad categories were formed. The first was mathematics, in which engineering and economics were included. The second was science, which includes those indicating premedical preparation. The third, fourth, and fifth were social sciences, humanities, and business or law. Analysis of the paired distribution of those enrolled in mathematical or science majors versus those in other areas was not significant. The trend, however, was for more boys than girls in either group to major in a mathematical or scientific area. Slightly more experimental girls were in mathematical majors than science areas, but control girls were divided

Never Enrolled (%)	Intellectualism Score[a]		Status Score[a]	
	Mean	Standard Deviation	Mean	Standard Deviation
4	53	14	55	10
4	56	14	55	10
0	61	12	58	12

twenty-one, and twenty-four colleges attended by the experimental girls, the control girls, and the control boys, respectively.

evenly between mathematical and scientific majors. Studies of large samples of college students typically find a higher attrition rate in mathematical majors for women than men (Melone 1980). In the present study, however, only one person in each group had already changed his or her major away from mathematics.

On the basis of the similarity in college majors, one might expect there to be little difference, or a slight difference in favor of the control boys, among the three groups in the mathematics courses taken in college. It is interesting to see that in terms of the number of semesters of mathematics studied, control boys and experimental girls were identical. As can be seen in table 7.6, they took more mathematics courses than did control girls. An analysis of variance for matched groups, however, was not significant.

With regard to attitudes held toward mathematics, no differences between the groups were detected. While in high school the control girls

TABLE 7.5. College Majors and Career Plans of Students
(by Group, in Percentages)

Group	N	M	S	SS	H	B/L	N
				College Major			
Experimental girls	22	32	14	18	18	18	0
Control girls	24	21	21	17	21	21	0
Control boys	24	42	21	13	17	8	0
				Career Plan			
Experimental girls	26	19	8	4	12	27	30
Control girls	26	15	23	19	15	19	9
Control boys	26	31	15	4	23	15	12

NOTE: M = Mathematics, engineering, and economics
  S = science
  SS = social sciences
  H = humanities
  B/L = business or law
  N = no response or undecided

TABLE 7.6. Mean College Semesters of Mathematics and Grade Point Average in the Mathematics Courses for Those Enrolled Full Time (by Group)

Group	N	Math Semesters	N	Grade Point Average
Experimental girls	20	3.25	17	3.24
Control girls	22	2.64	19	3.38
Control boys	20	3.20	16	3.34

rated their liking for mathematics more positively than the experimental girls, but the differences were not statistically significant. Moreover, the three groups, while in high school, did not differ in the perceptions of the usefulness of mathematics for their future careers.

Educational Aspirations and Career Goals.   The educational aspirations of students in all three groups are high, as one might expect given the fact that as seventh-graders they were all in the top 3 percent of their age group with respect to mathematical ability. There were no differences among the three groups, as can be seen in table 7.7. The mean of the educational aspirations for all three groups was somewhat more than a master's degree.

The distribution of students by category of career goal, by group, can be seen in table 7.5. No significant differences emerge when career interest in mathematical/scientific/medical careers are compared with all other career interests, and no clear trends appear. Experimental girls are oriented toward careers in business, law, or mathematics/science, with only a few interested in the social sciences or humanities. In contrast, the control girls are more evenly distributed among the options. Finally, control boys are very strongly oriented toward the careers in mathematics and science, followed by interest in business or law. The boys show less interest in careers in the humanities and social sciences than do the control girls but about the same degree of interest as the experimental girls.

PERCEIVED BARRIERS TO MATHEMATICAL OR SCIENTIFIC CAREERS

On the 1980 questionnaire each student was asked to rate eight possible barriers to careers in mathematics or science for women on a scale of zero to two. Zero was "no problem"; one was a "minor problem"; and two was a "serious problem." The results can be seen in table 7.8. There were no statistically significant differences among the three groups in their ratings of six of the eight factors.

Girls in both groups viewed the lack of appropriate role models and lack of information about careers in mathematics as more serious problems than did the boys. These differences in ratings were significant. Boys rated the "perception of women majoring in engineering and science as

TABLE 7.7. Highest Level of Educational Aspiration of Students
(by Group)

Group	N	High School	Some College or Vocational Training	B.S.	M.A.	Ph.D., etc.	Post-doctoral Study	Mean[a]	Standard Deviation
Experimental girls	25	0	8	4	56	28	4	4.2	0.9
Control girls	26	4	0	23	35	27	12	4.2	1.2
Control boys	25	0	4	20	36	32	8	4.2	1.0

[b] Educational aspiration was coded as follows: 1 = high school; 2 = some college; 3 = bachelor's degree; 4 = master's degree; 5 = doctorate degree; 6 = postdoctoral study.

unfeminine" as a more serious problem than did the girls, but the difference was not statistically significant.

A rank ordering from the greatest to the least problem, based on mean ratings, is similar for the two groups of girls. The lack of role models was viewed as the greatest problem; the perception of scientists as cold and impersonal was the least. Boys, however, viewed the problem of combining a career and family responsibilities as the most serious problem for women and the long years of preparation required as the least serious problem. It would seem that the boys did not perceive these possible barriers in the same way the girls did.

Since the lack of encouragement and support for mathematical and scientific careers for women was viewed as a problem by all three groups, it is interesting to look at how much encouragement and support the students in each group felt they had received. We had expected that the boys would have received the most. There were no statistically significant differences, however, among the three groups in their responses to a Likert-scale rating of encouragement and support received for their interest in and study of mathematics (see table 7.9). All three groups reported receiving "some," but not "much," encouragement.

On an open-ended question as to why they had or had not personally chosen to pursue a career in mathematics or science, the responses varied widely. For those who were interested in a mathematical or scientific career, the most frequent response was that they enjoyed the field. This was the most frequent response of experimental girls and control boys in particular. Control girls were more likely to mention the possibility of helping people as a major reason. This perhaps is related to the somewhat higher percentage of control girls in the medical science majors. The factor of having the ability was mentioned by one experimental girl and one control boy, but no control girls mentioned this. Only one experimental girl

TABLE 7.8. Rated Importance of Possible Factors Preventing Women from Pursuing Careers in Mathematics, Science, and Engineering (by Group)

Group	N	No Problem	Minor Problem	Serious Problem	Mean[a]	Standard Deviation
		Long Years of Formal Preparation				
Experimental girls	26	10	12	4	0.8	0.7
Control girls	26	11	11	4	0.7	0.7
Control boys	26	16	8	2	0.5	0.6
		Conflicts in Combining Career and Family				
Experimental girls	26	4	13	9	1.2	0.7
Control girls	26	2	17	7	1.2	0.6
Control boys	26	4	14	8	1.2	0.7
		Perception of Women Majoring in Engineering and Science as Unfeminine				
Experimental girls	26	15	9	3	0.5	0.6
Control girls	26	12	11	3	0.7	0.7
Control boys	26	9	11	6	0.9	0.8
		Lack of Encouragement				
Experimental girls	26	5	13	8	1.1	0.1
Control girls	26	9	9	8	1.0	0.8
Control boys	26	9	8	9	1.0	0.8
		Perception of Science and Math Work as Being Too Difficult				
Experimental girls	26	6	10	10	1.2	0.9
Control girls	26	12	8	6	0.8	0.8
Control boys	26	14	7	5	0.7	0.8
		Lack of Information about Careers in Science and Math				
Experimental girls	26	3	11	12	1.3	0.7
Control girls	25	3	13	9	1.2	0.7
Control boys	26	8	16	2	0.8	0.6
		Lack of Appropriate Role Models				
Experimental girls	26	1	13	12	1.4	0.6
Control girls	25	1	13	11	1.4	0.6
Control boys	26	5	16	5	1.0	0.6
		Perception of Scientists as Cold and Impersonal				
Experimental girls	26	19	4	3	0.4	0.7
Control girls	26	13	10	3	0.6	0.7
Control boys	25	12	12	1	0.6	0.6

[a] Responses were coded as follows: 0 = no problem; 1 = minor problem; 2 = serious problem.

TABLE 7.9. Encouragement and Support Received by Students for Interest in and Study of Mathematics (by Group)

Group	N	Degree of Support[a] (%)					Mean of Support[a]	Standard Deviation
		1	2	3	4	5		
Experimental girls	24	4	0	45	29	21	3.6	1.0
Control girls	24	0	0	54	25	21	3.7	0.8
Control boys	26	0	0	38	42	21	3.8	0.7

[a] Degree of support was coded as follows: 1 = much discouragement; 2 = some discouragement; 3 = neither support nor discouragement; 4 = some support; 5 = much support.

attributed her interest in a mathematical career to the fact that she had become accelerated in the study of mathematics. One control girl, but no experimental girls or control boys, cited direct encouragement from a significant other (in this case, the parents) as important.

Those who chose careers in other areas were often vague about their reasons for not choosing mathematics, citing only "other interest." Three experimental girls cited the difficulty of mathematics as a deterrent, but no others did so. On the ratings of barriers and reasons for not pursuing careers in mathematics or science, the experimental girls had rated difficulty as a more serious problem than had the other students.

If difficulty of science and mathematics majors deterred our students from entering them, we would expect that our boys would rate their mathematical ability as superior to that of the girls since more boys than girls pursued these majors. When students were asked to rate their mathematical ability relative to that of their high-school peers, however, the three groups did not differ significantly. Nineteen experimental girls, twenty-one control girls, and twenty-two control boys rated themselves as superior. It is of interest to note here that the students in each group had been initially matched on mathematical and verbal ability.

TREATMENT EFFECTS

When the total group of experimental girls was compared with the control groups on various outcome measures, such as acceleration, course-taking up through college, and college majors, there was only one statistically significant difference. The experimental girls were more accelerated than the control girls in their mathematics course-taking at the end of the ninth grade.

Not all of the experimental girls, however, completed the summer program, and some who did finish the summer course were not able to accelerate their course-taking in high school the following year. Therefore, it seemed desirable to look within the experimental group for effects of differential treatment. Three subgroups of the experimental girls were studied, and their progress relative to that of their matched counterparts was evaluated.

Subgroup A. The eleven girls who completed the summer program and completed an algebra II class during the eighth grade had the full benefit of the program. They continued to be accelerated in their mathematics course-taking in the ninth and tenth grades. Six of these students took calculus in the eleventh grade. Three others took college algebra in the eleventh grade and calculus in the twelfth grade. The eleven girls averaged 5.5 years of mathematics courses in high school.

Two girls never took high-school calculus. They were also the only two of the eleven who had not continued to attend college full time. One, a part-time student at the Peabody Institute of The Johns Hopkins University, majored in dance. The other, also at the Peabody Institute, dropped out of the music program.

Of the nine girls who were full-time college students in the spring of 1980, three majored in engineering, two in mathematics, one in business, one in English, and one in biology. One had an undeclared major but had previously been a physics major. She was contemplating a career in nursing. Considering the strong interest in mathematics and related areas, it is not surprising that this group of nine students took an average of 3.6 semesters of college mathematics courses in their first two years of college.

Of the eleven matched control girls, only two accelerated their mathematics course-taking in high school, but seven took a calculus course (compared to nine for the experimental girls). They averaged only 4.6 years of high-school mathematics, however. Nine of the eleven were enrolled full time in college and had averaged only 2.5 semesters of college mathematics. Two were majoring in engineering, two in science, two in business, two in the social sciences, and one in the humanities.

Of the eleven matched control boys, two had accelerated their course-taking and six took a calculus course in high school. They averaged 4.5 years of high-school mathematics. All eleven were enrolled full time in college and averaged 2.5 semesters of college mathematics. Seven majored in engineering, science, accounting, or economics. Three were social science majors and one was a fine arts major.

In summary, for these eleven matched triads, the only differences found were in favor of the experimental girls. The amount of mathematics studied by them in high school or college was greater. These data are summarized in table 7.10.

Subgroup B. This group consists of the seven girls who completed the summer course but who either did not enter or did not remain in an algebra II class in the eighth grade. They did not later accelerate their course-taking in mathematics, nor did any of them take a high-school calculus course. The average number of years of high-school mathematics studied by the group was four.

TABLE 7.10. Mathematics Course-Taking in High School and College and College Major (by Subgroups within Groups)

Subgroups[a]	Groups	N	Mean Number of Years of Mathematics in High School	Percentage Taking Calculus in High School	Percentage Enrolled in College Full-Time in 1980	Mean Number of Semesters of Mathematics in College[b]	Percentage Majoring in Mathematics/ Science Field[b]
A	Experimental girls	11	5.5	82	82	3.6	67
	Control girls	11	4.6	64	82	2.5	56
	Control boys	11	4.5	55	100	2.5	63
B	Experimental girls	6	4.0	0	83	1.4	40
	Control girls	7	4.2	0	100	1.6	29
	Control boys	7	4.2	29	43	2.7	29
C	Experimental girls	8	4.0	0	75	1.8	17
	Control girls	8	3.8	25	75	2.3	33
	Control boys	8	5.8	100	75	2.5	67

[a]Subgroups are composed as follows: A = experimental girls who completed algebra II in the eighth grade and their matched controls; B = experimental girls who did not enroll in or complete algebra II in the eighth grade and their matched controls; C = experimental girls who did not complete the program and their matched controls.
[b]Number of cases is those still enrolled full time in college at the end of their second year of college.

Of the seven girls, five were full-time college students in the spring of 1980. One had never enrolled, and one had dropped from a major in special education. The majors of those in college were accounting, business administration, political science, dental hygiene, and theater. The business administration major was interested in a career with a mathematical or statistical emphasis and had taken 3 semesters of college mathematics; the other four had each taken only 1 semester of mathematics in their first two years of college. (The average for the group was 1.4 semesters.)

In comparison, none of the seven matched control girls had accelerated her study of mathematics, and none took calculus in high school. Thus they were similar to their experimental counterparts in mathematics course-taking in high school and college. All were full-time college students but only two majored in a science area. With respect to the seven matched control boys, two of them had accelerated their course-taking in the ninth or tenth grade and had taken high-school calculus. The seven boys averaged 4.2 years of high-school mathematics. Only three of the seven were full-time college students. One was majoring in computer science, one in engineering, and one in business.

The differences among these triads were small. They can be seen in table 7.10.

Subgroup C.   Eight young women did not complete the summer algebra program and subsequently never became accelerated in their mathematics programs in school. Like the members of group B, they averaged four years of high-school mathematics, and not one of them took calculus in high school.

Six of the eight in this group were full-time college students in the spring of 1980. Three students had a business or economics major; one majored in psychology and education, another in political science, and one in horticulture. During the first two years of college a business major took 4 semesters of college mathematics, the horticulture major 1, and the political science major did not take any. The remaining three students took 2 semesters. For the group the overall average was 1.8 semesters.

None of the control girls who were matched with the eight program drop-outs had accelerated her mathematics progress, either, but two of them had taken high-school calculus. This group averaged 3.8 years of high-school mathematics. Two were pursuing college majors in mathematics, two in the social sciences, one in English, and one in nursing.

Four of the matched control boys had accelerated their study of mathematics in high school. Moreover, all eight took calculus in high school. These boys averaged 5.8 years of high-school mathematics. Six were full-time students in college and averaged 2.5 semesters of college mathematics. Four of the six were majoring in a mathematical or scientific career, and two were in the social sciences.

Thus it is within this triad that large sex differences emerge. The boys were more accelerated in mathematics in high school. They also took more courses, especially calculus. In college, however, the boys took only slightly more mathematics than the girls, even though more of these boys majored in a mathematics-related area. These data are also summarized in table 7.10.

Clearly, the nature of the treatment was important. It appears that at the time the achievement of the experimental females in mathematics and science was only enhanced if they received the full effect. Thus an early intervention strategy such as this can be effective in increasing the participation of females in mathematics and science, but girls participating must be successful in it. Moreover, providing only exposure to mathematics and role models is not enough to enhance achievement.

Conclusions

An experimental mathematics class with twenty-six seventh-grade female students was conducted during the summer of 1973. The purpose of this all-girls class was to enhance the participation in mathematics and science of moderately gifted females. For each girl in the study there was a control girl and a control boy who was matched with her on ability and parental background variable. The progress of the twenty-six experimental girls through high school and the first two years of college was studied and compared to the progress of the control boys and girls. It was hypothesized that this early intervention strategy would enhance the achievement of the experimental girls so that they would have participated more in mathematics than the control girls and at least at the level of the control boys. (Boys tend to participate more in mathematically related areas.)

If we view the students in the control groups as having had a "weak" treatment (only counseling by mail as to the benefits of accelerating their study of mathematics), and if we view the experimental girls as having had a "strong" treatment (a special class with exposure to role models and an immediate opportunity to accelerate their study of mathematics), one must conclude that for the moderately gifted, the "strong" treatment was not a significantly more effective treatment.

There were eleven girls in the experimental groups, however, who experienced success in the program. These students' participation in mathematics was later enhanced. Thus an early intervention strategy can improve the participation of girls in higher-level mathematics, but the girls have to be successful in the program.

Three factors may have confounded the results. First, the selection criteria for admission to the program was such that several students with very modest SAT scores were admitted to the class. Other special classes conducted at SMPY have used much higher criteria for admission than a

370 on the SAT-M. If the selection score had been 450, there would probably have been a higher success rate but also a very small class. The second
explanation is related to the first. Only eleven girls actually received the
full extent of the "strong" treatment. Therefore, comparisons in which all
twenty-six experimental girls are included actually involve fifteen girls who
had a moderate treatment or a failure experience. The eleven girls who did
experience the total program were more accelerated, took more mathematics courses in high school and college, and scored higher on the SAT-M
in high school than any other group. Third, the numbers were so small that
the selection of the control groups was such as possibly to bias the results
in that the students were from a variety of different school systems. Some
of these school systems may have encouraged more acceleration in
mathematics than did the school system in which the experimental girls
were enrolled. For example, some of the control boys were enrolled in an
accelerated program in a Baltimore City school. Several control boys and
girls were enrolled in schools in Maryland's Howard and Montgomery
counties, where accelerated programs for the gifted were later developed
along the lines of the SMPY model.

On the basis of this study and the results of the evaluations of other
accelerated classes conducted by SMPY for both boys and girls, we can
draw two major implications for programs for the gifted. First, intensive
intervention programs during the summer by an outside-of-school agency
such as SMPY are more necessary and effective for the highly gifted than
for the moderately gifted. Second, what may be most beneficial for the
moderately gifted is the provision of flexible scheduling in the junior and
senior high schools to allow these students to accelerate their study of
mathematics at a moderate rate within the existing school program.

Perhaps the most encouraging result of the present study is that boys
and girls who were matched on measures of ability and socioeconomic
backgrounds in grade seven did not differ strikingly in terms of educational experiences, aspirations, and career goals. While one may still conclude that mathematically apt girls may need encouragement to take
calculus in high school, it is gratifying to see that most of these gifted
students, male and female, are continuing their education beyond high
school and aspire to professional careers.

Notes

We thank Julian C. Stanley for helpful comments on an earlier draft of this
chapter.

1. These differences are even more remarkable because most of the students
eligible for the mixed-sex classes were considerably apter mathematically than were
these thirty-four girls.

References

Admissions Testing Program of the College Board. 1981. *National report: College-bound seniors, 1981.* Princeton, N.J.: Educational Testing Service.

Astin, A. W. 1965. *Who goes where to college?* Chicago: Science Research Associates.

College Entrance Examination Board. 1975. *Summary report of 1975 Advanced Placement examinations.* Princeton, N.J.

Dearman, N. B., and Plisko, V. W. 1979. *The condition of education,* pp. 232–33. Washington, D.C.: National Center for Education Statistics.

Educational Testing Service. 1962. *Cooperative Mathematics Tests: Algebra I.* Princeton, N.J.

Fox, L. H. 1974. A mathematics program for fostering precocious achievement. In *Mathematical talent: Discovery, description, and development,* ed. J. C. Stanley, D. P. Keating, and L. H. Fox, 101–25. Baltimore: Johns Hopkins University Press.

———. 1976. Sex differences in mathematical talent: Bridging the gap. In *Intellectual talent: Research and development,* ed. D. P. Keating, 183–214. Baltimore: Johns Hopkins University Press.

George, W. C., and Denham, S. A. 1976. Curriculum experimentation for the mathematically talented. In *Intellectual talent: Research and development,* ed. D. P. Keating, 103–31. Baltimore: Johns Hopkins University Press.

Melone, F. 1980. *Mathematics as a barrier to career success for women.* Paper presented at the Annual Meeting of the American Association for the Advancement of Science, San Francisco, Calif.

Sells, L. W. 1980. The mathematics filter and the education of women and minorities. In *Women and the mathematical mystique,* ed. L. H. Fox, L. E. Brody, and D. H. Tobin, 66–76. Baltimore: Johns Hopkins University Press.

APPENDIX 7.1: 1980 Follow-Up Questionnaire Used Only for Summer, 1973, Study

THE JOHNS HOPKINS UNIVERSITY • BALTIMORE, MARYLAND 21218

STUDY OF MATHEMATICALLY PRECOCIOUS YOUTH (SMPY)

Please reply care of: DEPARTMENT OF PSYCHOLOGY

PROFESSOR JULIAN C. STANLEY, Director of SMPY

Ms. LOIS S. SANDHOFER, B.A., Administrative Assistant

127 Ames Hall, (301) 338-7087

Mr. WILLIAM C. GEORGE, Ed.M., Associate Director

125 Ames Hall, (301) 338-8144

Ms. CAMILLA P. BENBOW, M.A., Assistant Director

126 Ames Hall, (301) 338-7086

QUESTIONNAIRE ON FACTORS IN MATHEMATICS ACHIEVEMENT

Please fill out carefully and completely all of the questions below that apply to you. Please print or type all answers and send the completed questionnaire as soon as possible to SMPY, Dept. of Psychology, The Johns Hopkins University, Baltimore, Md. 21218. All information will be kept strictly confidential; you will not be publicly identified with the information herein in any way.

NAME: _____
      First   Middle   Last   (Maiden, if applicable)

Permanent address: _____ Telephone ( ) _____
               Street   City   State   Zip   Area Code

Temporary address if different from above: _____
                                       Street

_____Telephone ( )_____
  City   State   Zip   Area Code

1. Are you currently employed full-time? (circle)   yes   no

   If yes, please supply the following information about your present and past post high-school occupations in chronological order.

Type of Occupation	Duties Involved	Employer	Dates of Employment
1)			
2)			
3)			

2. Please check the box that applies to you with regard to attendance in an institution of higher education.

   ☐ I am currently a full-time student.

   ☐ I have graduated.

   ☐ I am currently a part-time student after having attended full-time.

   ☐ I am a part-time student.

   ☐ I am not currently enrolled but was previously.

   ☐ I am not and have not been enrolled. (Go to question 3.)

a. Which school are your currently or were you attending? (Do not list schools you may have transferred from.) _____

b. Dates of attendance: _____
   Month/Year   to   Month/Year

c. If you have been graduated, date of graduation: _____
                                             Month/Year

d. What is your major field of study? _____

e. If you have switched majors in your undergraduate career, please list your previous major(s) in chronological order: _____

f. Please list the titles of the mathematics courses you have already taken in college, your grades in these courses, and when they were taken.

Mathematics Course	Grade	Dates of Attendance
1.		
2.		
3.		
4.		
5.		

   If you have taken more mathematics, please continue on a separate sheet of paper.

g. Please list the titles of the science courses you have already taken in college, your grades in these courses, and when they were taken.

Science Course	Grade	Dates of Attendance
1.		
2.		
3.		
4.		
5.		

   If you have taken more science courses, please continue on a separate sheet of paper.

3. Please list the college-level mathematics courses you are planning to take in the future: _____

4. Please describe your career goal (i.e., a professor of mathematics or a practicing pediatrician): _____

a. If this career is in the field of science or mathematics, why did you choose this career goal? _____

133

b. If this career is <u>not</u> in the field of science or mathematics, why did you not pursue a career in those areas? _____

5. Have you been accelerated in your educational progress?   Yes   No   (Circle.)

a. If no, do you wish you would have been?   Yes   No   (Circle.)

b. If yes, please circle the letter of the applicable sentences to you and then complete them.

   1) I skipped the following grades: _____

   2) I took Advanced Placement Program (APP) examinations for which I received _____ credits of advanced placement in college.

   3) I was accelerated in subject-matter placement in _____ subjects.

   4) I took college courses on a part-time basis as a high-school student for which I received _____ credits of advanced standing in college.

   5) Other. (Please specify.) _____

c. If you were to reconsider your acceleration, which one of the following would best describe your thoughts (check the box)?

   ☐ I would not accelerate my education at all.

   ☐ I would accelerate my education somewhat but not as much as I have done.

   ☐ I would accelerate my education to the degree which I have already done.

   ☐ I would accelerate my education somewhat more than what I have already done.

   ☐ I would accelerate my education much more.

6. In general terms, how would you describe the amount of encouragement and support that you have received for your interest in and study of mathematics?

   ☐ Much support   ☐ Some support   ☐ Neither support nor discouragement   ☐ Some discouragement   ☐ Much discouragement

7. How important do you think mathematics will be for your future career?

   (Circle.)   Very   Fairly   Slightly   Not very   Not at all

8. Relative to students who went to high school with you, how well do you feel that you rank in general mathematical ability?

   ☐ Much superior to my peers

   ☐ Somewhat superior to my peers

   ☐ About as well as my peers

   ☐ Less well than my peers

   ☐ Much less well than my peers

9. In the past, fewer women than men have pursued careers in mathematics, science, and engineering. The reasons listed below have been mentioned as factors contributing to this. Indicate whether you think these reasons constitute serious problems, minor problems, or no problem to most mathematically talented girls today by placing a (√) in the appropriate column.

	NO PROBLEM	MINOR PROBLEM	SERIOUS PROBLEM
Long years of formal preparation required			
Possible conflicts combining a career and family responsibilities			
Perception of women majoring in engineering or sciences as unfeminine			
Lack of encouragement from teachers and counselors			
Perception that the work will be more difficult than they can handle			
Lack of information about careers in science and mathematics			
Lack of contact with women employed in those fields			
Perception of scientists and engineers as cold and impersonal			

I hereby certify that I have read over my responses carefully and thoroughly. They are as complete and accurate as I can make them.

_____
Signature

Please return this questionnaire to:

Ms. Camilla P. Benbow
SMPY
Department of Psychology
The Johns Hopkins University
Baltimore, Maryland 21218

APPENDIX 7.2: Intercorrelations of Talent Search and High-School SAT Scores for the Three Groups

	Talent Search SAT-M Control Girls	Talent Search SAT-M Control Boys	Talent Search SAT-V Experimental Girls	Talent Search SAT-V Control Girls	Talent Search SAT-V Control Boys	High School SAT-M Experimental Girls	High School SAT-M Control Girls	High School SAT-M Control Boys	High School SAT-V Experimental Girls	High School SAT-V Control Girls	High School SAT-V Control Boys
Talent Search SAT-M Experimental Girls (N)	.9491[c] (26)	.9592[c] (26)	.0426 (26)	.1763 (26)	.1661 (26)	.4863[a] (20)	.7427[c] (23)	.5263[b] (25)	-.0382 (20)	.2607 (23)	.2573 (25)
Talent Search SAT-M Control Girls		.9514[c] (26)	.1038 (26)	.2506 (26)	.2112 (26)	.5023[a] (20)	.7329[c] (23)	.5083[b] (25)	.0417 (20)	.3381 (23)	.1706 (25)
Talent Search SAT-M Control Boys			.0900 (26)	.2149 (26)	.1805 (26)	.3943[a] (20)	.7512[c] (23)	.5267[b] (25)	.0070 (20)	.3455 (23)	.1641 (25)
Talent Search SAT-V Experimental Girls				.9001[c] (26)	.9176[c] (26)	.4638[a] (20)	-.0465 (23)	.1407 (25)	.8527[c] (20)	.6006[c] (23)	.4773[b] (25)
Talent Search SAT-V Control					.9401[c] (26)	.4764[a] (20)	.0479 (23)	.0583 (25)	.7083[c] (20)	.6685[c] (23)	.5384[b] (25)

	Talent Search SAT-M Experimental Girls	Talent Search SAT-M Control Girls	Talent Search SAT-M Control Boys	Talent Search SAT-V Experimental Girls	Talent Search SAT-V Control Girls	Talent Search SAT-V Control Boys	High School SAT-M Experimental Girls	High School SAT-M Control Girls	High School SAT-M Control Boys	High School SAT-V Experimental Girls	High School SAT-V Control Girls	High School SAT-V Control Boys
Talent Search SAT-V Control Boys							.3993[a] (20)	-.0330 (23)	.0754 (25)	.7853[c] (20)	.5183[b] (23)	.5290[b] (25)
High School SAT-M Experimental Girls								.4757[a] (18)	.3956[a] (20)	.3004 (20)	.5737[b] (18)	.5239[b] (20)
High School SAT-M Control Girls									.5837[b] (22)	-.0071 (18)	.4742[a] (23)	.1289 (22)
High School SAT-M Control Boys										.1486 (20)	.4123[a] (22)	.4973[b] (25)
High School SAT-V Experimental Girls											.4592[a] (18)	.3146 (20)

	Talent Search SAT-M Experimental Girls	Talent Search SAT-M Control Girls	Talent Search SAT-M Control Boys	Talent Search SAT-V Experimental Girls	Talent Search SAT-V Control Girls	Talent Search SAT-V Control Boys	High School SAT-M Experimental Girls	High School SAT-M Control Girls	High School SAT-M Control Boys	High School SAT-V Experimental Girls	High School SAT-V Control Girls	High School SAT-V Control Boys
High School SAT-V Control Girls												.5610[b] (22)
High School SAT-V Control Boys												

[a] $p \le .05$.
[b] $p \le .01$.
[c] $p \le .001$.

8

A Case for Radical Acceleration: Programs of the Johns Hopkins University and the University of Washington

HALBERT B. ROBINSON

Abstract

Common arguments for and against accelerated pacing are presented. The conclusion is reached that educational programs must be adapted to fit the needs of the intellectually talented student. SMPY at The Johns Hopkins University and the Child Development Research Group at the University of Washington, both of which espouse curricular flexibility and emphasize radical acceleration, are described and exemplified by individual case studies. The description of the Washington program stresses the Radical Acceleration Group of the Early Entrance Program (EEP). This aspect of the program involves early entrance to the University of Washington for those students 14 years old and under, not yet in the tenth grade, who score better than college freshmen on the Washington Pre-College Test. Providing a structured support system, the program aids in the transition from junior-high to college-level work. Although some problems have been encountered, overall the students have made satisfactory academic and social progress in college.

The purpose of this paper is to discuss arguments for and against the accelerated pacing of intellectually precocious children in the educational system and to describe the experience of two programs that promote radical acceleration of highly talented young people.

139

It is customary to refer to the practice of permitting intellectually talented children to move to more difficult levels of a curriculum as "educational acceleration." This phrase implies that the advancement is a result of educational practice, as though somehow an educational method had been discovered that can speed up the inherent rate of a child's development. At the opposite end of the continuum, one does not refer to "educational retardation" but to "mental retardation," a description of the slowed pace of intellectual development. It would be more accurate, similarly, to refer to "mental acceleration" and to acknowledge that educational adaptations are responsive to, but usually are not largely responsible for, the mental advancement of gifted children.

A central conclusion of the present paper is that the pace of educational programs must be adapted to the capacities and knowledge of individual children. In a few instances, the appropriate fit of child and program calls for placement several levels above the child's age-mates and is termed "radical acceleration." The rationale behind the position to be advanced is grounded in the bedrock of developmental psychology as it has evolved, theoretically and empirically, during the past century. The propositions that follow may seem so obvious that they are no longer worth stating. Their triteness, however, is of particular significance because of the regularity with which they are ignored by educators of gifted students.

Premise 1.   Learning is a sequential, developmental process. Attainment of skills, understanding in domains of knowledge, and strategies for solving problems are all acquired gradually and in sequences that are more or less predictable (Hilgard & Bower 1974). The learning of language, reading, and mathematics, and the understanding of logical and scientific relationships, proceed in orderly patterns that have been well described, if not altogether understood (Gagné 1965; Rohwer 1970).

Premise 2.   Effective teaching must involve a sensitive assessment of the individual's status in the learning process and the presentation of problems that slightly exceed the level already mastered. Too-easy tasks produce boredom; too-difficult tasks cannot be understood. This is what Hunt (1961) referred to as "the problem of the match," which is based on the principle that learning occurs only when there is "an appropriate match between the circumstances that a child encounters and the schemata that he has already assimilated into his repertoire" (p. 268). Hunt notes that "this principle is only another statement of the educator's adage that 'teaching must start where the learner is'" (p. 268).

Premise 3.   There are substantial differences in learning status among individuals of any given age. Acquisition of knowledge and the development of patterns of cognitive organization follow predictable sequences, but the rates with which children progress through these sequences vary considerably (Bayley 1955, 1970; George, Cohn, & Stanley 1979; Keating 1976; Keating & Stanley 1972; Robinson & Robinson 1976). Individual differences characterize both the rate of overall cognitive development (i.e., general intelligence) and the acquisition of specific skills (e.g., reading).

Despite the axiomatic character of these truisms, current educational "wisdom" about the education of gifted children flies baldly in their face. If it is true that learning is a sequential process, that effective teaching must be grounded where the learner is, and that there are striking differences in developmental rate among individuals of the same age, then how do we justify an educational system that ignores competence and utilizes age to place students for the purpose of educating them?

In the schools of all fifty of the United States, classes are organized by age of pupils, and deviation from age-graded placement is disapproved of. Children who are slow learners are socially promoted until their deviance from the class mean becomes intolerable; exceptionally precocious children are advanced with their age-mates no matter what their deviance from the class mean. Even most special programs for gifted children tend to assume that students will advance one grade per year.

Most teachers, however, do try their best to accommodate to the different learning rates of their pupils. They may create smaller subgroups within the classroom, allowing students to do special projects or even to study a more advanced textbook on their own. These adjustments, however, tend to be piecemeal, inconsistent from one year to the next, and sometimes conflicting (as when children who have mastered a more advanced level of reading or mathematics must repeat the curriculum when they reach "the right age for it"). Seldom do schools take the very sensible step of utilizing their own resources — existing classes at more advanced grade levels — for academically advanced children.

The rigid correspondence between age and grade placement is a new phenomenon in American education and rarely characterizes programs outside the large bureaucracy that constitutes the present-day educational establishment. Not only the fabled one-room schoolhouse but also larger school districts formerly permitted a considerable degree of flexibility in advancing or holding back students in order to achieve a reasonable match between placement and competence (Kett 1974). Prior to World War II one typically found some mixture of ages represented in the classroom. In Terman's study (Terman & Oden 1947, 1959), for example, most of the children with IQs of 140+ were accelerated one or more grade levels by the time of graduation from high school.

In many realms of education we easily accept the principle of placement according to competence. Music and sports instructors, for example, clearly place higher value on skill and attainment than on age. Child prodigies in the performing arts and athletics have always been recognized and applauded, while adult pupils in many skill areas have been welcomed as beginners at any age. Even the most bureaucratic school systems often support orchestras in which children advance according to talent and competence, sports programs in which age is a minor consideration, and science and art fairs that reward excellence, not seniority. The age-graded system is not inevitable or preordained; it is a modern invention motivated largely by egalitarian goals. In the process of equalizing educational opportunity, however, the rights of many children to an appropriate education have been abrogated.

Rationale for the Age-Graded System of Education

What are the fundamental reasons for an age-graded educational system? The one most often proposed is that advancing students according to their demonstrated mastery of subject areas fails to take into consideration the level of their social competencies and their emotional strengths and weaknesses (Hildreth 1966; Hollingworth 1929). Social and emotional maturity is thought to correspond rather specifically to chronological age (Gold 1965; Rothman & Levine 1963). It is argued that intellectual and academic accomplishments indicate very little about social and emotional development and that to advance individuals according to their progress in one domain may seriously jeopardize healthy progress in the other areas and impair the child's immediate adjustment as well as his or her future mental health (see, e.g., Congdon, 1979).

More than two hundred articles that I have examined report experiences of students who have, in one way or another, been advanced in school because they appeared to be academically ready for a challenge beyond their years. Some reported on students who were granted early admission to kindergarten or first grade, others on students who skipped one or more grades, and still others on students who earned college credit while in high school or who entered college early. Not one of these studies lends credence to the notion that such practices lead to major difficulties for the students involved. It is, indeed, much easier from the available evidence to make the case that students who are allowed to move ahead according to their competencies are benefited in their social and emotional development than it is to make the case that they are harmed. Reviewers who have examined this issue (Daurio 1979; Gallagher 1975; Newland 1976) have arrived at essentially the same conclusion. As Keating (1979) observed, "As for the socio-emotional concerns, it seems time to abandon them unless and until some solid reliable evidence is forthcoming that indicates real dangers in well-run programs" (p. 218).

A second objection to allowing academically advanced students to progress at their own pace stresses the importance of the academic experiences that would be lost if they were moved ahead of their age peers. Grade skipping is said to produce gaps in knowledge because students miss important learning experiences (Hildreth 1966). The argument is not entirely specious. There is a danger that gaps may occur when significant portions of a curriculum are omitted. Few children are likely to invent logarithms and few are likely on their own to memorize the multiplication tables. Although skipping grades may not be the best alternative, there is little evidence to support the position that bright students who do skip are afflicted with substantial lacunae in their knowledge base (Keating 1976; Stanley, Keating, & Fox 1974). Specific gaps that do appear can usually be handled by brief, targeted, individual tutoring. Missed subject matter in nonsequential subjects, such as history and English, can be acquired at many different levels in elementary and secondary schools, as well as through college work and by independent study.

A third argument against acceleration, which is closely related to the second, is that valuable nonacademic experiences will be eliminated by rapid advancement through the system (Rothman & Levine 1963). One cannot, of course, be president of the junior class if one skips the junior year, and it does seem very unlikely that a 12-year-old will be able to play with his high-school football team. It is not clear, however, just how far this argument should be extended. A student who is younger than his or her classmates may well be permitted to edit the school paper, participate in the debate club, or go out for noncontact sports. The available evidence suggests, in fact, that age *per se* is not an important determiner of extracurricular activities. Indeed, in a study of high-school performance of individuals who were younger than average because they had been admitted to kindergarten at an early age, Hobson (1963) found that underage students "engaged in a significantly larger average number of extracurricular activities over a four-year period. Their activity participation was not overly weighted with activities of a scholastic nature. Athletic and social honors and elective positions came in for their full share of underage participation. . . . In the matter of honors, awards, and distinctions at graduation the underage boys and girls exceeded their fellows by a ratio of about two to one" (p. 168).

Many other arguments have been advanced to support the practice of keeping children with their chronological age peers, but the evidence for or against them is difficult to marshal. It has been proposed, for example, that the fact that a child is accelerated in intellectual development and the attainment of academic skills at one age does not guarantee that he or she will be similarly advanced at a later age. It is also asserted that young people who are pushed ahead will be robbed of a carefree childhood and that they will likely "burn out" before they can produce anything worthwhile. Furthermore, there are those who contend that to allow academically talented young people to move ahead deprives their nongifted age peers of valuable role models.

The available research evidence does not justify any of these concerns. Indeed, the available data tend to suggest the opposite conclusion. Stability in rate of intellectual development from one age to another cannot, of course, be guaranteed, but longitudinal studies indicate that, on the whole, individuals who are significantly advanced at one age tend to be similarly advanced at subsequent ages (Burks, Jensen, & Terman 1930; Terman 1925; Terman & Oden 1947, 1959). As is well known, the older the child, the greater the stability. Even for children whose academic achievement does not keep pace, however, it is quite possible that retention in age-grade has exerted a dampening effect on development. All of the evidence we have suggests that, as a group, gifted children who are educationally accelerated tend to experience satisfying childhoods and that they are productive and relatively content with their positions as adults (Burks, Jensen, & Terman 1930; Terman & Oden 1947, 1959).

Finally, nongifted children may indeed be deprived of role models when their gifted age-mates are placed in special classes. When the gifted children are simply moved to other, higher-level classes, however, they can continue to provide models of high achievement and motivation to their (somewhat older) classmates. Presumably, talented children will make a greater contribution to their classmates when they are challenged than when too little is demanded of them.

Rationale for a Competency-Based System of Education

Perhaps the most cogent reason for an age-graded system of education is the lack of hard evidence conclusively demonstrating that any other system produces more beneficial results. Even though acceleration does not lead to the evils that have been attributed to it, there is little evidence as yet which indicates that children who are denied the opportunity to move ahead according to their abilities and academic attainments are harmed. Indeed, evidence that acceleration produces benefits lasting into adulthood is sparse as well.

Yet, despite the lack of hard data concerning the consequences of accelerating or decelerating academically gifted children, there is good reason to believe that forcing them to conform to a rigid age-graded system may have harmful consequences. Those who have worked with precocious children have often noted their boredom and frustration (Hollingworth 1942; Newland 1976; Terman 1925). Whatever one's theoretical view, it is clear that a child exposed to a too-easy curriculum day after day has little alternative but to "tune out" and "turn off."

Perhaps more serious is the fact that gifted children in an age-graded educational system are seldom encouraged to develop good study habits, habits of application and perseverence in the face of difficulty. The child for whom everything comes easily may learn to expect that everything *should* come easily. He or she may be made anxious and discouraged when faced with a degree of challenge or even a minor failure that a less capable student would take in stride. Encounters with adversity may have devastating effects, including avoidance of difficulty, feelings of self-abasement, and even withdrawal from college or graduate study.

It is obvious that academically advanced young people are required to waste time. Enrichment programs can help them fill up time, of course, and expand their horizons, but in a typical enrichment program there is likely to be a wide range of children, from those with capabilities several months to several years beyond those of their age-mates. Almost inevitably, then, the enrichment class suitable for the mean of that class will be little better suited to some children than the program of the "regular" class from which they came. The problem of the match will not have been solved.

Many gifted children who are deviant in their school situation are isolated and lonely, particularly those with very precocious capabilities (Hollingworth 1942). Such children seldom become class presidents, cheerleaders, or editors of their school paper. They are likely, rather, to be regarded by teachers and classmates as "smart alecks," "class clowns," or "misfits." The social consequences of engaging all day with their "peers" (actually, their age-mates) are negative rather than positive.

In summary, gifted children are deviant and therefore they are at risk. Doing nothing — failing to accelerate children who seem ready for more advanced educational placement — is not necessarily the safest course. Using their best judgment on behalf of the individual child, courageous educators need to try to adapt the system to the child with special needs. One cannot expect them to do so perfectly. One can only ask them to try in the best-informed ways feasible.

Programs of Radical Acceleration

The outcome of such reasoning implies that matching the competencies of many children to the learning environment may demand extraordinary measures. On the one hand, children may be educated individually by tutors or, worse yet, given no guidance while left to pursue academic goals on their own. On the other hand, they may be permitted to attend classes with older students, with a teacher, the "props," and the social facilitation that only classroom learning can provide. Choosing the latter alternative, at least two investigators during the early 1970s became convinced that accelerated educational experiences can be appropriate for some gifted children, and that for extraordinarily precocious children acceleration may well be essentially mandatory.

THE STUDY OF MATHEMATICALLY PRECOCIOUS YOUTH

In 1971 Julian C. Stanley, professor of psychology at The Johns Hopkins University, initiated his Study of Mathematically Precocious Youth. He sought to identify and recognize the achievements of a large number of young people who were significantly advanced in mathematical reasoning ability and to give special assistance to those with extraordinary talent. His program was designed to facilitate the appropriate education of such talented young people. Under the auspices of SMPY he has been influential in the lives of many thousands of mathematically talented young people.

Many of the children thus identified have undergone accelerated educational programs, some with the aid of special, preparatory "fast-math" programs provided under Dr. Stanley's direction on the campus of Johns Hopkins (see Benbow, Perkins, & Stanley, chapter 4 of this volume). Many have skipped grades or have taken advanced mathematics and related courses while pursuing other studies in settings with students closer to their age. A good many of the students identified by Professor Stanley have entered The Johns Hopkins University, thereby assuring the personal support of Professor Stanley and his staff, though no formal program especially for them has been undertaken.

A few of Professor Stanley's protégés have been radically accelerated, i.e., they have become full-time college students when only 10 to 13 years old. A description of a few of these students will provide a sense of the kind of youngster involved in radical acceleration.

C-B.C. is one of the brightest students identified by any SMPY talent search. In December, 1975, one month after his tenth birthday, he took the SAT in a regular administration and scored 600 Verbal and 680 Mathematical; one year later he raised these scores to 710 and 750, respectively. A variety of intelligence test scores indicated an IQ of about 200. A Chinese-American youngster whose father is a professor of physics and whose mother has a master's degree in psychology, C-B. has two younger siblings who are also very bright. He attended a private school in Baltimore, where he was given some special opportunities.

It was discovered that, although C-B. had taken only first-year high-school algebra (as a fifth-grader), he had acquired by age 11 the subject matter of algebra II, algebra III, and plane geometry. Trigonometry took him a few weeks to learn, as did analytic geometry. At age 12, while his father was doing research using the linear accelerator at Stanford University, C-B. completed his high-school career in Palo Alto while simultaneously taking demanding calculus courses at Stanford. In the fall of 1978, when still 12 years old, C-B. entered The Johns Hopkins University with sophomore standing. He had been accepted at Harvard and California Institute of Technology as well. He received his baccalaureate in May of 1981, at age 15, with a major in physics, general and departmental honors, the physics award, a Churchill Scholarship for a year's study at Cambridge University, and a National Science Foundation three-year graduate fellowship to work toward his doctorate in physics at the California Institute of Technology.

C.F.C., born in 1959, completed his doctorate in finance before his twenty-second birthday at the University of Chicago Graduate School of Business, after earning his MBA there when he was 19. C.'s father, a college graduate, is a sales manager; his mother, a high-school graduate, is an executive secretary. C. skipped grades seven, nine, ten, and twelve and entered Johns Hopkins with sophomore standing through Advanced Placement Program course work and college credits earned while attending the eighth and eleventh grades. He held a variety of jobs while in college, including summer jobs as a staff writer on a weekly publication and a junior security analyst covering publication stocks. His hobbies include skiing, tennis, golf, horseracing, and writing. Several letters written during graduate school reflect not only the substance but also the style of a student well into his twenties. With several research publications already to his credit, he joined the faculty of the Graduate School of Management of Northwestern University in the fall of 1981.

B.J.T. was born in 1967, one of four children of the owner of a dataprocessing company. In May, 1979, while still only 11 years old, he achieved high marks on the AP mathematics examination (Calculus Level BC) and on both of the difficult Level C AP physics examinations (Mechanics, and Electricity and Magnetism). One year later he scored extremely well on the AP chemistry examination. On the calculus examination he was, indeed, one of the highest scorers in the country. At age 10 years 7 months he scored 770 on the SAT-Mathematics and 590 on the SAT-Verbal tests. Later that year he took a fast-paced mathematics program at Johns Hopkins for brilliant ex-seventh-graders. B.'s family lives in New Jersey, where in the fall of 1980, shortly after his thirteenth birthday, he entered Princeton University as a full-time student. Princeton does not award sophomore-class standing for AP scores, and he therefore entered as a freshman but with advanced standing in mathematics, physics, and chemistry. Apparently he is doing well academically and also from a social/emotional perspective as well.

A final example from the SMPY program is L-H.R., a young woman born in 1967 who in January of 1980 earned SAT scores of 760 on the Verbal segment and 790 on the Mathematics segment. She hopes to be a medical researcher. During the summer of 1980 she carried a full-time course-load at Johns Hopkins by taking organic chemistry. At 13 years of age she became a full-time resident student there with sophomore-class status. She is doing well.

Many more boys than girls have achieved extremely high SAT-M scores in the SMPY talent searches (Benbow & Stanley 1980, 1981), and an even smaller proportion of young women have entered college as radical accelerants from that program (Daggett, chapter 9 of this volume). L-H. appears to be one of the most intellectually talented of the girls identified so far.

One of the most remarkable students in Johns Hopkins's history is N.T.M., a first-generation American from Oklahoma whose parents immigrated there from Japan. She skipped the twelfth grade of her public high school and came to Johns Hopkins with full sophomore-class standing via five AP examinations taken in one week during May of her eleventh-grade year on which she had earned four 5s and one 4 on the 1-to-5 grading scale. By taking heavy course-loads of difficult courses, she completed the B.A. degree in mathematics in a total of four semesters with nearly all *A*s and was elected to membership in Phi Beta Kappa. Besides earning her baccalaureate at age 18 with both general and departmental honors, she became one of the youngest persons ever to win a Rhodes Scholarship with which to study for two years at Oxford University and a Churchill Scholarship with which to study for one year at Cambridge University. Having to make a choice between the two scholarships, she chose the Rhodes.

N.T. had won the state piano competition as a tenth-grader, competing with eleventh- and twelfth-graders. While at Johns Hopkins she minored in piano at the Peabody Institute. She plays the flute excellently and also the violin. At the end of the eleventh grade she attended Girls' State, a political-experience camp, in Oklahoma and was elected president of it. At Johns Hopkins she was a member of the varsity women's fencing team. In addition to these accomplishments, she is a skilled teacher of fast-paced mathematics through the calculus to SMPY's youths who reason extremely well mathematically. Also, during the summer of 1982, after graduation from Johns Hopkins, she worked as a junior researcher in mathematics and physics at the Bell Telephone Laboratories.

These examples give a flavor of the outstanding students located by Professor Stanley and his co-workers at Johns Hopkins. These young people not only appear appropriate for marked acceleration in their studies, but indeed would very probably be seriously handicapped by the requirement that they complete their regular schooling at the ordinary, prescribed pace.

THE CHILD DEVELOPMENT RESEARCH GROUP

Shortly after Professor Stanley established SMPY, efforts were begun at the University of Washington, under my directorship, to investigate aspects of intellectual precocity. In 1973 the Child Development Research Group was established and undertook a formal study of the identification and nurturance of very young, highly precocious children. This group has now established a broad spectrum of research and educational programs, including: (1) a longitudinal study of some 500 gifted youngsters identified by the age of five as exhibiting precocious development, (2) a preschool serving a segment of these youngsters, (3) an accelerated educational program in the Seattle Public Schools intended for children achieving four grades or more above their age-mates, (4) a diagnostic and counseling center serving families with children who seem to be experiencing school and/or behavioral problems related to markedly advanced intellectual development, and (5) a program of early entrance to the University of Washington for very academically talented young people.

For the purposes of the present paper, the Radical Acceleration Group of the Early Entrance Program, which accepts students to the University of Washington who are age 14 or younger and/or who have not yet entered the tenth grade, will constitute the focus.[1] This program began in the spring of 1977 with two students, a 12-year-old girl and a 14-year-old boy, each of whom enrolled part time while attending junior high school. By 1981 it had grown to twenty students who were taking part-time or full-time academic loads. Two of these students transferred to a small, residential college, but the other eighteen were located on the university campus in Seattle.

To qualify for admission to the EEP a student must be 14 years old or younger and/or not yet in the tenth grade, have demonstrated high academic achievement, and have attained scores on the Washington Pre-College Test (Noeth 1979) that compare favorably with those of high-school juniors who subsequently enter four-year colleges. Specifically, the applicant must attain a score at the eightieth percentile or better of that group on either the verbal or the quantitative portion of the test and a score at least at the fiftieth percentile on the other segment. Applicants are thus being compared with norms appropriate for college-bound students, who are at least four years, and sometimes as much as eight years, older. Applicants must also be judged strongly motivated to enter the program and be prepared to exert the effort and maturity needed to succeed in college courses.

Having qualified, students are invited to enroll in University of Washington courses concurrently with the pursuit of their elementary- or junior-high-school programs. Having succeeded at a few such courses, the student can attend a summer quarter at the university, taking a variety of college courses (not just "favorites"). Thirty-two students have entered the EEP; eleven of them opted during the gradual screening process to return to their former schools, and one other was required to do so, with the possibility of returning to the program at a more propitious time. The majority of those who started the process have, however, entered the university on a full-time basis, at ages which thus far have ranged from 10 to 14 years.

The following is a presentation of our experience up to January 1, 1981; the left-hand column indicates the number of students in that category.

172   Took the Washington Pre-College Test
46   Qualified for the Early Entrance Program
32   Entered the EEP and took one or more courses
20   Were still students in good standing in the EEP
8   Dropped out after attempting only one university course
4   Dropped out after attempting two or more courses

About one-quarter of those who were nominated by a teacher, counselor, or parent qualified to try out for the EEP by taking college classes. Approximately two-thirds of those who qualified elected to take at least one university course, and more than one-half of these actually proceeded through the probationary period and became full-time university students.

The deficiencies in the education of EEP students when the students enter the university make it necessary to add required courses to their programs. For this reason, and because students are encouraged to explore a variety of potential career options and to obtain a broad, well-rounded education, a typical program will take about five academic years.

The EEP provides guidance and a home base for these young students, acting far more actively in loco parentis than is the custom in colleges today. This is particularly true of the first two years of the students' college lives, after which many begin to feel that they have "outgrown" the program. During their beginning college years the students are required not only to use the various departmental and college advising offices, but also to check programs and program changes with EEP counselors. Their own talents and the special university requirements must be carefully intermeshed. Progress in their courses is monitored by mid-quarter student interviews, end-quarter contact with professors, and written course evaluations by the students. Group meetings are held twice weekly; at these, attendance is mandatory during the first year and is encouraged during the second. The group meetings are used to furnish an orientation to the university community and the study/social skills needed in this setting. They also provide an opportunity for students to share the problems (and the solutions) they are experiencing. A lounge provided serves as a "home base." Conferences are held with parents as needed. The program plays an important role in the lives of the students, at least at times of crisis and/or decision. For the most part, however, youngsters are simply University of Washington students. They attend regular classes, eat at university facilities, participate in the extracurricular activities they choose, and assume responsibility for their own scholastic achievement. All are required to live with their families (or, occasionally, in some nonfamily home setting) when they enter the program, but approximately 85 percent of the undergraduate population of approximately 36,500 students also live off campus. The EEP students have done well. Table 8.1 presents in capsule form the standing and academic progress of the group through 1980.

By far the majority of the EEP students who have made the transition to full-time status are progressing handily through their college careers, taking a variety of courses, meeting university requirements, choosing (and often rechoosing) majors, and generally acquitting themselves with success, poise, and an air of optimistic self-confidence. All the students have made friends not only within the program but also with college classmates, though the extent of these friendships varies, of course, from one student to another. As a group they appear to be socially skilled, committed to their own endeavors, and making satisfactory progress. Such matters are hard to quantify, but the overall situation appears to be quite salutary.

This is not to say that these young people have experienced no problems. Many of them were socially rather isolated when they applied to the program, having been considered very different from their classmates and having had a difficult time finding compatible friends. Some have been at times less mature than they needed to be in the university milieu.

One set of problems stems from conditions inherent in the lock-step educational system from which the young people come. Few of them, for example, had previously learned to take good notes. A few who skipped the third and fourth grades still print rather than write cursively. More serious, most of them have not learned to manage time well because they have never had to do so. Indeed, with regard to schoolwork, they have generally had a great deal of time to waste; they have almost never had to study at home.

The structure of our young students' lives tended to have been imposed by others — parents who have determined when they should go to bed and how much TV they should watch, for example. Students who have engaged in demanding activities such as competitive athletics or serious study of a musical instrument, drama, or dance seem to have learned to use their time better and to expect (and even relish) challenges.

A few students have not handled the freedom of the university well. They spent too much time playing with the computer or chatting with

TABLE 8.1. Status of EEP Students after Autumn Quarter, 1980

Level	N	Total Credits	Grade Point Average
Freshman (- to 44 credits)	4	169	3.49
Sophomore (45 to 89 credits)	7	322	3.45
Junior (90 to 134 credits)	4	291	3.53
Senior (135 to - credits)	3	394	3.62

friends, or they simply did not apply themselves to their studies. They expected to complete the university courses as they have always completed their school requirements — easily, "without opening a book." When this tactic proved unsuccessful, some became discouraged, cut classes, and tended to sink deeper into failure. Program staff try to help students to monitor their time and their school progress, particularly during the first year. This task, however, has been difficult with some students to whom everything has always come so easily and whose parents have so willingly taken responsibility for providing the "good life."

Perhaps surprisingly, the social maturity of these young people has tended to exceed by a considerable degree that of their age-mates. The important variable here seems to be the age at which the youngster enters puberty. All of the female students who have been full-time students at the university were post-pubescent. Their social maturity has tended to be fully adequate to handle the campus situation. Most of these girls, in fact, made close female friends within the program and, in addition, established male (and sometimes female) friendships with their non-EEP classmates. Some have dated and some have not, but their friendship patterns have seemed to be mature and gratifying to them.

A number of our boys, on the other hand, were prepubescent, still "children" in appearance as well as demeanor. They have not blended into the campus setting as did the more mature EEP students. They did not tend to make friends outside the program as did the post pubescent boys For the most part, however, they seemed to be quite content with their lifestyles. A few have continued their neighborhood friendships and athletic activities outside the university. Our young boys have tended to rely on their parents for transportation and for structuring their lives; this in turn has postponed their assumption of responsibility for themselves and has led to a high degree of involvement of their parents with EEP staff. As the boys reach puberty this state of affairs has diminished and a natural progression can be seen.

With the girls and the postpubescent boys, issues of dependence-independence have tended to become rather critical. Some students have manifested a strong desire to become more a part of the college community by moving away from home. Of the nine girls in the program, two transferred to a small, residential college in Oregon and one lived in a campus cooperative; of the eleven boys in the program, one lived in a dormitory. The youngest of this subgroup was 15, and the others were 16 or 17. The parents in each case agreed reluctantly to permit their child to move from home. The recognition that their age-role expectations must be determined in part by the circumstances in which their child functions has come easily to few of the parents.

Any group of adolescents has its share of crises and conflicts, and our group is certainly not atypical in this respect. There have been, as far as we know, practically no problems with some hazards originally anticipated, such as alcohol or drug use, psychiatric disorders, or sexual encounters exceeding the student's capacity to handle them. Staff members have, however, been called to mediate between child and parents and make themselves available for that purpose. Parent meetings are held quarterly and often become "rap" sessions at which parents share their experiences and provide mutual support. Indeed, in some ways the problems that have been encountered have been more acute for parents than for their children.

On the whole, both the academic and the social progress of this group of highly capable young people has been very satisfactory. The following sketches introduce a few of our group and provide a multifaceted picture of the kind of young person who enrolls in the EEP. As this diverse group indicates, each student is so distinctive an individual that it is almost impossible to pick a "typical" one.

F.M.Q. was one of the first students to enter the program, in spring quarter, 1977. She is the youngest of four children of two university faculty members. At age 12 years she enrolled in college calculus and astronomy courses while attending a private middle school in Seattle; she had had only introductory algebra at this point. She earned *A*s in both courses and experienced no difficulties in adjusting to the university. Her parents, though, were apprehensive about her becoming a full-time college student and enrolled her in a private high school with high academic standards. She was skipped a grade but still remained insufficiently challenged; she consequently took a second calculus course at the university during spring quarter, 1978. She entered the EEP as a full-time student that summer. F.'s Washington Pre-College Test at the age of 12 years 8 months yielded a Verbal composite of 55 (sixty-fifth percentile) and a Quantitative composite of 66 (ninetieth percentile). Her SAT scores at the age of 13 years 7 months were 630 Verbal and 750 Mathematics. As a youngster who had long been interested in physics and mathematics, she enrolled in the undergraduate honors program and undertook a major in each of these areas. During the summer of 1979 she worked at the Nuclear Physics Laboratory, and as a sophomore she was appointed as a teaching assistant for the first-year physics program. At the end of the 1979–80 academic year she had attained a grade point average (G.P.A.) of 3.72 and senior status. She and a close friend within the program transferred to Reed College in 1980, where she decided to stay for two years in order to obtain an enriched liberal arts background in addition to a combined physics-mathematics major. Socially poised and mature beyond her years, she experienced some conflicts with her parents over her new independence. For the most part, however, she had a relatively smooth and certainly a successful academic career.

T.G., the oldest of four children of a Chinese-born physician father and biochemist mother, was 10 years old in 1978 when he entered the university as a part-time student. He had been a very unhappy first-grader in public school and had been enrolled the following year in an ungraded private school. After only one year he returned to a public school as a fifth-grader and then proceeded to advance rapidly through junior-high-school and high-school subjects, particularly in the mathematics and science areas. T.'s Washington Pre-College Test taken at the age of 9 years 4 months yielded a Verbal score of 63 (eighty-seventh percentile) and a Quantitative score of 58 (sixty-fifth percentile). The SAT taken at the age of 9 years 10 months produced scores of 550 Verbal and 630 Mathematics. A very serious boy in general demeanor, T. illustrates the prepubescent student who does not easily blend into the university student body. He had difficulties in learning to budget his time and to accept responsibility for completing his work independently. He would rather work at a computer terminal than finish an English theme or read a history assignment. His intellectual competence, however, was sufficient that he made satisfactory grades despite these problems. Taking notes was particularly difficult for him. At the end of autumn quarter, 1980, he had completed 76 credits with a G.P.A. of 3.56, not the academic level of which he is basically capable, but a record that shows steady progress. He had begun also to exhibit the capability of succeeding at university classes aside from the sciences and mathematics, which he so clearly preferred.

M.B. is not one of our success stories, at least not in the short run. The older of two sons of a widowed father, he entered the university when he was 13. His scores on the Washington Pre-College Test taken when he was 13 years 3 months old, were 67 Verbal (ninety-fifth percentile) and 62 Quantitative (seventy-seventh percentile). He was enthusiastic about all aspects of university life except studying. Weighing at the time less than ninety pounds, he was welcomed as a coxswain on the freshman crew, an activity that he pursued not only during practice hours but socially, at the crew house, during most of every day. A somewhat troubled youngster to begin with, he never managed to apply himself to his courses. Eventually he ceased attending university classes and finally transferred to an alternative public high school. He did not achieve a distinguished record there and remains somewhat troubled. It is clear that his acceptance by EEP and other university students was a distinctly positive experience for him, and the recognition of his considerable academic competence was important to him as well. On balance, perhaps the EEP was neither particularly helpful nor harmful to M.

E.V.C. was 12 years old when she entered the EEP in the summer of 1978. The oldest of seven children of an intellectually outstanding but economically troubled family, she initially showed a strong preference for the study of classic languages and literature but soon began to explore other areas such as mathematics and science. Her test scores on the Washington Pre-College Test at age 12 years 4 months were 70 Verbal composite (ninety-seventh percentile) and 58 Quantitative composite (sixty-fifth percentile); on the SAT at age 13 years 5 months her scores were 610 Verbal and 540 Mathematics. E. is one of those students who had previously been challenged to assume responsibility and to handle her time well. She is a highly trained dancer, a participant in local dramatic companies, and for several years held paid jobs such as housecleaner and assistant in campus laboratories. She continued to fill her life with these activities, including highly rigorous dancing instruction. At the same time she achieved a G.P.A. of 3.35 for 142 total units. E. generated considerable conflict with her parents over issues concerned with her bids for more independence. These were exacerbated by the fact that she had no clear goals and had not been able to work out a well-defined plan for her education.

N.C. qualified for the program at age 11, as a junior-high-school student. Her Washington Pre-College Test scores included an 87 Verbal composite (eighty-seventh percentile) and a 55 Quantitative composite (fifty-fifth percentile). Her father is an engineer and her mother is a teacher. She has one younger sister, who also is very bright. Entering the program rather gradually, she took courses concurrently at the university and at her junior high school for more than a year. She finally entered the university full time in 1979 and subsequently earned a G.P.A. of 3.55 with a total of 82 units. She is outstanding for her social poise and articulate manner. Clearly mature beyond her years, she established a wide circle of friends, both male and female, within the EEP and among her regular classmates. Her instructors rate her consistently among the brightest in their classes, and several have noted that her ability to express her insights in writing "is extraordinary." In addition to taking a demanding course-load, N. taught French to youngsters in the Transition Component (see note number 1). She assumed all the responsibilities of a course instructor and did an exceptional job. Her pupils were delighted with her and learned very rapidly. N's current major is political science, and she may well be headed for a career in the public arena.

O.P., whose poise and maturity remind one very much of N.C., qualified for the EEP at age 13. She was at that time attending a private parochial high school as a ninth-grader. Her Washington Pre-College Test scores placed her significantly above the ninety-ninth percentile on the

Verbal composite and at the seventy-third percentile on the Quantitative composite. O.'s father is a U.S. prosecuting attorney and her mother has had a varied career in advertising, public relations, and film production. O. began reading at 30 months of age and was academically advanced throughout her school career. She skipped kindergarten altogether and was consistently given difficult work by all her teachers. She was among the most capable students in the program, having accumulated a G.P.A. of 3.79 for 100 units of work. At the same time, she taught German to some of the students in the Transition Component, as N.C. taught others French, and with equal success. Her career plans are in the area of foreign service. She was one of two students nominated by the University of Washington to compete for the coveted Truman Scholarship. With the reluctant support of her parents, she moved into the university's Russian House and handled very well this opportunity for independence and self-determination.

B.J. qualified for the program in 1977, just before his thirteenth birthday, with scores on the Washington Pre-College Test at the eighty-fifth percentile on the Verbal composite and at the fifty-fifth percentile on the Quantitative composite. A dedicated musician with strong interest in composing he recognized that the university offered the major local possibility for formal education in his chosen field. His father is a faculty member at the university, his mother works with an import firm, and his older sister is a university student. They all supported his application to the EEP and have continued to encourage him in his music studies. In winter and spring quarters, 1978, B. took courses in German at the university. Then transferring from junior high school, in which he was doing well, and giving up his activities in the Seattle Little Symphony and the Junior Wind Ensemble, he entered the university full time in autumn, 1978. By the end of the 1979–80 academic year he had accumulated 153 credits, with a cumulative grade point average of 3.75. B. did well in all his classes, which represented a variety of liberal arts and social sciences in addition to his music courses. It is in the music courses that he really distinguished himself, however. To be accepted as a music major, a highly competitive situation at this university, he had to present a folio of his compositions and audition for the faculty. He accomplished this by winter quarter, 1979, when he was barely 14 years old. Most of B.'s friends were regular university students who were also music majors. Much of his time was spent with them, studying, practicing, and composing.

CONCLUSIONS

Here, then, are two programs, one in Maryland and one in Washington, which demonstrate that for some children a radically accelerated educational approach is both appropriate and successful. The two programs differ somewhat in orientation. The SMPY program has emphasized the discovery and recognition of youngsters talented in a particular area. The University of Washington program has searched far less systematically, but it has provided a somewhat more structured support system to students who have entered the university in their early teens with a variety of talents. The common orientation is, however, very striking. Each program is designed to provide the most appropriate match between learner and environment, using for the most part classes already available in the educational system. The components specific to these programs — the fast-math classes at Johns Hopkins, the Transition Component at the University of Washington — were not undertaken to replace the regular classroom, but to aid the transition, which is difficult in the lock-step age-graded Carnegie-unit educational system today.

In a sense it is unfortunate that case studies involving such unusually precocious and high-achieving youngsters have been presented. This can be misleading. In fact, there are a great many talented young people who are also in need of adjustment in their programs. Although there are many more of the very bright than one would anticipate from the normal curve (see Robinson 1981), there are a great many other youngsters whose precocity is not quite so outstanding but whose needs are being ill served by age-graded practices.

If the school system permitted a significantly greater degree of flexibility, our society might well find itself returning to the "good old days," when children actually passed and failed in school according to their competencies and when, therefore, a mix of ages was to be found in most classrooms. While there would still be a need for radical acceleration of a few students in such a system, these radical accelerants would be less conspicuous in age-heterogeneous classes. No grade-placement system will ever handle entirely the "problems of the match" created by inter- and intraindividual differences (e.g., see Stanley 1980). Flexibility in the system and recognition of the problem, however, might advance us a significant step toward meeting the educational needs of gifted and talented youngsters.

Notes

In March, 1981, shortly after completing this chapter, Professor Robinson died tragically. His program, which is outlined in this chapter, is continuing at the University of Washington under the direction of Professor Nancy Robinson, his widow. Although the program has changed and matured, it is largely along the plans that Halbert Robinson outlined but did not see come to fruition.

1. Before his death, Dr. Robinson had initiated a new component of the EEP – the Transition Component. It is a self-contained program stressing academic preparation for university work and allowing students older than 14 years to take courses as part-time University of Washington students while they acquire necessary basic skills and an orientation to the intellectual life of the university. As of February, 1983, there are nine students currently in the program, thirty-eight who were in the program but have now become full-time students at the University of Washington, six who have now graduated and gone to graduate school (three at the University of Washington and one each at Brown, California Institute of Technology, and MIT), and four who transferred to other schools.

References

Bayley, N. 1955. On the growth of intelligence. *American Psychologist* 10:805–18.
_____. 1970. Development of mental abilities. In *Carmichael's manual of child psychology,* vol. 1, ed. P. H. Mussen. 3d ed. New York: Wiley.
Benbow, C. P., and Stanley, J. C. 1980. Sex differences in mathematical ability: Fact or artifact? *Science* 210:1262–64.
_____. 1981. Mathematical ability: Is sex a factor? *Science* 212:118, 121.
Burks, B. S.; Jensen, D. W.; and Terman, L. M. 1930. *The promise of youth: Follow-up studies of a thousand gifted children.* Vol. 3 of *Genetic studies of genius.* Stanford, Calif.: Stanford University Press.
Congdon, P. J. 1979. Helping parents of gifted children. In *Gifted children: Reaching their potential,* ed. J. J. Gallagher, 347–63. Jerusalem: Kollek and Son.
Daurio, S. P. 1979. Educational enrichment versus acceleration: A review of the literature. In *Educating the gifted: Acceleration and enrichment,* ed. W. C. George, S. J. Cohn, and J. C. Stanley, 13–63. Baltimore: Johns Hopkins University Press.
Gagné, R. M. 1965. *The conditions of learning.* New York: Holt, Rinehart, and Winston.
Gallagher, J. J. 1975. *Teaching the gifted child.* 2d ed. Boston: Allyn and Bacon.
George, W. C.; Cohn, S. J.; and Stanley, J. C. 1979. *Educating the gifted: Acceleration and enrichment.* Baltimore: Johns Hopkins University Press.
Gold, M. J. 1965. *Education of the intellectually gifted.* Columbus, Ohio: Merrill.
Hildreth, G. H. 1966. *Introduction to the gifted.* New York: McGraw-Hill.
Hilgard, E. R., and Bower, G. H. 1974. *Theories of learning.* 4th ed. Englewood Cliffs, N.J.: Prentice-Hall.
Hobson, J. R. 1963. High school performance of underage pupils initially admitted to kindergarten on the basis of physical and psychological examinations. *Educational and Psychological Measurement* 23(1): 159–70.
Hollingworth, L. S. 1929. *Gifted children: Their nature and nurture.* New York: Macmillan.

_____. 1942. *Children above 180 IQ, Stanford-Binet*. Yonkers-on-Hudson, N.Y.: World Book.

Hunt, J. M. 1961. *Intelligence and experience*. New York: Ronald Press.

Keating, D. P. 1979. The acceleration/enrichment debate: Basic issues. In *Educating the gifted: Acceleration and enrichment*, ed. W. C. George, S. J. Cohn, and J. C. Stanley, 217–20. Baltimore: Johns Hopkins University Press.

_____, ed. 1976. *Intellectual talent: Research and development*. Baltimore: Johns Hopkins University Press.

Keating, D. P., and Stanley, J. C. 1972. Extreme measures for the exceptionally gifted in mathematics and science. *Educational Researcher* 1(9): 3–7.

Kett, J. 1974. History of age grouping in America. In *Youth: Transition to adulthood: A report to the panel on youth of the president's Science Advisory Committee*, ed. J. S. Coleman et al. Chicago: University of Chicago Press.

Newland, T. E. 1976. *The gifted in socioeducational perspective*. Englewood Cliffs, N.J.: Prentice-Hall.

Noeth, R. J. 1979. *The 1980–81 Washington pre-college counselors guide*. Seattle: Washington Pre-College Test Program.

Robinson, N. M. 1981. The uncommonly bright child. In *The uncommon child*, ed. M. Lewis and L. A. Rosenblum. New York: Plenum.

Robinson, N. M., and Robinson, H. B. 1976. *The mentally retarded child*. 2d ed. New York: McGraw-Hill.

Rohwer, W. D. 1970. Cognitive development in education. In *Carmichael's manual of child psychology*, vol. 1, ed. P. H. Mussen, 57–81. 3d ed. New York: Wiley.

Rothman, E., and Levine, M. 1963. From little league to ivy league. *Educational Forum* 25:2–34.

Stanley, J. C. 1980. On educating the gifted. *Educational Researcher* 9(3, Mar.): 8–12.

Stanley, J. C.; Keating, D. P.; and Fox, L. H., eds. 1974. *Mathematical talent: Discovery, description, and development*. Baltimore: Johns Hopkins University Press.

Terman, L. M. 1925. *Mental and physical traits of a thousand gifted children*. Vol. 1 of *Genetic studies of genius*. Stanford, Calif.: Stanford University Press.

Terman, L. M., and Oden, M. H. 1947. *The gifted child grows up: Twenty-five years' follow-up of a superior group*. Vol. 4 of *Genetic studies of genius*. Stanford, Calif.: Stanford University Press.

_____. 1959. *The gifted group at mid-life: Thirty-five years' follow-up of the superior child*. Vol. 5 of *Genetic studies of genius*. Stanford, Calif.: Stanford University Press.

The Effects of Acceleration on the Social and Emotional Development of Gifted Students

LYNN DAGGETT POLLINS

Abstract

From the two perspectives of a literature review and a longitudinal comparison of accelerants and non-accelerants, an examination of the potential effects of acceleration on the social and emotional development of gifted students revealed no identifiable negative effects. The literature review discusses several major studies with respect to issues central to the problem: the differential effects of varying methods of acceleration, the definition of the "social and emotional development" construct, and the identification of appropriate reference groups. The longitudinal comparison presents the results of a study of twenty-one male radical accelerants and twenty-one nonaccelerants matched on age and ability at the time of the talent search. A comparison on several variables revealed that the two groups were very similar at age 13. Five years later, however, differences favoring the accelerants were found in educational aspirations and in the perceived use of educational opportunities, amount of help they reported having received from SMPY, and their evaluation of SMPY's influence on their social and emotional development.

Daurio (1979) argues that opposition to acceleration of gifted students is justified primarily by concern for its effect on the students' social and emotional development. This report examines the merits of this argument from two perspectives. First, the results of several major studies of the social and emotional development of accelerants are reviewed in the context of a core of issues central to the problem. Second, the social and emotional development of gifted radical accelerants and the social and emotional development of nonaccelerants identified through the Study of Mathematically Precocious Youth are compared. Neither the review of the literature nor the comparison of the SMPY gifted students identified any negative effects of acceleration on social and emotional development. Indeed, any effects of this sort seem to be positive. The validity of the claim that acceleration is somehow detrimental to the social and emotional development of accelerants must thus be seriously questioned.

Research on the Social and Emotional Development of Gifted Students

The social and emotional development of accelerated gifted students has been the subject of much attention from psychologists and educators. The belief that acceleration somehow inhibits social and emotional development appears so widespread that arguments over the advantages and disadvantages of acceleration "seem to hinge on the relative weights that should be given to social and intellectual values in the educative process" (Terman & Oden 1947, p. 264). This section discusses a cluster of issues whose resolution is central to research in this area and reviews the results of several major studies in this context.

ISSUES CENTRAL TO THE STUDY OF THE SOCIAL AND EMOTIONAL DEVELOPMENT OF ACCELERATED STUDENTS

There are several problems inherent in studying the effects of acceleration on the social and emotional development of gifted youths. First, acceleration may be achieved by one or more of a variety of methods. Stanley (1979) has delineated some types of acceleration: grade skipping, early part-time college study, college graduation in fewer than four years (by entering college with sophomore standing, taking heavier-than-average course-loads, attending summer school, and/or concurrent graduate study), and bypassing the bachelor's degree. While all of these methods follow Pressey's (1949, p. 2) definition of *acceleration* as "progress through an educational program at rates faster or ages younger than conventional," they may affect the social and emotional development of the students choosing them in different ways. It is not difficult, for example, to imagine that studying calculus on one's own at age 13 and taking the Advanced Placement exam to get college credit for it affects the student differently than does taking a regular college calculus course at the same age. Despite the basic nature of this concern, many studies of the social and emotional development of accelerated students do not report the method by which the students became accelerated (see, for example, Terman & Oden 1947). The degree of acceleration, as well as the method used to achieve it, may also differentially affect the social and emotional development of gifted students. Six years of acceleration quite probably affects a gifted student differently than does one year of acceleration. Most research in the area has focused on "moderate" acceleration of one to two years.

Another definitional problem involves the "social and emotional development" construct. Consensus among investigators on the meaning of this phrase is low. In various studies the construct has been equated with participation in extracurricular activities (Pressey 1949; Hobson 1963), presence of leadership qualities (Morgan 1959; Keys 1938), degree of interpersonal effectiveness (Worcester 1956; Birch 1954), and absence of psychopathology (Elwell 1958). That these and other specific, relevant concepts are themselves difficult to define precisely and even more difficult to measure accurately complicates the situation further. Clearly, a thorough study would measure several of these facets of "social and emotional development."

A third problem lies in the definition of reference groups. Many studies have compared the accelerants with their older, more average-ability classmates (Hobson 1963; Pressey 1949). If the question to be addressed is how well the accelerants fit in with their older classmates, this approach seems worthwhile. It does not, however, speak to the more important issue of how acceleration affects the development of gifted students. A bright youth may choose either to accelerate or to opt for some other educational path and still remain equally bright. The most appropriate comparison is thus between the social and emotional development of two groups of equally gifted youths – accelerants and nonaccelerants (as in Terman & Oden 1947; Fund for the Advancement of Education 1953).

A number of investigators have examined the effects of acceleration on the social and emotional development of gifted youths with varying degrees of consideration of the issues just discussed. A large group of educators recommended exercising extreme caution when considering acceleration as an educational alternative for gifted students. Most of these recommendations were based on intuition or on case studies that did not involve comparison with any reference groups (Zorbaugh 1937; Edelston 1950).

FINDINGS OF RESEARCH ON THE SOCIAL AND EMOTIONAL DEVELOPMENT OF ACCELERATED STUDENTS

Among the scientific investigations in this area, a review of the literature confirmed Daurio's (1979) finding that not one study has found acceleration to harm the social and emotional development of gifted students permanently or severely. The following is a discussion of the results of several of the major studies in this area.

Terman (1925–59) investigated longitudinally, descriptively, and observationally the development of more than 1,000 gifted children. In chapter 20 of the fourth volume of the *Genetic Studies of Genius* series, Terman and Oden (1947) divided their sample into three groups according to age at high-school graduation. The routes by which these students had come to be accelerated were not specified. The three groups were compared longitudinally on a number of measures of social adjustment, including ratings by parents, teachers, and fieldworkers, extracurricular participation in high school and college, and scores on a marital adjustment test. Terman and Oden found that "the influence of school acceleration in causing social maladjustment has been greatly exaggerated. There is no doubt that maladjustment does result in individual cases, but our data indicate that in a majority of subjects the maladjustment consists of a temporary feeling of inferiority which is later overcome. The important thing is to consider each child as a special case" (ibid., p. 275).

Terman and Oden also found that the accelerants had a higher probability of furthering their education, had greater occupational success, had higher marital satisfaction, and had suffered no negative effects on their physical maturation.

Keys's (1938) carefully controlled study compared a group of gifted accelerated students with a sample of equally bright nonaccelerants. Further, two subgroups of accelerants were defined according to I.Q.; one group of accelerants had IQs below 120 and another had IQs greater than 136. The effects of acceleration could thus be analyzed in terms of both intelligence and chronological age. Keys found that the accelerants participated in more extracurricular activities, had better study habits, held more offices, and won more scholarships than did the equally intelligent nonaccelerants. Sociability appeared more related to intelligence than to age. The highest self-estimated happiness was reported by the very bright accelerants.

Hobson (1963) followed up underage students admitted to school on the basis of mental, rather than chronological, age. The underage pupils participated in more extracurricular activities than their normal-aged classmates. Worcester (1956) also examined the social and emotional development of underage students admitted on the basis of test scores. Peers and teachers rated the underage students as being as well or better adjusted socially and emotionally as their older classmates. Worcester concluded that "the younger ones had gained a year of school time without a loss in social adjustment" (ibid., p. 28).

Pressey (1949) studied underage college students at Ohio State University matched with a control group of equally bright, older students. He found that a larger percentage of the underage students worked part time and that more of the underage students participated in extracurricular activities.

The Ford Foundation (Fund for the Advancement of Education 1953) compared a group of accelerated Ford Scholars with an equally able, nonaccelerated group of comparison students. The social and emotional development of the Scholars was evaluated with respect to problems resulting directly from acceleration. No social maladjustment directly attributable to acceleration was found. "The Scholars encountered more initial difficulties in adjusting to campus life than their older Comparison students, but most of the difficulties were minor and were soon overcome" (ibid., p. 10).

Finally, Keating, Wiegand, and Fox (1974) examined the behavior of five precocious boys aged 12 to 15 in a college course. In addition to outperforming their older classmates, these young students interacted as much as their older classmates and often were not even identified as being young.

This by no means complete summary of the relevant literature is intended only to give the reader the flavor of the research in this area. For a more thorough review the reader is directed to Daurio (1979).

Data available from SMPY provide an opportunity to investigate the social and emotional development of accelerated students in a way that is unique with respect to the issues delineated here. Gifted radical accelerants (students accelerated three years or more) and nonaccelerants were longitudinally studied. Measurements for a number of the facets of the social and emotional development construct were available. The findings of this study are in accord with those of the investigations previously mentioned — that is, the social and emotional development of gifted students choosing to accelerate is not harmed by that choice and may in fact be enhanced.

Mathematically Talented Radical Accelerants and Nonaccelerants: Their Social and Emotional Development

Over 2,500 mathematically talented seventh- and eighth-graders took the College Board's Scholastic Aptitude Test in SMPY's 1972, 1973, and 1974 talent searches. The SMPY students' scores on this test were superior to those of a national sample of high-school juniors and seniors. High-scoring participants were encouraged to consider acceleration as one means of developing their talents. Many youths did choose to accelerate and entered college at an age between one and six years younger than that of the average college freshman. Other equally high-scoring youths chose different educational paths. The data SMPY has collected on these youths provide an opportunity to investigate the effects of acceleration on the gifted students' social and emotional development that is unique for three reasons. First, the social and emotional development of the accelerants may be compared with that of equally bright nonaccelerants. As pointed out earlier, several studies (e.g., Hobson 1963; Pressey 1949) have compared the social and emotional development of accelerated students with that of their postacceleration classmates — that is, older students of more average ability. That kind of investigation does not address the effects of acceleration on the social and emotional development of the gifted child. Second, the development of both accelerating and nonaccelerating high scorers has been longitudinally monitored by SMPY (Benbow 1981). A retrospective comparison of the two groups both before and several years after acceleration occurred can thus be made. This kind of comparison deals with the issue of potential self-selection factors that might bias results. In other words, any differences in the two groups before any of the students accelerated which might account for postacceleration differences can be ascertained and evaluated. Finally, a significant number of the students who accelerated have done so radically (i.e., are three or more years ahead of their age-mates). It is these radical accelerants who have been the subject of the most concern over social and emotional development (e.g. Maeroff 1977; Nevin 1977) and whose development has been chosen for investigation.

METHOD

Subjects

Twenty-one male radical accelerants were found in the ranks of talent-search participants between 1972 and 1974.[1] Two female radical accelerants were also found; they are not included in the analyses. It is interesting that so few girls chose to accelerate their education radically. This finding may be partially attributed to the smaller number of girls who scored high in the talent searches (Stanley, Keating, & Fox 1974; Keating 1976), but probably also results from other considerations such as sex differences in social interests and interest in mathematics and science (Fox 1976; Fox, Brody, & Tobin 1980).

Radical accelerants were defined as those students who at some point are at least three years ahead of their age-mates in educational placement. This may be accomplished via one or more of the accelerative methods previously delineated. Thus any youth who is a college freshman at age 15 or younger, a college sophomore at 16 or younger, a baccalaureate recipient at 19 or younger, a master's degree recipient at 21 or younger, a law degree recipient at 22 or younger, or a four-year professional degree (M.D., Ph.D., etc.) recipient at age 23 or younger is considered a radical accelerant no matter how he or she has achieved that acceleration. Once a student acquires radical accelerant status he is always treated as such, even if he slows down his educational pace. Most of the radical accelerants in this study accelerated by skipping grades and by subject matter acceleration.

These twenty-one male radical accelerants were matched with other talent-search participants who were of approximately the same age and who had scored about as well on the SATs. The results of this matching can be seen in table 9.1. The two groups seem well-matched, with respect to both age and verbal and mathematical abilities. Further, it is clear that both the accelerant and the nonaccelerant groups are extremely able, averaging 691 and 690, respectively, on SAT-M and 543 and 536, respectively, on SAT-V. These scores represent the ninety-sixth percentiles on SAT-M and seventieth percentiles on SAT-V for college-bound seniors (Admissions Testing Program 1979).

An interesting problem arose during the matching process. It became increasingly difficult to find nonaccelerated youths of ability equal to that of the radical accelerants as the matching progressed. While most of the high-scoring talent-search participants did not radically accelerate their educations, neither did most of them avoid acceleration altogether. For this reason it was decided to include as nonaccelerants some youths who had accelerated their education to a minimal extent (e.g., had entered college with AP credits).

Data Set and Analysis Protocol

With the available data, the social and emotional development of the subjects in one group was compared with that of the subjects in the other group at two points: first, at the time of the talent search, prior to acceleration, when the subjects were roughly 13 years old, and, second, five years later, when the subjects were of high-school graduation age. Comparison of available data for the two groups at the first measurement point addresses potential dissimilarities between the two groups which might have affected the acceleration decision and/or the social and emotional results of acceleration. Differences at the second measurement point can therefore more confidently be attributed to the acceleration itself rather than to any prior social/emotional characteristics.

The results of three relevant standardized affective measures were available for most of the subjects. All three of these tests had been administered when the subjects were of seventh- or eighth-grade age. The three

TABLE 9.1. Talent-Search Performance on SAT-M and SAT-V

Measure	SMPY Radical Accelerants (N = 21)		SMPY Nonaccelerants (N = 21)	
	Mean	Standard Deviation	Mean	Standard Deviation
SAT-M*	691.0	44.8	690.0	36.3
SAT-V**	542.9	70.8	535.7	64.7
Age (year-month)	12-11	0.95 year	13-3	1.00 year

*rSAT-M radical accelerants, nonaccelerants = .76 $p < .001$.
**rSAT-V radical accelerants, nonaccelerants = .91 $p < .001$.

measures are the California Psychological Inventory (CPI) (Gough 1969), the Strong-Campbell Interest Inventory (SCII) (Strong & Campbell 1974), and the Study of Values (SOV) (Allport, Vernon, & Lindzey 1970).

These three measures address different aspects of the social and emotional development construct. The CPI purports to measure "personality characteristics important for social living and social interaction" (Gough 1969, p. 5). The device is composed of eighteen scales clustered into four groups. "The profile obtained gives a good indication of the general social functioning of an individual" (Weiss, Haier, & Keating 1974, p. 128). Furthermore, the CPI has been successfully used with gifted junior-high-school students (Lessinger & Martinson 1961). A variety of reference groups are thus available. Means and standard deviations for each of the eighteen scores were computed separately for the two groups, and a linear discriminant analysis was performed using the SPSS package (Nie et al. 1975).

The SCII, on the other hand, has as its goal the measurement of vocational interests. Six occupational categories (realistic, investigative, enterprising, artistic, social, and conventional), as well as academic orientation and introversion-extroversion are ranked for each individual. Holland (1973), whose vocational preference scales are incorporated in the SCII, believes that vocational interests and personality are closely linked. He feels that within an occupational category, people's interests and values tend to be similar. Various personality types are thus associated with different occupational category ratings. As with the CPI, means and standard deviations for each category were computed separately for the two groups and a discriminant analysis was performed.

The SOV is an ipsative measure of evaluative attitudes based on Spranger's (1928) theory of types of men. He posited six types: the theoretical, truth-seeking man; the economic, practical man; the aesthetic, beauty-seeking man; the social, altruistic man; the political, power-seeking man; and the religious, mystical man. SOV profiles have also been shown to be related to traits such as creativity (Hall & MacKinnon 1969). The analysis protocol was the same as that for the CPI and the SCII.

The final piece of available data on the subjects when they were of seventh- or eighth-grade age was self-rated liking for school and for mathematics. These ratings were obtained from the questionnaire required for participation in the talent search on a 5-point scale (with 1 equalling strong like and 5 equalling strong dislike). The same analysis protocol was used. Approximately five years after each talent search (i.e., when its participants were of high-school graduation age) each participant was sent a detailed questionnaire about his or her progress as part of another study (see Benbow, chapter 2, Appendix 2.1). Thus the group as a whole was followed up at age 18, when the radical accelerants were, on the average, seniors in college, and the nonaccelerants were college freshmen. The questionnaire was aimed primarily at identifying the academic accomplishments and status of former talent-search participants; however, questions about high-school and college activities, liking for college, educational aspirations, and self-perceived social and emotional development were also included. The two groups' answers to these questions were compared via discriminant analysis. Unfortunately, this questionnaire represents the only data SMPY yet has on the social and emotional development of the students subsequent to their acceleration.

Results

California Psychological Inventory.   In figure 9.1 and table 9.2 can be seen the mean CPI profiles for four groups: the SMPY radical accelerants, the SMPY nonaccelerants, and Lessinger and Martinson's (1961) eighth-grade gifted and eighth-grade random groups. It is clear that the two SMPY groups differ very little if at all in their CPI profiles. The SMPY groups are also similar to the eighth-grade gifted group. All three of these groups seem to be functioning more effectively than the eighth-grade random group. The largest differences, not surprisingly, are in the achievement potential/intellectual efficiency cluster composed of the achievement via conformance (Ac), achievement via independence (Ai), and intellectual efficiency (Ie) scales.

Profiles of the two SMPY groups show them to be well adjusted and interpersonally effective. The generally high scores of the SMPY group members, compared with those of the random eighth-grade sample, indicate that the gifted radical accelerants and nonaccelerants are mature, academically advanced, and interpersonally effective. The relatively high scores on flexibility (Fx) and psychological-mindedness (Py) point toward a group of insightful individuals, while the rather low scores on well-being (Wb) and good impression (Gi) suggest a cautious group.

A discriminant analysis performed on the CPI data for the two SMPY groups (see table 9.6) revealed no differences between them.

Strong-Campbell Interest Inventory.   In table 9.3 are presented the means and standard deviations for the radical accelerants and nonac-

FIGURE 9.1.   Profile Sheet for the California Psychological Inventory: Male [1] — Comparison of profiles in the CPI for four groups: the radical accelerants, non-accelerated SMPY students, 8th-grade gifted group, and an 8th-grade random sample

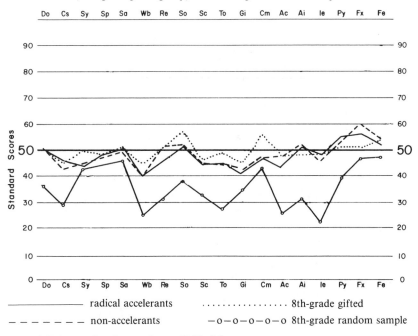

——————— radical accelerants   · · · · · · · · · · · · · · · 8th-grade gifted

— — — — — — — non-accelerants   —o—o—o—o—o 8th-grade random sample

[1] *For definitions of various scales see Table 9.2.*

celerants on eight SCII scales. Both groups' scores on the six occupational themes fall into the average range (40 to 60), but there are some large intra-profile differences. Both groups scored highest on investigative and in the low range on artistic and social themes. Surprisingly, both groups fell within the average range on the academic orientation scale — that is, working with people was not preferred to working with things or vice versa. Both groups achieved rather high scores on the introversion-extroversion scale — that is, they seem to be rather introverted. The two groups thus appear to be investigative in outlook. People who prefer investigative activities are described by Holland (1973) as scholarly, independent, cautious, introverted, and rational. This description seems to correspond well with the impression of the two groups gleaned from the CPI.

The results of a discriminant analysis performed on this data are non-significant (see table 9.6). It thus appears that the vocational interests of the two groups do not differ.

Study of Values.   Means and standard deviations for each of the six SOV scores for the two SMPY groups and for high-school students are reported in table 9.4. Again, the radical accelerants and nonaccelerants appear quite similar. Both groups scored highest on theoretical, second

TABLE 9.2. CPI Scales

CPI Scale	SMPY Radical Accelerants (N = 16)		SMPY Non-accelerants (N = 13)		Eighth-Grade Gifted (N = 94)		Eighth-Grade Random (N = 82)	
	Mean	Standard Deviation	Mean	Standard Deviation	Mean	Standard Deviation	Mean	Standard Deviation
Do (Dominance)	27.1	6.7	27.6	5.1	27.0	5.5	19.5	4.9
Cs (Capacity for status)	18.0	3.7	16.8	4.2	17.6	3.7	11.3	3.5
Sy (Sociability)	21.8	5.1	22.0	5.2	24.4	5.0	20.7	4.2
Sp (Social presence)	33.3	6.8	32.8	7.7	32.9	5.7	30.6	6.2
Sa (Self-acceptance)	19.7	3.6	19.2	3.5	19.6	3.5	17.6	3.8
Wb (Well-being)	33.2	4.0	33.2	5.3	35.6	4.8	27.2	6.1
Re (Responsibility)	28.9	4.0	31.2	3.3	31.7	4.3	21.5	5.8
So (Socialization)	37.3	5.2	37.9	4.8	40.8	4.9	29.9	5.3
Sc (Self-control)	26.8	4.7	28.5	6.9	28.2	8.8	18.0	7.2
To (Tolerance)	20.2	4.8	20.0	6.3	22.4	4.4	12.1	4.8
Gi (Good impression)	14.4	4.6	15.9	5.3	16.9	6.8	10.3	4.7
Cm (Communality)	24.4	2.8	24.7	2.2	26.4	1.8	23.6	3.5
Ac (Achievement via conformance)	24.8	3.3	26.5	4.3	26.3	4.2	16.4	4.4
Ai (Achievement via independence)	18.9	3.6	19.5	3.7	18.0	3.9	10.9	3.5
Ie (Intellectual efficiency)	38.8	4.9	37.4	4.1	38.7	4.4	26.0	5.3
Py (Psychological-mindedness)	12.3	3.1	11.8	3.4	11.2	2.7	7.9	2.7
Fx (Flexibility)	11.0	4.3	12.4	4.7	9.4	3.4	7.7	2.7
Fe (Femininity)	16.9	3.0	17.8	4.5	17.4	3.2	15.1	3.4

TABLE 9.3. Strong-Campbell Interest Inventory (SCII) Scales

SCII Scale	SMPY Radical Accelerants (N = 19)		SMPY Non-accelerants (N = 20)	
	Mean	Standard Deviation	Mean	Standard Deviation
Realistic	47.7	13.7	49.5	9.2
Investigative	59.9	4.5	56.1	7.2
Artistic	40.8	8.4	41.9	8.4
Social	40.1	12.3	42.3	8.9
Enterprising	43.7	8.1	44.9	7.1
Conventional	50.4	10.3	52.0	9.1
Academic orientation	54.4	11.3	51.6	11.5
Introversion-extroversion	59.3	12.3	59.3	12.0

TABLE 9.4. Allport, Vernon, and Lindzey's Study of Values

SOV Scale	SMPY Radical Accelerants (N = 21)		SMPY Non-accelerants (N = 20)		High-School Students (N = 12,616)	
	Mean	Standard Deviation	Mean	Standard Deviation	Mean	Standard Deviation
Theoretical	52.6	5.8	50.4	6.9	40.2	7.4
Economic	42.6	7.0	41.8	8.4	40.5	7.0
Aesthetic	35.2	7.3	33.3	6.8	36.7	7.6
Social	36.3	9.0	39.9	7.8	40.2	6.9
Political	46.7	5.6	45.7	7.2	41.1	6.3
Religious	27.0	10.9	29.1	11.1	40.9	8.7

highest on political, and lowest on religious values. Both groups obtained "high" scores on theoretical, "low" scores on religious, and fell within the average range on the other four scales compared with high-school students (Allport, Vernon, & Lindzey 1970, p. 24). Allport, Vernon, and Lindzey also claim that a theoretical type is "inclined to actively seek truth in a logical, often scientific manner." The political scale, on which the two SMPY groups scored second-highest, denotes "a concern for power." These findings also correspond well with those of the other standardized measures.

A discriminant analysis performed on the SOV data for the two groups again resulted in a nonsignificant discriminant function (see table 9.6).[2] There is no evidence that at age 13 the values of the two groups differed.

Liking for School and Math.   The data presented in table 9.5 concern liking for school and for math for the radical accelerants and nonaccelerants. Both groups reported a strong liking for math and a fairly strong liking for school. In this respect, too, the two groups appear quite similar.

The Composite Profiles for the Two Groups at Age 13.   At age 13 there is no evidence of any dissimilarity, favoring either group, between

TABLE 9.5. Liking for School and Mathematics

Reported Liking for	SMPY Radical Accelerants (N = 21)		SMPY Nonaccelerants (N = 21)	
	Mean	Standard Deviation	Mean	Standard Deviation
School	1.67	0.80	2.05	0.74
Mathematics	1.29	0.46	1.29	0.46

NOTE: Liking was coded as follows: 1 = strong liking; 2 = slight liking; 3 = neutral; 4 = slight dislike; 5 = strong dislike.

the radical accelerants and nonaccelerants. This was true with respect to age, academic ability, and social and emotional development (general social functioning, vocational interests, and values). None of the three discriminant analyses performed on this data resulted in significant discriminant functions (see table 9.6).

Considering the diversity of the measures used, the composite profile is remarkably consistent. Subjects from both groups seem best described as solid, well adjusted, socially mature, and interpersonally effective individuals who are also rather cautious and introverted. Both groups also seem to prefer academic/intellectual pursuits to social ones. It may be surprising that the group profile is so consistently positive. The manner in which subjects were selected may have influenced this. All of the subjects volunteered to participate in a difficult contest and in the follow-up testing sessions. Thus there is a potential positive bias in the profile.

If some kind of self-selection factor is operating for the two groups, it does not appear to be operating differentially for the radical accelerants and nonaccelerants. This finding is in itself interesting. Thus any differences between the two groups after acceleration may be attributed with some confidence to the acceleration and not to a priori differences between the two groups.

The Questionnaire: Five Years Later.   In table 9.7 the means and standard deviations of the two groups' answers to the follow-up questionnaire can be seen. It is clear from this table that the radical accelerants and nonaccelerants differ in a number of respects at age of high-school graduation. In high school the radical accelerants participated in slightly more types of activities than did the nonaccelerants, but the nonaccelerants took part in a greater number of activities. This was true even though the number of activities was corrected for the number of years spent in high school. The nonaccelerants held more jobs than did the radical accelerants. Many of the radical accelerants, however, were too young to work in high school. The nonaccelerants participated in more college activities than did the radical accelerants, although the radical accelerants had been in college longer. The nonaccelerants reported a slightly greater liking for college than did the radical accelerants. Whether these last two findings are

TABLE 9.6. Discriminant Analysis for the SMPY Radical Accelerant and Nonaccelerant Groups

Discriminant Functions	Measure			
	CPI	SCII	SOV	Questionnaire
Eigenvalue	0.89	0.17	0.08	2.89
Canonical correlation	0.69	0.39	0.29	0.86
Wilks' Lambda	0.53	0.85	0.92	0.26
Chi-square, d.f., sig.	14.68, 1, NS	5.80, 1, NS	3.06, 1, NS	48.94, 8, $p < .001$
Centroids ⟨ radical accelerants	0.61	0.39	0.21	0.85
nonaccelerants	−0.75	−0.37	−0.20	−0.85

Unstandardized discriminant function:

CPI		SCII		SOV		Questionnaire	
Capacity for status	0.16	Investigative	0.16	Social	0.12	Kinds of high-school activities	0.21
Responsibility	−0.24	Social	−0.06	Constant	−4.44	Total in-school activities	−0.42
Self-control	−0.11	Constant	−6.98			Total out-of-school activities	0.15
Tolerance	0.10					Number of Jobs	−0.30
Communality	−0.19					Educational aspirations	0.20
Achievement via conformance	−0.08					Use of educational opportunities	0.27
Flexibility	−0.22					Helped by SMPY	−0.89
Femininity	0.12					Acceleration's effect on social/emotional development	0.24
Constant	12.54					Constant	−0.47

173

TABLE 9.7. Follow-Up Questionnaire Responses Obtained Five Years after
Talent-Search Participation

Questionnaire Item	SMPY Radical Accelerants (N = 21)		SMPY Non-accelerants (N = 21)	
	Mean	Standard Deviation	Mean	Standard Deviation
Kinds of in-school activities	2.0	1.5	2.1	1.7
Number of in-school activities	2.3	1.7	3.0	1.5
Kinds of out-of-school activities	3.6	2.6	3.1	2.0
Number of out-of-school activities	3.0	1.9	3.2	2.2
Number of jobs held in high school	0.4	0.6	1.5	1.1
Number of college activities	1.3	1.1	2.0	1.6
Liking for college[a]	1.9	0.9	1.4	0.8
Educational aspirations[b]	8.1	0.4	7.2	1.8
Use of educational opportunities[c]	1.8	0.9	2.7	1.1
How SMPY has helped[d]	1.3	0.7	2.7	0.7
How SMPY has affected social/ emotional development[d]	2.4	1.1	3.0	0.8
How acceleration has affected social/ emotional development[d]	2.2	1.1	2.5	1.2

Responses were coded as indicated for each item.

[a] 1 = strong liking
2 = moderate liking
3 = neutral
4 = moderate dislike
5 = strong dislike
[b] 7 = master's degree
8 = doctoral degree
[c] 1 = extremely well

2 = rather well
3 = about average
4 = rather poorly
5 = extremely poorly
[d] 1 = extremely positively
2 = slightly positively
3 = no effect
4 = negatively

the result of a real difference or are the artifactual product of freshman
enthusiasm on the part of the nonaccelerants is unknown.

The radical accelerants had higher educational aspirations than did the
nonaccelerants; the radical accelerants planned, on the average, to obtain
a doctoral degree, while the nonaccelerants aspired, on the average, to
obtain a master's degree (table 9.7).

The final section of the follow-up questionnaire presented perhaps the
most important and interesting questions, since they deal with the students'
perceptions of their own academic and social/emotional development.
More specifically, they asked each subject how well he had used his educational opportunities, how much SMPY had helped him, how SMPY had
affected his social and emotional development, and how acceleration had
affected his social and emotional development. The two groups answered
these questions quite differently. The radical accelerants felt that they had
used their educational opportunities rather well compared with the nonaccelerants, who thought they had used them "about average." The radical
accelerants felt that SMPY had helped them very much, while the nonaccelerants thought that SMPY had given them very little help. The radical

accelerants thought that their association with SMPY had positively influenced their social and emotional development, while the nonaccelerants perceived no influence. Interestingly, both groups felt that acceleration (if any) had influenced their social and emotional development in a slightly positive way (table 9.7).

A discriminant analysis performed on the questionnaire data resulted in a discriminant function of considerable power. The results of this analysis can be seen in table 9.6. Eight of the original twelve variables were retained in the discriminant function, which had a chi-square value of 48.9, with 8 df ($p < .001$).

While the significance of the discriminant function indicates clear differences between the radical accelerants and the nonaccelerants, the nature of the measurement instrument makes it difficult to explain precisely this difference. The data on participation in extracurricular activities are equivocal — neither group consistently outperformed the other in that respect. The best interpretation of these data is perhaps that no differences in extracurricular participation exist between the two groups. The nonaccelerants held more jobs in high school than did the radical accelerants, but this is attributable to the fact that the radical accelerants were too young to work in high school.

The last five questions are more easily interpretable. The radical accelerants had higher aspirations than the nonaccelerants. The radical accelerants report that they have used their educational opportunities better than the nonaccelerants have. The radical accelerants report being helped more by SMPY. The radical accelerants report that SMPY has influenced their social and emotional development more positively than do the nonaccelerants. Interestingly, both groups reported that acceleration had positively influenced their social and emotional development. Thus it appears that the effects of acceleration on the social and emotional development of gifted students are not negative and might in fact be positive. A more thorough follow-up of the social and emotional development of talent-search participants would shed light on this question.

Conclusions

The potential effects of acceleration on the social and emotional development of gifted students were examined from two perspectives: (1) a review of the relevant literature, and (2) a longitudinal comparison of the social and emotional development of equally bright radical accelerants and nonaccelerants identified by SMPY. The literature survey resulted in the identification of three dimensions along which research in this area may be classified and evaluated: method and degree of acceleration of the subjects, the definition of "social and emotional development," and the identification of an appropriate reference group. No study, regardless of its orientation on these dimensions, has demonstrated any permanent or significant negative effects of acceleration on social and emotional development. The present study, which is unique in its combination of orientations along the three dimensions, also found no negative effects of acceleration on social and emotional development. In fact, some evidence of positive effects is presented. The similarity of findings of these two approaches is strong support for the claim that there is no validity to the argument that acceleration is harmful to the social and emotional development of gifted youths. A more extensive longitudinal investigation of the social and emotional development of SMPY accelerated and nonaccelerated gifted students would be worthwhile.

Notes

1. Two of the subjects were not formal talent-search participants, since they lived outside the search region, but they have otherwise been treated as such by SMPY and are thus incorporated into this study.
2. The SOV data were ipsative. Since no significant differences were found this should not affect the results.

References

Admissions Testing Program of the College Board. 1979. *National report: College-bound seniors, 1979.* Princeton, N.J.: Educational Testing Service.
Allport, G. W.; Vernon, P. E.; and Lindzey, G. 1970. *Manual for the Study of Values: A scale for measuring the dominant interests in personality.* 3d ed. Boston: Houghton Mifflin.
Benbow, C. P. 1981. Development of superior mathematical ability during adolescence. Ph.D. diss., Johns Hopkins University.
Birch, J. W. 1954. Early school admission for mentally advanced children. *Exceptional Children* 21:84–87.
Daurio, S. P. 1979. Educational enrichment versus acceleration: A review of the literature. In *Educating the gifted: Acceleration and enrichment,* ed. W. C. George, S. J. Cohn, and J. C. Stanley, 13–63. Baltimore: Johns Hopkins University Press.

Edelston, H. 1950. Educational failure with high intelligence quotient: A clinical study. *Journal of Genetic Psychology* 77:85–116.

Elwell, C. 1958. Acceleration of the gifted. *Gifted Child Quarterly* 2(Summer): 21–23.

Fox, L. H. 1976. Sex differences in mathematical precocity: Bridging the gap. In *Intellectual talent: Research and development,* ed. D. P. Keating, 183–214. Baltimore: Johns Hopkins University Press.

Fox, L. H.; Brody, L. E.; and Tobin, D. H., eds. 1980. *Women and the mathematical mystique.* Baltimore: Johns Hopkins University Press.

Fund for the Advancement of Education of the Ford Foundation. 1953. *Bridging the gap between school and college.* New York: Research Division of the Fund.

Gough, H. G. 1969. *Manual for the California Psychological Inventory.* 3d ed. Palo Alto, Calif.: Consulting Psychologists Press.

Hall, W. B., and MacKinnon, D. W. 1969. Personality inventory correlates of creativity among architects. *Journal of Applied Psychology* 53(4): 322–26.

Hobson, J. R. 1963. High school performance of underage pupils initially admitted to kindergarten on the basis of physical and psychological examinations. *Educational and Psychological Measurement* 23(1): 159–70.

Holland, J. L. 1973. *Making vocational choices: A theory of careers.* Englewood Cliffs, N.J.: Prentice-Hall.

Keating, D. P., ed. 1976. *Intellectual talent: Research and development.* Baltimore: Johns Hopkins University Press.

Keating, D. P.; Wiegand, S. J.; and Fox, L. H. 1974. Behavior of mathematically precocious boys in a college classroom. In *Mathematical talent: Discovery, description, and development,* ed. J. C. Stanley, D. P. Keating, and L. H. Fox, 176–85. Baltimore: Johns Hopkins University Press.

Keys, N. 1938. The underage student in high school and college. *University of California Publications in Education* 7:145–271.

Lessinger, L. M., and Martinson, R. A. 1961. The use of the CPI with gifted pupils. *Personnel and Guidance Journal* 39: 572–75.

Maeroff, G. I. 1977. The unfavored gifted few. *New York Times Magazine,* August 21, 1977, pp. 30–32, 72ff.

Morgan, A. B. 1959. Critical factors in the academic acceleration of gifted children: A follow-up study. *Psychological Reports* 5:649–53.

Nevin, D. 1977. Young prodigies take off under special program. *Smithsonian* 8(7): 76–81, 160.

Nie, N. H.; Hull, C. H.; Jenkins, J. G.; Steinbrenner, K.; and Bent, D. H. 1975. *SPSS: Statistical package for the social sciences.* 2d ed. New York: McGraw-Hill.

Pressey, S. L. 1949. *Educational acceleration: Appraisal and basic problems.* Bureau of Educational Research Monographs, no. 31. Columbus, Ohio: Ohio State University Press.

Spranger, E. 1928. *Types of men: The psychology and ethics of personality.* New York: Johnson Reprint, 1966.

Stanley, J. C. 1979. The study and facilitation of talent for mathematics. In *The gifted and the talented: Their education and development,* ed. A. H. Passow, 169–85. Pt. 1 of *The seventy-eighth yearbook of the National Society for the Study of Education.* Chicago: University of Chicago Press.

Stanley, J. C.; Keating, D. P.; and Fox, L. H., eds. 1974. *Mathematical talent: Discovery, description, and development.* Baltimore: Johns Hopkins University Press.

Strong, E. K., and Campbell, D. P. 1974. *Strong-Campbell Interest Inventory.* Stanford, Calif.: Stanford University Press.

Terman, L. M. 1925. *Mental and physical traits of a thousand gifted children.* Vol. 1 of *Genetic studies of genius.* Stanford, Calif.: Stanford University Press.

Terman, L. M., and Oden, M. H. 1947. *The gifted child grows up: Twenty-five years' follow-up of a superior group.* Vol. 4 of *Genetic studies of genius.* Stanford, Calif.: Stanford University Press.

———. 1959. *The gifted group at mid-life: Thirty-five years' follow-up of the superior child.* Vol. 5 of *Genetic studies of genius.* Stanford, Calif.: Stanford University Press.

Weiss, D. S.; Haier, R. J.; and Keating, D. P. 1974. Personality characteristics of mathematically precocious boys. In *Mathematical talent: Discovery, description, and development,* ed. J. C. Stanley, D. P. Keating, and L. H. Fox, 126–39, 191–202. Baltimore: Johns Hopkins University Press.

Worcester, D. A. 1956. *The education of children of above average mentality.* Lincoln: University of Nebraska Press.

Zorbaugh, H. 1937. Is instability inherent in giftedness and talent? *Proceedings of the Third Conference on Education and Exceptional Children,* Langhorne, Pa., pp. 17–24.

10 Statewide Replication in Illinois of the Johns Hopkins Study of Mathematically Precocious Youth

JOYCE VAN TASSEL-BASKA

Abstract

After the successful pilot testing of a program modeled after the SMPY approach, Illinois began in 1978 a statewide mathematics search using as a selection criterion for educational facilitation a score of 420 or better on the School and College Ability Test-Mathematics. Special fast-paced mathematics classes were established in areas where there were enough high scorers. Although these classes varied in number of students and amount of material covered, a large percentage of their participants completed the program successfully. Because of this success a verbal program was begun in 1979. Following brief descriptions of the verbal and mathematics classes, several problems and concerns encountered in the functioning of the classes are presented. The author concludes with the positive implications of such a program.

After approximately ten years of research under the direction of Dr. Julian C. Stanley at The Johns Hopkins University, the Study of Mathematically Precocious Youth program has firmly established itself as a viable approach to working with highly gifted children in the field of mathematics. The evidence of student growth in this program is compelling and has been well documented (Stanley, Keating, & Fox 1974; Keating 1976; Stanley, George & Solano 1977; George, Cohn, & Stanley 1979; Fox, Brody, & Tobin 1980; Bartkovich & George 1980).

In 1977 the state of Illinois utilized federal funds from PL 93-380 to

pilot the Hopkins project at two sites within the state, the northern suburban area of Chicago (Bethalto) and the southern metro-east area of
Chicago (Niles). The results (see table 10.1) of that pilot activity were
highly successful and thus led the way to a statewide effort toward identifying and serving highly gifted children (Van Tassel 1977).

The pilot replication was considered successful for several reasons.
Foremost, of course, was that a large number of gifted students were identified and then subsequently facilitated in their education. But, in addition,
the pilot program demonstrated that different geographical regions of the
state had sufficient talent pools to warrant regionalized identification procedures and that there was adequate student/parent interest. Furthermore,
school officials were made cognizant of the potential of the identified
students to handle a more accelerated mathematics class; in the following
year, they allowed their junior-high-school students to take high-school-
level mathematics course-work (ibid.). Press coverage of the event was
somewhat remarkable and included a front-page story in the Sunday edition of the *Chicago Tribune.*

Based on the success of the project in three pilot sites, the state agency
decided to copy the SMPY talent-search concept (George & Solano 1976)
on a statewide basis. In July, 1978, the Illinois Office of Education
negotiated with the nine Gifted Area Service Centers (regional service
delivery units) to implement a mathematics talent search for their respective regions of the state. Most centers limited participation to the public
schools within each region that were currently participating in the state
gifted program. This included 465 districts in the state of Illinois and the
city of Chicago.

Program Implementation

A portion of state funding in Illinois has been set aside since 1971 to
fund nine regional centers for facilitating the education of the gifted. Each
center is staffed by two full-time professionals in the field. Historically, the
major role of the centers has been to provide technical assistance in program development for the gifted to the districts participating in the state-
funded program. Thus natural linkages were already in place to regionalize
the math talent search, since each center already had responsibility for and
contact with between forty-five and ninety-five districts in their
geographical area through district-designated program coordinators. Further, as a part of its contract, each center had the potential to carry out the
talent search and the follow-up educational facilitation work by utilizing
existing staff.

Beginning in 1978 this network of Area Service Centers became
organized to implement the program statewide. The implementation was
accomplished through the following processes:

1.   Area Service Centers solicited names of students in participating

TABLE 10.1. Results of the Illinois Pilot Program and the SMPY January, 1978, Program

	Bethalto (Dec., 1977)	Niles (Oct., 1977)	SMPY (Jan., 1978)
	Identification Phase		
Percentile used for cut-off score for talent search	96	98	97
Grade level(s) included in talent search	7th & 8th	7th	7th
Number of students nominated for testing as part of talent search	85	510	3,333
Number of students taking test	7th grade 43 8th grade 34	320	2,798
Highest SAT-M score[a]	760	780	790
Lowest SAT-M score	290	260	220
Mean SAT-M score[b]	7th grade 406 8th grade 501	390	432
Mean SAT-V score[b]	358	338	374
Median SAT-M score	450	380	Males 427 Females 396
Median SAT-V score	340	330	Males 363 Females 366
	Development Phase		
Number of students eligible for fast-math class	35	55	
Number of students taking class	25	48	
Number of students completing class	24	35	
Mean score on ETS Algebra I (reference)			
Pre-test	18.4	18.3	
Post-test	33.4	35.8	
Mean score on ETS Algebra II (reference)	Not given	33.6	
Mean score on ETS Algebra III (reference)	Not given	30.9	

[a] All SAT scores are converted from the SCAT with the exception of the data reported from SMPY. Scores above 740 are extrapolated.
[b] Mean SAT-M and SAT-V scores for college-bound twelfth-grade males are 491 and 428, respectively.

districts of the Illinois Gifted Program who scored at the ninety-fifth percentile or higher on a standardized achievement test in mathematics.

2.   These students were invited to take a test comparable to the College Board's Scholastic Aptitude Test, the School and College Ability Test Form 1C-Mathematics (SCAT-M) and -Verbal (SCAT-V) (ETS 1955), at a specific place and time scheduled by the center.

3.   Those students scoring 420 or better on SCAT-M were invited to participate in a special fast-paced mathematics class in their regional area.

4.   Special classes were set up as the talent search revealed enough students in the same geographical area.

5.   In regions where special classes were not established, special intervention strategies were shared with appropriate school personnel.

Data from the first two years of the search can be seen in tables 10.2 and 10.3. It should be noted that over 6,000 students were tested in this period; thirty-four special courses were structured as a direct result of the

TABLE 10.2. 1978–79 Illinois Talent-Search

Coordinating Center	Number of Students Tested[a]	Cut-Off Score on SCAT-M Utilized for Facilitation	Number Qualifying	Top Score on SCAT-M	Facilitation Offering (classes)
City of Chicago	1011	450	376	800 (2)	5 algebra I, II, and computer programming; 7 special math seminars for all tested
Area I: north	800 (97%)	500	100	780	2 at Niles West (algebra I & II)
Area I: south	388	500	31	590	2 enrichment for 8 weeks
Carthage	175	450	30	800	no classes; individual acceleration
Illinois State University	79	400	31	580	none
Benton	166	420	52	650	none
Belleville	100	470	24	760	1 8th-grade algebra I at community college
Northern Illinois University	156	450	28	740 (2)	1 regional algebra I & II
University of Illinois	140	500	30	740	none
Total	3,015		702		11

[a] All regions utilized a ninety-fifth percentile cut-off on standardized achievement to derive students tested – except region I: north.

TABLE 10.3. 1979–80 Illinois Talent-Search

Coordinating Center	Number of Students Tested [a]	Cut-Off Score on SCAT-M Utilized for Facilitation	Number Qualifying	Top Score on SCAT-M	Facilitation Offering (classes)
City of Chicago	487 (7th)	420	49	720	3 algebra I & computer programming; 1 (advanced) geometry & computer programming
Area I: north	800 (97%)	470	90	780	1 algebra I & II, geometry, & part of trigonometry
Area I: south	515	420 Math 420 Verbal	100 25	720 Math 580 Verbal	1 pilot verbal Latin I; 3 7th-grade algebra I & II; 2 8th-grade algebra II & geometry
Carthage	225	450 Math	32	760	1 7th-grade algebra, geometry, & logic
Illinois State University	298				none
Benton	160	420	40	640	3 8th-grade algebra I (2 in district and 1 at a junior college)
Belleville	125	450	70	800	3 8th-grade algebra I
DeKalb	262	440	74	700	4 8th-grade algebra I & II
Rantoul	159	430	106	640	1 8th-grade algebra I & II
Total	3,031		586		23

[a] All regions utilized a ninety-fifth percentile cut-off on standardized achievement to derive students tested — except region I: north.

183

testing. Awards ceremonies were held regionally in all areas. In addition, in June, 1979, the Illinois Office of Education sponsored a statewide awards luncheon for students scoring 600 or better on the SCAT-M. The following year, in June, 1980, a four-day residential program for students scoring 500 or better on SCAT-M was held on the campus of Illinois State University.

Fast-Math Classes

Statewide, the fast-math classes varied to some extent in the number of students served and the amount of material covered. The northern suburban area of Chicago classes covered the most: algebra I and II in the seventh-grade and plane and solid geometry and trigonometry in the eighth-grade year. High schools in the area provided Advanced Placement Calculus, Level AB, and two universities (Oakton Community College and Northwestern) provided linear algebra, calculus II, and differential equations to complete the sequence.

The southern suburban area of Chicago offers algebra I and II in the seventh and the eighth grade, respectively, with high schools providing two additional years of mathematics instruction. Prairie State College then offers the students advanced mathematical instruction in their junior and senior years of high school.

Other areas of the state, including Chicago, facilitate through fast-math classes only at the eighth-grade level in algebra I, along with some exposure to other mathematics. Thus students begin their high-school sequence with algebra II and thereby save one year of traditional instruction.

For the northern and southern suburban areas of Chicago, 65 percent of the students continue with the fast-math program beyond the first year. Approximately 18 percent enroll in university mathematics courses while still in high school. Where facilitation occurs in the eighth grade only, 80 percent of the students successfully complete the program. The ETS Algebra Cooperative Tests are utilized to confirm proficiency and placement decisions.

1979–80 Pilot Verbal Program

Because of the great success in mathematics, a pilot class in the verbal area was begun for the 1979–80 school year. The students met for two hours of instruction per week. In twenty-six sessions they completed the high-school Latin I text, *Latin for Americans* (Ullman, Henderson, & Henry 1968).

Students were exposed to the following routine during the two hours of instructional time: Latin vocabulary work, review of new concepts from the preceding week, homework discussion, introduction of new concepts, practice and application of new concepts, sight translations, discussion of Roman myths, and assignment for the next week. Assignments consisted of learning vocabulary and doing exercises in the new material covered. A second text, titled *Myths and Their Meanings* (Herzberg 1978), was utilized for enrichment purposes. The class was grouped into three sections to provide for individualization of progress.

A proficiency examination developed by high-school Latin teachers in the area was given to the students at the end of the course, in June. Placement and credit options were then discussed with those high schools to which the students would matriculate. Table 10.4 is an overview of the student progress in the pilot program. Twelve of the fourteen students completed the program. Ability on the SCAT-V did not seem to relate strongly to later performance in the class, but it must be kept in mind that there was little variance in SCAT-V scores (see table 10.4). The best predictor of class success was related to motivational factors surrounding completion

TABLE 10.4. Latin Pilot Class: Selection Scores and Results, 1979–80

Student	Sex	Pre-SCAT (Sept., 1979) V	M	Post-SCAT-V (June, 1980)	Proficiency Test (% Correct)	Recommendation
1	M	530	720	610	84	Pass to Latin II (class grade: *A*)
2	M	500	380	610	51	Qualify for regional program (combined Latin I, II) (class grade: *C*)
3	F	460	480	570	70	Pass to Latin II (class grade: *A*)
4	M	460	380	610	67	Pass to Latin II (class grade: *B*)
5	M	460	350	450	50	Qualify for regional program (combined Latin I, II) (class grade: *C*)
6	M	430	340	450	76	Pass to Latin II (class grade: *B*)
7	M	420	470	520	54	Qualify for regional program (combined Latin I, II) (class grade: *C*)
8	M	420	450	540	59	Qualify for regional class in Latin II (class grade: *B*)
9	F	420	390	460	65	Qualify for regional program (combined Latin I, II) (class grade: *B*)
10	F	420	340	470	51	Qualify for regional program (combined Latin I, II) (class grade: *C*)
11	F	420	330	470	Not taken	Other options in verbal areas
12	F	420	320	560	Not taken	Other options in verbal areas
13	F	420	300	480	79	Pass to Latin II (class grade: *A*)
14	F	390		450	63	Try in Latin II (class grade: *B*)
		Mean				
		441	404	518	64	
		Standard Deviation				
		38	111	64	12	

of homework and eagerness to learn evidenced during class sessions. Also, students who showed high concentration ability succeeded in the program.

1980–81 Academic Talent Search

Buoyed by the results of the 1979 pilot program in Latin, two Illinois sites proceeded to conduct full-fledged searches for students scoring at the ninety-fifth percentile or higher on a standardized achievement test in the verbal or the mathematics areas. This yielded 625 participants for the spring testing of seventh-graders in Chicago Public Schools and 750 in the southern suburbs of Chicago. The SCAT was again utilized for identification at the second level. Arbitrary cut-off points of SCAT-M ≥ 420 for mathematics facilitation and SCAT-V ≥ 400 for verbal facilitation were set for purposes of recommending students for special city or regional classes. In Chicago, 320 scores qualified for facilitation in mathematics, verbal, or both, accounting for 51 percent of all students tested. In the southern suburbs of Chicago, 187 scores qualified in a similar manner, which represented 21 percent of all students tested. In Chicago, 33 percent qualified for the verbal classes and 67 percent for mathematics classes. The respective figures for the southern suburbs were 39 percent and 61 percent. For further data on these two regional talent searches, consult tables 10.5 and 10.6.

Sex differences were apparent in the talent search, paralleling what SMPY has found in its program (Benbow & Stanley 1980, 1981). For example, for every female scoring at least 500 on the SCAT-M there were 2.6 males. On the SCAT-V the proportions were almost equal.

1980–81 Facilitation Efforts

Chicago

Educational facilitation for students in the city of Chicago occurs at the eighth-grade level. Three semesters of algebra instruction including algebra I and a part of algebra II were offered through classes taught by university professors at the University of Illinois (Circle Campus) and Chicago State University. Approximately eighty students were enrolled.

In the verbal area, Chicago State University offered one writing class for eighteen students; Loyola University offered a class, serving twenty-two students, in Latin and Greek languages and cultures.

Southern Suburban Area of Chicago

The mathematics sequence offered through the regional programs provided two semesters of algebra I at the seventh-grade level and two

TABLE 10.5. 1980–81 Ranges of Scores for Chicago and Area I: South on the SCAT-M and SCAT-V

Range	Chicago (N = 625 ending seventh-graders)	Area I: South (N = 750 beginning seventh-graders)
SCAT-M		
700–800	2	0
600–699	7	2
500–599	51	14
400–499	187	109
SCAT-V		
700–800	0	0
600–699	4	1
500–599	10	4
400–499	92	68

TABLE 10.6. 1980–81 Academic Talent Search and Development for Two Sites in Illinois

Location, Number Tested, and Date	Qualifying Score	Number of Students Qualifying for Facilitation		Top Qualifying Score		Number of Facilitation Classes	
		M	V	M	V	M	V
Chicago N = 625 ending seventh-graders May, 1980	420 Math 400 Verbal	214	106	760	690	4 8th-grade	2 8th-grade
Area I: south N = 750 beginning seventh-graders October, 1980	420 Math 400 Verbal	114	73	680	640	3 7th-grade 2 8th-grade	3 7th-grade

semesters of algebra II in eighth grade. The after-school classes consisted of twenty-six two-hour sessions. High-school placement and/or credit allowed able students to complete calculus by the end of their sophomore year and pursue advanced mathematical topics at area colleges for the third and fourth years of high school.

The 1980 mathematics facilitation in the southern suburbs consisted of three algebra I classes and two algebra II classes. All were taught by high-school instructors with training, experience, and interest in working with gifted children. Approximately sixty-five students were enrolled in these five regional mathematics programs.

In the verbal area, three classes of Latin I were offered to eligible students. The sequence of classes was Latin I and II in the regional programs followed by Latin III and IV in the first two years of high school *or* four years of another foreign language in high school. High-school Latin teachers acted as instructors in all three programs, which were held at geographically determined subregional sites. Approximately thirty-five students were enrolled in the Latin program.

Summary

The Illinois replication of The Johns Hopkins University's SMPY project had over 7,000 students participating during its first three years. Special regional facilitation, established by the Area Service Centers, had allowed over 650 students to take special fast-paced classes. Selection of students followed the Hopkins two-step process; cut-off points for facilitation range from the sixtieth percentile to the eightieth percentile of the combined-sex high-school sample. A pilot effort in the verbal area of Latin in 1979–80 resulted in academic talent searches to identify and facilitate those students precocious in verbal areas as well as mathematics. Appendixes 10.1 and 10.2 present step-by-step identification and facilitation protocols.

Problems and Concerns

For other states and groups interested in a replication program such as the one described here, it might be useful to share major problem areas Illinois experienced in its efforts.

1.   There have been problems generated around issues of placement following and credit for work completed in the fast-paced classes. Some schools will not accept the ETS Algebra Cooperative Tests as evidence of high proficiency. Therefore, additional testing has occurred at the high-school mathematics department level in order to assure placement. Additionally, some high schools have a school-board policy prohibiting the awarding of credit for such classes.

2.   In some cases, articulation of the classes with the home-school mathematics program has been difficult.

3.   Lack of teachers in the junior high schools trained to meet the needs of our students is another problem area. Many cannot provide assistance even with algebra I homework.

4.   The need for effective communication in this program is vital, yet it is difficult to effect because of the bureaucratic organization in school districts.

5.   Since early entrance to university mathematics classes is both a natural and an intended result of the program, problems emerge in terms of tuition payments, transportation, and scheduling around other high-school subjects.

6.   For Illinois, the use of the SCAT has created a problem in test administration and uniformity in procedures. Also, test security and the age of the test have been called into question. Yet control over testing procedures is deemed important for establishing facilitation efforts. On the basis of the experience in Illinois, it is recommended that the College Board's Scholastic Aptitude Test (SAT) be used, as it has been by SMPY.

Positive Implications

It is fair to assume that the replication of the Johns Hopkins model in mathematics and, later, in verbal areas has had a profound effect on the state program in Illinois and has served the needs of a large number of gifted students. Perhaps the most notable of these effects are as follows:

1.   The drama associated with younger children's scoring very high on difficult tests has created a positive public-relations furor, with school districts clamoring to take credit for good results. Newspaper and television coverage has been better for this project than for any other ever attempted in the state.

2.   The project has forced better articulation between junior high schools and high schools. Where little or no communication existed before, now real planning, albeit in specific areas, is occurring for these highly gifted students.

3.   The project has forced practicing professionals in the field of education for the gifted to focus on serving those students who clearly demonstrate giftedness as opposed to haggling over who might be gifted in a particular district.

4.   The project has displayed brilliantly the need for matching the nature of the giftedness to a specific and appropriate program intervention strategy.

5.   The identification protocol provides a pool of students for whom a variety of intervention techniques could be tried.

6.   Junior high schools are offering more appropriate mathematics curricula. A few are following the algebra I and II sequence at seventh and eighth grade, respectively, within their own districts. Thus mathematics acceleration becomes integrated into their regular course offerings.

7.   Because of the successful mathematics intervention, experimentation in other content areas is being conducted.

References

Bartkovich, K. G., and George, W. C. 1980. *Teaching the gifted and talented in the mathematics classroom.* Washington, D.C.: National Education Association.

Benbow, C. P., and Stanley, J. C. 1980. Sex differences in mathematical ability: Fact or artifact? *Science* 210:1262–64.

———. 1981. Mathematical ability: Is sex a factor? *Science* 212:118, 121. Letters section; response to seven letters there and an editorial that had appeared in the 16 Jan., 1981, issue of *Science.*

Educational Testing Service. 1955. *School and College Ability Tests.* Princeton, N.J.

Fox, L. H.; Brody, L. E.; and Tobin, D. H., eds. 1980. *Women and the mathematical mystique.* Baltimore: Johns Hopkins University Press.

George, W. C.; Cohn, S. J.; and Stanley, J. C., eds. 1979. *Educating the gifted: Acceleration and enrichment.* Baltimore: Johns Hopkins University Press.

George, W. C., and Solano, C. H. 1976. Identifying mathematical talent on a statewide basis. In *Intellectual talent: Research and development,* ed. D. P. Keating, 55–89. Baltimore: Johns Hopkins University Press.

Herzberg, M. 1978. *Myths and their meanings.* Boston: Allyn and Bacon.

Keating, D. P., ed. 1976. *Intellectual talent: Research and development.* Baltimore: Johns Hopkins University Press.

Stanley, J. C.; George, W. C.; and Solano, C. H., eds. 1977. *The gifted and the creative: A fifty-year perspective.* Baltimore: Johns Hopkins University Press.

Stanley, J. C.; Keating, D. P.; and Fox, L. H., eds. 1974. *Mathematical talent: Discovery, description, and development.* Baltimore: Johns Hopkins University Press.

Ullman, B. L.; Henderson, C.; and Henry, N. E. 1968. *Latin for Americans.* New York: MacMillan.

Van Tassel, J. 1977. Illinois plans a state-wide talent search. *Intellectually Talented Youth Bulletin* 4(1): 1–2.

Notes

I would like to acknowledge gratefully the assistance of William C. George in establishing the Illinois program.

APPENDIX 10.1: Illinois Academic Talent Search: Identification Protocol

Step 1.   Find all students scoring 95 percent or higher on standardized achievement test in verbal and/or mathematics areas.

Step 2.   Administer to this population an aptitude test that correlates well with the SAT.

Step 3.   Share results of testing with all students taking the test; recommend special classes for those scoring better than 60 percent of college-bound seniors on a similar instrument.

APPENDIX 10.2: Illinois Academic Talent Search: Facilitation Protocol

Step 1.   Set up fast-paced classes (algebra I–II) for high-scoring math students. Set up fast-paced classes (Latin I–II or other appropriate options) for high-scoring verbal students.

Step 2.   For students who wish to take the classes, create a class within their geographic region, if enrollment permits.

Step 3.   Administer a program of fifty-two hours of instruction in two-hour classes once a week after school in the specified content area.

Step 4.   Evaluate the classes semiannually in respect to proficiency levels, attitudes, and other evidences of growth gains.

Step 5.   Provide for articulation of the program with participating school districts, high schools, and local universities.

11 Eclecticism: A Comprehensive Approach to Education of the Gifted

JOHN F. FELDHUSEN

Abstract

The argument is advanced that an eclectic, or integrative, approach, utilizing all possible resources, is most appropriate for meeting the needs of gifted students. Characteristics of the integrative approach and descriptions of classes utilizing it are provided. The Program for Academic and Creative Enrichment (PACE) and the Individual Educational Program for the Gifted (IEPG), both based on the author's three-stage model for educating the gifted, are presented. The author concludes that since "gifted, creative, talented, and high-ability students have diverse needs, they should have individual counseling and guidance."

The major purpose of this paper is to discuss educational provisions for the gifted, especially the intellectually and artistically gifted, and to argue that acceleration is a vital ingredient of all effective programs. An argument is also advanced that the concept of acceleration may be too narrow for a suitably comprehensive approach to the education of the gifted. Concepts derived from enrichment, acceleration, and extended learning opportunities are all essential for the development of a full-scale concept of education for the gifted. The term *eclectic* sums up and defines this process, since the new concept is derived from several current approaches to gifted education. The key terms describing the eclectic or integrative approach to acceleration are faster pace, higher level, greater depth, cognitive complexity, challenge, higher cognitive processes, and more information.

Various definitions of giftedness have been proposed. The most widely held conception, promulgated in Public Law 95–561, suggests five different categories of ability: (1) intellectual, (2) academic, (3) creative, (4) leadership, and (5) artistic. This view, perpetuated from the time of the Marland Report (1972), has little support from research or any theory of human abilities. A more parsimonious and yet inclusive conception of the fundamental areas of giftedness might be the following:

1. *Intellectual,* academic, curriculum-related aptitudes (e.g., abilities such as those measured by the Differential Aptitude Test);
2. *Artistic* talent;
3. *Social,* leadership, affective; and
4. *Motor,* athletic, movement, dance.

Each of these categories is subject to numerous divisions, but overall they define fundamental areas of human performance fairly well. Creativity in itself is an unlikely area of unique performance, even though it has been recently suggested that one may be creatively gifted (Khatena 1978; Willings 1980). Alternatively, as Renzulli (1978) suggested, creative ability may be a fundamental aspect of excellent performance in any area.

The concern of this paper is chiefly with the intellectually and/or academically gifted, and secondarily with the artistically gifted. Intellectual giftedness was defined as curriculum-related because giftedness in this category most likely manifests itself in and becomes nurtured in one or more of the broad curricular areas such as science, mathematics, language arts, or social science. Most of the concepts presented are also relevant to the education of those who are artistically gifted.

ENRICHMENT VERSUS ACCELERATION

One of the most unfortunate dichotomies in the field of education is the enrichment-acceleration conflict (George, Cohn, & Stanley 1979). It has led to extreme narrowness in conception on the part of advocates on both sides of the controversy and to crystallization of programs that fall far short of meeting the needs of gifted students. Our current state of knowledge about how best to provide for the gifted should lead educators to be eclectic with reference to both enriching and accelerating instruction. The single experimental study that has compared enrichment and acceleration found that a combination of the two provided the best educational benefits for the gifted (Goldberg et al. 1966). It should be acknowledged, however, that the preponderance of solid evidence supports acceleration (George, Cohn, & Stanley 1979).

Perhaps the best way to approach the problem of how to educate the gifted appropriately is in terms of needs of the gifted. Feldhusen and Wyman (1980) and Van Tassel (1980) have argued that gifted, creative, and talented (GCT) students have special needs. The needs of the gifted as delineated by these researchers can be seen in table 11.1 It should be noted that the *first* two needs on the Feldhusen and Wyman (1980) list call for accelerated learning experiences. Acceleration or some closely related concepts characterize pursuit of most of the other needs on this list (see Feldhusen & Wyman 1980). For example, needs 3, 4, and 5, even if pursued in a so-called enrichment program, would have to be taught at an appropriately challenging level and at a more rapid pace to be suitable in educational programs for the gifted. Similarly, needs 7, 8, 11, and 12 imply a need for instruction at a level appropriate for the gifted. Stimulation in reading, for example, ought surely to be at levels appropriate to the gifted child's achievement level. Furthermore, nine of the ten needs statements on the Van Tassel (1980) list contain the word *challenge*. Challenge is developed through appropriate acceleration.

Acceleration refers to all those activities that involve the gifted youngster in instruction outside the normal or regular school-grade placement and involve a relatively bold advancement of pace and level of instruction. Stanley's (1976) definitions of *enrichment* and *acceleration* may further clarify the distinction. "Enrichment," he says, "is any educational procedure beyond the usual ones for the subject or grade that does not accelerate or retard the student's placement in the subject or grade" (p. 66). In contrast, he says, "Academic acceleration is vertical because it means moving the student up into the higher school level of a subject in which he or she excels, or into a higher grade than the chronological age of the student would ordinarily warrant" (p. 68).

A list of accelerative options for the gifted includes eleven appropriate types.

1. Early admission to nursery school
2. Early admission to kindergarten or first grade
3. Grade-level advancement
    Midyear advancement
    Grade skipping
4. Access to junior-high-school courses at the elementary level
5. Condensation of junior high school or high school from three years to one or two years
6. Access to high-school courses in junior high school
7. Access to advanced courses in junior or senior high school, including Advanced Placement Program courses meant to lead to college credit by examinations conducted nationwide each May
8. Access to college courses in high school or junior high school
9. Admission to college early and/or with advanced standing
10. Earning a bachelor's degree in fewer than four years
11. Earning a master's degree concurrently with a bachelor's degree

TABLE 11.1. Two Concepts of the Needs of Gifted Students

Feldhusen and Wyman (1980)	Van Tassel (1979)
1. Maximum achievement of basic skills and concepts	1. To be challenged by activities that enable them to cooperate cognitively and affectively at complex levels of thought and feelings
2. Learning activities at appropriate level and pace	2. To be challenged through opportunities for divergent production
3. Experience in creative thinking and problem solving	3. To be challenged through group and individual work that demonstrates process/product outcomes
4. Development of convergent abilities, especially in logical deduction and problem solving	4. To be challenged by discussions among intellectual peers
5. Stimulation of imagery, imagination, spatial abilities	5. To be challenged by experiences that promote understanding of human value systems
6. Development of self-awareness and acceptance of own capacities, interests, and needs	6. To be challenged by the opportunity to see interrelationships in all bodies of knowledge
7. Stimulation to pursue higher level goals and aspirations (models, pressure, standards)	7. To be challenged by special courses in their area of strength and interest which accelerate the pace and depth of the content
8. Development of independence, self-direction and discipline in learning	8. To be challenged by greater exposure to new areas of learning within and without the school structure
9. Experience in relating intellectually, artistically and affectively with other gifted, creative and/or talented students	9. To be challenged by the opportunity of applying their abilities to real problems in the world of production
10. A large fund of information about diverse topics	10. To be taught the following skills: (a) critical thinking, (b) creative thinking, (c) research, (d) problem solving, (e) coping with exceptionality, (f) decision making, and (g) leadership
11. Exposure to a variety of fields of study, art, professions, and occupations	
12. Access and stimulation to reading	

Sources: J. F. Feldhusen and M. B. Kolloff, "A Three-Stage Model for Gifted Education," *Gifted/Creative/Talented* 4 (1978): 3–5, 53–57; and J. Van Tassel, "A Needs Assessment for Gifted Education," *Journal for the Education of the Gifted* 2 (1979): 141–48.

Any combination of those options can be appropriate for the highly gifted. These options make up in part the "smorgasbord of special educationally accelerative options" used successfully by the Study of Mathematically Precocious Youth (Stanley 1978). A student is considered "radically" accelerated if by the end of high school or college his or her educational placement has been speeded up by three or more years (Stanley 1980).

METHODS OF ACCELERATION

In the Gifted Education Resource Institute at Purdue University several major forms of educational activity for gifted students which can be characterized as "acceleration" are utilized. For example, highly gifted children are encouraged to advance in grade at the elementary- or junior-high-school level. A child's readiness for acceleration is assessed through individual diagnostic testing of his or her intellectual ability, achievement levels, and personal-social adjustment. The general rule for positive signs for acceleration is that the IQ should be at or above 130, achievement levels three or more years advanced beyond current grade placement, and adjustment essentially normal.

If the child and his or her parents are positive in their motivation to proceed and the psychological evidence is positive, a meeting of the child's current teacher, the teacher who would receive the child, the principal, and the parents is set up. At this meeting it is proposed that the child spend the first half of the year in his or her normal grade placement and move midyear to the next higher grade. The teachers are asked to cooperate in making sure that essential elements of curriculum are not missed. If the grade advancement involves skipping a grade, receipt by the student of summer tutoring by a teacher of the grade to be skipped may be desirable.

Another form of acceleration promoted by the institute is to introduce college-level courses into the high-school curriculum. Professors from nearby universities come to the high school each semester and offer juniors and seniors college-level courses for college credit. Thus these students become accelerated in subject-matter content. A model program is offered at Gary, Indiana. In the 1979–80 school year ninety-two gifted students were enrolled in six English composition courses taught by Purdue or Indiana University professors. Twenty-three students earned As, forty-three earned Bs, and twenty-one earned Cs, while none earned a D; two students withdrew, one received an F, and three took incompletes. The overall grade point average (G.P.A.) of these classes was 3.0 on a scale where $A = 4$, $B = 3$, etc.

The three-credit university course offered on the Purdue campus during the summer of 1980 for highly gifted students in grades seven to twelve illustrates further the institute's use of acceleration. The subject matter, PASCAL programming, was presented in a fast-paced lecture format by a staff member from the computer science department of Purdue University. Of the fourteen high-ability youth who entered this class, five earned *A*s, six earned *B*s, and three earned *C*s. The G.P.A. for the class was 3.1. Their grade levels were as follows: seven in grade seven, two in grade eight, three in grade nine, and two in grade ten. None of the students who registered dropped the course. The distribution of grades earned by students' grade level in school was as follows:

Grade in School	A	B	C
seventh	3	3	1
eighth		2	
ninth		1	2
tenth	2		

It can be seen that the seventh-graders performed better than the eighth- and ninth-graders. All of these seventh-graders had had two years in a special mathematics enrichment program prior to this university course (Hersberger & Wheatley 1980).

These forms of acceleration are clearly appropriate for highly gifted students. While their focus was certainly on the academically gifted, similar acceleration occurs in Suzuki violin classes for three- to five-year-olds and in dance classes for children at the same age levels. In most art forms it is crucial for children with high-potential talent to start instruction early.

Integrative Acceleration

To meet the needs of a wide spectrum of gifted students, however, an alternate or extended conception of acceleration is needed. Although it appears that acceleration deals merely with pace, in reality it implies undertaking instruction at advanced levels commensurate with students' achievement. Aspects of the extended conception of acceleration, called the *integrative approach to acceleration,* are listed here.

Characteristics

1. Rapid pace
2. Compression of content
3. Advanced level of material
4. Extended diversity of topics or curriculum
5. Objectives, questions, or activities at higher levels of cognitive processing
6. Greater amounts of information
7. Intellectually challenging
8. Requiring complex, full formal operations

9. Less didacticism, more inquiry
10. More independence
11. Greater depth of investigation

Activities

1. A pull-out program meeting two or three periods per week or one-half or one full day per week
2. Cluster grouping of gifted students in one classroom with a teacher who can find special time for their instruction
3. Enrichment in the regular classroom by the regular teacher
4. Special topic classes as electives in such areas as logic and foreign languages
5. A full-time class for gifted students

In contrast to the accelerative options listed earlier, integrative acceleration includes all the forms of providing for the gifted without altering students' grade placement and without formal advancement of the subject matter to a higher-level book or specified curriculum. The net effect, however, of integrative enrichment is to involve the student in learning activities characteristic of grade levels considerably above his or her current grade-level placement. An example is a class on research methods for fifth- and sixth-graders in the institute's Saturday program (Feldhusen & Wyman 1980). Twelve students were enrolled, and all achieved satisfactory ratings of their performance. While the approach in this course is viewed largely as enrichment, it is nevertheless accelerating, since the content of research methods often is not taught until high school or college.

Integrative acceleration is a term synonymous with *enrichment.* Yet the concept of acceleration is vital in education for the gifted because it provides challenge. The most important elements of integrative acceleration are:

1. rapid pace,
2. compression of content,
3. advanced levels of material,
4. extended diversity of topics,
5. greater amounts of information, and
6. intellectual challenge.

Major approaches to integrative acceleration include the so-called "accelerated" classes that are used in many schools from the elementary level upward. The Gifted Education Resource Institute designed a special mathematics curriculum for fifth- and sixth-graders (Hersberger & Wheatley 1980). A group of about twenty high-ability students are identified through administration of the junior-high-school level of the Stanford Achievement Test at the end of the fourth grade. They are required to have grade-equivalent scores at or above the 6.0 level in math concepts and 8.0 in math application. Then, beginning in fifth grade, the students meet one period daily as a special group and pursue a unique mathematics curriculum that stresses topics beyond those usually covered at the grade level. Probability, estimation, and problem solving are some of the special topics. The students use calculators, and with microcomputers they learn how to use the computer language BASIC for programming and solving problems. Traditional mathematics topics are compressed, and the general pace of the class is fast. The entire approach used in this class fits the concept of integrative acceleration. Others, however, might see it as an essentially enriching approach to mathematics.

During the 1978–79 school year this class's pre-test and post-test scores in grade equivalents on the junior-high level of the Stanford Achievement Test were as follows.

	Mean Grade Level, Math Concepts	Mean Grade Level, Problem Solving
Pre-test (end of fourth grade)	8.1	8.7
Post-test (end of fifth grade)	10.1	10.1

These students were far advanced in achievement at the end of fourth grade, and they still made substantial gains during the special fifth-grade mathematics program.

A Three-Stage Model

The major efforts of the Gifted Education Resource Institute in designing curricula for gifted, creative, talented, and high-ability students are embodied in a three-stage model developed for educating the gifted at the elementary- and junior-high-school levels (Feldhusen & Kolloff 1978). This model operates within a format of integrated acceleration or enrichment, aspects of which are listed here.

Stage 1	Stage 2	Stage 3
Basic convergent and divergent thinking skills	Inquiry skills	Independent projects
	Research methods	Inquiry activities
	Creative problem solving	Self-directed research
Essential curriculum content	Convergent problem solving	
	Synectics	
	Morphological analysis	
	Logical analysis and deduction	
	Brainstorming	

In stage 1 basic knowledge and thinking skills are taught. In stage 2 special cognitive processing strategies are taught within each discipline. In stage 3 students learn techniques of independent inquiry and investigation.

The basic concepts of our three-stage model have been elaborated in two other papers (Feldhusen & Kolloff 1979; OrRico & Feldhusen 1979) and in a substantially funded project in the elementary schools of the Tippecanoe School Corporation in Indiana. The project is titled PACE (Program for Academic and Creative Enrichment). While considered essentially an enrichment model, PACE's title connotes a penchant for an underlying accelerative approach to gifted education. It serves students in grades three to six.

Students are selected for the PACE program on the basis of Metropolitan Achievement Test scores, teacher nominations, teacher ratings on the Scale for Rating the Behavioral Characteristics of Superior Students (Renzulli et al. 1976), and teacher ratings on the Checklist of Creative Positives (Torrance 1969). Nominees must score at or above the ninetieth percentile on one major area of the Metropolitan Achievement Test and have high scores on the two rating scales. Local norms are used for the rating scales.

In the PACE program itinerant resource teachers meet with students outside their regular classroom two class periods per week in groups of eight to twelve at a grade level. All of the instruction follows our three-stage model. Some of the special features of PACE are as follows:

1. close cooperative working relationships between the regular classroom teachers and resource teachers;
2. substantial in-service training for resource and regular teachers;
3. a curriculum guide for regular teachers providing activities for the regular classroom to support the program for the gifted and other children;
4. close liaison with parents;
5. periodic student evaluation reported to students and parents; and
6. comprehensive program evaluation.

For the independent inquiry work of stage 3 a special project planning form called IEPG (Individual Educational Program for the Gifted) was developed. It can be seen in figure 11.1. This format provides excellent guidance to the gifted student, the teacher, and the parents in planning an independent inquiry project.

An intensive experimental evaluation of the PACE program focusing on school achievement, creative abilities, self-concept, and higher-level thinking skills was carried out. The evaluation involved experimental and control groups, both of which were drawn from a group identified as eligible for the program. The results show that the PACE program is highly successful in increasing the creative abilities of gifted children.

FIGURE 11.1. IEPG: Individual Educational Program for the Gifted

NAME _____ *Tommy Ames* _____ TEACHER _____ *M. Smith* _____ DATE ___ *3/17* ___

Child's Major Interests

1. _____ *Dinosaurs* _____ 3. _____ *Camping* _____

2. _____ *Circuses* _____ 4. _____ *Stamp collecting* _____

Major Strengths

Skills _____ *Reading* _____ _____ *Computation* _____

Concepts _____ *Science* _____ _____ *Math concepts* _____

Major Needs (assessment results)

Skills _____ *Reading speed* _____ *Spelling* _____

Concepts _____ *None* _____ *None* _____

Plan for Study or Project

Will do an in-depth study of North American dinosaur regions.

Reading and Study Sources

Dinosaurs, Guided Discovery Program, Educational Progress,

informational books on dinosaurs in school library.

What is to be Produced? (e.g.: a report, a model, a set of worksheets, a drawing, a play, problems, a presentation)

Will produce a written report, a bulletin board display, and an

illustrated oral report.

With Whom Will He Work, If Anyone?

Might work with Sally Thomas.

Approximate Date to Complete Project?

May 8, 1981.

Plan for Teacher Contribution and Consultation

Will meet with teacher once a week.

Role for Other Resource People

Will meet with Peter Lewis, a professor of paleontology, and Robert Drew,

a professor of geology.

Parent Role and Contribution

Parents will assist in taking field trip to Natural History Museum.

In all applications of the three-stage model, and especially in PACE, the need for the resource teachers to provide challenge, increase the pace, compress routine learning at stage one, press for high-level thinking, and, above all, induce challenge is stressed. Without these emphases the program would degenerate into routine and boring enrichment activities.

Different activities are appropriate for moderately gifted students than for highly gifted ones. PACE and the three-stage model best serve moderately gifted students. Acceleration, sometimes radical acceleration, is necessary for the highly gifted. Thus the guide in table 11.2 was developed to meet the differential needs of moderately able and highly gifted students.

Conclusion

Because gifted, creative, talented, and high-ability students have diverse needs, they should have individual counseling and guidance. The schools can do a great deal, but members of the broad community, especially parents, should be utilized in developing educational experiences and opportunities. Acceleration of learning experiences is essential, but, for the present, program coordinators should be eclectic and utilize all possible resources in trying to meet the needs of these students.

Some parents and teachers worry about the gifted students' emotional development and even advocate neglecting their intellectual and artistic needs. Many parents and teachers assert that they just want the gifted student to grow up "normal" and "happy." They seem not to realize that forcing a gifted person to be like an average person is forcing him or her to be abnormal. Giftedness is a total package of high potential, intellectually (and/or artistically) and emotionally. Ability and emotion are inextricably linked.

The best and happiest balance for the gifted student is attained by finding emotional fulfillment in high-level intellectual or artistic activities. The world provides many examples of disgruntled, dissatisfied people who had the talent or ability to achieve at a very high level but did not get the opportunity to do so. Thus it appears that through appropriately accelerated and enriched learning experiences we can help the gifted individual achieve intellectual and/or artistic fulfillment, a strong self-concept, and good emotional adjustment.

Perhaps the major issue is to plan educational programs for the gifted carefully and to provide the individual counseling necessary to meet their diverse needs. Enrichment *versus* acceleration is probably a false dichotomy. The following quotation from Keating (1979, p. 188) seems an appropriate way to conclude this discussion: "Thoughtless acceleration can be harmful, and unplanned enrichment can turn out to be mostly busy-

TABLE 11.2. Programming Guide for Use in Educational Planning for the Gifted

Ability Level	Program Needs
I. Highly Gifted	I. Acceleration

I.Q.s 130 and above
Achievement: 3 or more grade levels
   advanced
Grade average in top 5 percent
Achievement test scores at or above
   the ninety-fifth percentile
	Individual psychological and
	   ability testing
	Individual counseling
	Several forms of acceleration
	Integrated acceleration

II. Moderately Gifted	II. Integrated Acceleration or Enrichment

I.Q.s 120 and above
Achievement: 1–3 grade levels
   advanced
Grade average in top 10 percent
Achievement test scores at or above
   the ninetieth percentile
	Careful identification but no individual
	   psychological testing
	Might be candidate for some forms
	   of acceleration
	Integrated acceleration or
	   enrichment activities

work. Good educational acceleration is always enriching, however, and solid enrichment programs always advance the student's learning of new and relevant material."

References

Feldhusen, J. F., and Kolloff, M. B. 1978. A three-stage model for gifted education. *G/C/T,* no. 4, pp. 3–5, 53–57.

———. 1979. An approach to career education for the gifted. *Roeper Review* 2:13–17.

Feldhusen, J. F., and Wyman, A. R. 1980. Super Saturday: Design and implementation of Purdue's special program for gifted children. *Gifted Child Quarterly* 24(1, Winter): 15–21.

George, W. C.; Cohn, S. J.; and Stanley, J. C., eds. 1979. *Educating the gifted: Acceleration and enrichment.* Baltimore: Johns Hopkins University Press.

Goldberg, M. L.; Passow, A. H.; Camm, D. S.; and Neill, R. D. 1966. A comparison of mathematics programs for able junior high school students. Vol. 1. Project no. 3-0381. Washington, D.C.: U.S. Office of Education, Bureau of Research.

Hersberger, J., and Wheatley, G. 1980. A proposed model for a gifted elementary school mathematics program. *Gifted Child Quarterly* 24(1, Winter): 37–40.

Keating, D. P. 1979. Secondary school programs. In *The gifted and the talented: Their education and development,* ed. A. H. Passow, 185–98. Pt. 1 of *The seventy-eighth yearbook of the National Society for the Study of Education.* Chicago: University of Chicago Press.

Khatena, J. 1978. *The creatively gifted child.* New York: Vantage Press.

Marland, S. P. 1972. *Education of the gifted and talented.* Vol. 1: *Report to the Congress of the United States by the U.S. Commissioner of Education.* Washington, D.C.: U.S. Government Printing Office.

OrRico, M. J., and Feldhusen, J. F. 1979. Career education for the gifted, creative and talented. *G/C/T,* no. 10, pp. 37–40.

Renzulli, J. S. 1978. What makes giftedness? *Phi Delta Kappan* 60: 180–84.

Renzulli, J. S.; Smith, L. H.; White, A. J.; Callahan, C. M.; and Hartman, R. K. 1976. *Scales for rating the behavioral characteristics of superior students.* Mansfield Center, Conn.: Creative Learning Press.

Stanley, J. C. 1976. The case for extreme educational acceleration of intellectually brilliant youth. *Gifted Child Quarterly* 20(1, Spring): 41, 66–75.

———. 1978. Educational non-acceleration: An international tragedy. *G/C/T,* no. 3, pp. 2–5, 53–64, 60–64.

———. 1980. On educating the gifted. *Educational Researcher* 9(3): 8–12.

Torrance, E. P. 1969. Creative positives of disadvantaged children and youth. *Gifted Child Quarterly* 13:71–81.

Van Tassel, J. 1979. A needs assessment for gifted education. *Journal for the Education of the Gifted* 2(3): 141–48.

Willings, D. 1980. *The creatively gifted.* Cambridge: Woodhead-Faulkner.

12 An Eight-Year Evaluation of SMPY: What Was Learned?

CAMILLA PERSSON BENBOW and
JULIAN C. STANLEY

In 1971 the concept of systematic, annual mathematics talent searches was born because the number of talented students found through informal means was insufficient and because the staff of the Study of Mathematically Precocious Youth wanted to discover how many exceptionally mathematically able students there were within a given locale.

Six talent searches were conducted by SMPY from March, 1972, to January, 1979. The first search attracted participants chiefly from the greater Baltimore area, but the fourth one (December, 1976) extended over the Mid-Atlantic region. In 1979 the Johns Hopkins Office of Talent Identification and Development, now called the Center for the Advancement of Academically Talented Youth, was established to conduct the talent searches, seeking not only students with high mathematical ability but also those with high verbal and/or general ability. In 1980 Assistant Provost Robert N. Sawyer of Duke University adopted the SMPY model (Sawyer & Daggett 1982). Sanford J. Cohn also conducts an annual talent search from his center at Arizona State University at Tempe, as does Joyce Van Tassel-Baska of Northwestern University in Illinois. Many other efforts are based at least somewhat on the SMPY-CTY model. The concept of a talent search has spread and has been adopted across the country since 1972. In this way more than 85,000 students have been identified as talented. Currently, approximately 70,000 talented students are expected to be identified each year by the talent searches. This necessitates determining the validity and reliability of this identification protocol.

The goal of SMPY and of the programs conducting talent searches, however, is not only to identify talented students early but also to provide educational opportunities that make it more likely for these gifted students to become effective, productive adults. SMPY's model is an attempt to capitalize on Zuckerman's (1977) finding that accumulation of advantages characterized the backgrounds of Nobel Laureates in the United States.

Such advantages can be, or are for the most part, various educational opportunities. SMPY and the other programs try to provide these opportunities to their students. Accumulating educational advantage, SMPY predicts, will increase and enhance talented students' creative contributions as adults. This may be especially true if their education proceeds at a faster rate, since, based on Lehman's (1953) conclusion, an individual's greatest creative accomplishments tend to be concentrated within a few years when the scholar, scientist, or inventor is young.

Thus SMPY's model relies heavily on acceleration. The educational development procedures involve making the school curriculum flexible enough for intellectually talented students instead of developing new curricula (Stanley & Benbow 1982a, in press b). Furthermore, the staff of SMPY believes that offering intellectually talented students a varied assortment of accelerative possibilities and letting them choose an optimum combination of these to suit the individual's situation is far superior to so-called "special academic enrichment" (Stanley 1977).

Additional justification of acceleration was discussed by Robinson in this volume from the developmental psychological perspective. His central conclusion was that the pace of educational programs must be adapted to the capacities and knowledge of individual children. For a few students the appropriate fit involves placement several levels above the child's age-mates and is termed "radical acceleration." For others it may involve only moderate acceleration. The key point is that the curriculum is adapted so that each child can be learning at the level at which he or she is functioning. This is based on the premise that learning occurs only when there is "an appropriate match between the circumstances that a child encounters and the schemata that he has already assimilated into his repertoire" (Hunt 1961, p. 268). A class for high-IQ children could not possibly provide this match for every child.

Operating under its principle that SMPY should work with the school using its already available curricula or supplementing them with classes outside of school, SMPY formed special fast-paced mathematics classes that met on weekends or during summers and also encouraged its students to accelerate their education by skipping grades, taking college courses on the side while still a high-school student, entering college early, or taking Advanced Placement (AP) examinations for college credit. Although this procedure was flexible, it created some problems. For example, parents had to spend countless hours driving their children from high school to college, from junior high school to high school, or to summer or weekend classes; some children had to live double lives — as high-school student and as college student; a calculus course taken at an evening college may not be as beneficial as a calculus course taken in the day school of a university. Many other compromises are involved. Thus SMPY's smorgasbord of educationally accelerative opportunities (Benbow 1979; Stanley 1978a) should be viewed as a series of compromises between what may be ideal for a precocious child and the opportunities or circumstances that exist.

On a short-term basis the accelerative opportunities offered by SMPY were successful, as has been extensively documented (e.g., Stanley, Keating, & Fox 1974; Keating 1976; Stanley 1978c; Stanley & Benbow 1982b). A purpose of the research described in this volume was to discover how effective these compromises were over an eight-year period for the students who made them. Another goal was to characterize the students who participated in the talent searches. What has happened to the students identified by SMPY as being mathematically precocious? How many took SMPY's advice and accelerated their programs as they deemed best? In essence, the chapters in this volume provide the necessary data to be used in evaluating the long-term effectiveness of the SMPY model.

Most of the data for this evaluation were obtained from SMPY's first major follow-up of its students who had reached high-school graduation age (Benbow 1981). From 1972 to 1974 SMPY had identified over 2,000 students who as seventh- or eighth-graders had scored on the SAT-M or SAT-V as well as a random sample of high-school-junior or -senior females.

Identification Procedure

The first questions raised in this evaluation were these: How effective is SMPY's primary screening measure (i.e., the SAT)? What type of students are identified by looking for high scorers on the SAT in the seventh or eighth grade? The general conclusion was that SMPY's identification measure selects students in the seventh grade who achieve academically at a superior level in high school, especially in mathematics and science. The SAT-M score of an intellectually talented seventh- or eighth-grader has much predictive validity.

SAT-M scores, supplemented by SAT-V scores, are proving to be excellent in finding special talent in the area of mathematics. CTY showed how effective initially the SAT also is in the verbal areas. Long-term validity needs to be determined, however, for areas besides mathematics.

Certainly the SAT is not appropriate for everyone. SMPY and CTY work with extremely academically talented students who can demonstrate their precocity. In so doing, however, compromises have to be made. Some students, it was realized, are unable to demonstrate academic precocity because they lack facilitative environments and opportunity. Some are "late bloomers." Moreover, there are many types of giftedness. Obviously the SAT may tell little about leadership potential. Neither will the SAT be useful for identifying the moderately gifted in the seventh grade; it is too difficult. Thus use of the SAT in a talent-search protocol is appropriate only if it fits the goals of a particular program for gifted children. Where the aim is to provide better educational opportunities for students of demonstrably great academic aptitude, however, the SAT can be a highly effective identification instrument.

CREATIVITY

Much attention in the field of educating the gifted is focused on creativity. Moreover, SMPY's aim is to increase for many of its students the number of years during which their greatest creative contributions are made. Thus manifestation of creativity among the SMPY students was studied. Inconclusive and indecisive results were found by Michael in this volume, partly because of difficulty in defining creativity operationally. Moreover, it was hard to specify accomplishments in mathematics and science that by the end of high school should be considered creative. Consequently, it was found that questions in the follow-up survey were inadequate. The staff of SMPY is investigating this question further in its after-college follow-up and in the follow-up after high-school graduation of selected students from the last SMPY talent searches. Clearly, most of the SMPY students achieve well academically. When the SMPY students become about 50 years old, we shall know if for some of them their academic achievement is translated into creative achievement. The signs to date indicate that this will probably occur (see Stanley & Benbow 1982b, in press a).[1]

Educational Development

FAST-PACED CLASSES

The second set of questions concerns the educational facilitation procedures specified by the SMPY model, especially its fast-paced mathematics classes. What are the long-term effects of having attended one of these? Is educational acceleration of mathematically able youths justifiable? Do the facilitated students show a higher level of achievement? These issues were covered in chapters four through nine.

Findings from the eight-year follow-up of the participants in SMPY's first fast-paced precalculus classes and equally able nonparticipants revealed that the most successful students in the mathematics classes achieved much more in high school and college than the equally able students who had not participated. The students were satisfied with their acceleration, which they felt did not detract from their social and emotional development. Furthermore, there appeared to be no evidence to justify the fear that accelerated rate of learning produces gaps in knowledge or poor retention. Later, when the College Board's achievement tests were taken in high school, the accelerated students had not scored lower on those exams than the nonaccelerated students. Even though the accelerated students had gone to college at an earlier age, this was not at the expense of the quality of the institution they attended, as was judged by the Astin (1965) ratings. Thus learning mathematics at an accelerated rate appears to have had distinctly beneficial effects.

The rate at which mathematics is taught by SMPY's methods depends upon the student. In the first fast-paced classes, it was taught at a pace geared to the ablest members in the class. This approach necessitated splitting up the classes into a faster and a slower section, because some students could not keep up with the initial rate of instruction. This early approach to teaching mathematics has been altered from experience. Students are no longer taught as a class, which involves lecturing and group participation. Instead, SMPY and CTY utilize the Diagnostic Testing followed by Prescriptive Instruction (DT → PI) model (Stanley 1978b, 1979). Through diagnostic testing the student's placement in mathematics is determined. Moreover, testing allows the instructor to determine what the student knows and does not know about precalculus. The student then learns, at his/her individual rate, only the subject matter not known. Progress is certified by use of standardized tests. Thus instruction has become quite individualized, accommodating a wide range of students from the moderately gifted to the highly gifted. The initial success of the new approach has been documented (Bartkovich & Mezynski 1981). The long-term effects remain to be evaluated but are not expected to be less positive than the results from the evaluation of the first fast-paced mathematics classes.

SMPY's accelerated classes have not been limited to the domain of precalculus. They have been conducted successfully in calculus (Mezynski & Stanley 1980; Mezynski, McCoart, & Stanley, in this volume) and also in college chemistry and physics (Mezynski, McCoart, & Stanley, in this volume). During the summer of 1982 fast-paced high-school biology and chemistry were taught to extremely academically able students in three weeks each. At the end of the three weeks the class's mean score on the College Board's biology achievement test was 730 (the ninety-sixth percentile of a select group of students who had taken one or more years of high-school biology) and 743 on the chemistry achievement test (the ninety-fourth percentile of the norm group). Initially the fast-paced classes have been highly successful. Students have received a solid background in the subject matter of these classes. The long-term effects remain to be evaluated, however. SMPY will do so.

Mathematics and the sciences are subjects more dependent for their mastery on manifest intellectual talent than on chronological age and associated life experiences. The Program for Verbally Gifted Youth (PVGY) in CTY at Johns Hopkins, however, adapted the fast-paced approach for teaching courses in the verbal area (Durden 1980). In its writing skills courses PVGY helps students achieve the following: (1) an expository writing style that is both accurate and imaginative; (2) knowledge of the syntactical possibilities of English and naturalness of diction; (3) understanding and appreciation of the semantic, structural, and rhetorical resources of the English language; and (4) basic library and research skills. The staff of PVGY also offers courses such as German, Latin, Etymology, and Critical Readings in Literature. These classes are offered during the academic year and during the summer in a residential setting. Initial results are very positive, but longitudinal evaluation of PVGY's programs remains to be done.[2]

SEX DIFFERENCES

Although the fast-paced model of instruction is effective and has lasting impact, it may be that the mathematics and science classes are more appropriate for 11- to 14-year-old boys than for girls that age. Many mathematically talented girls seem to have different needs from most mathematically talented boys. This lack of suitability may be a major component in determining the sex difference in mathematics achievement among SMPY students. It is well known that many females prefer to work with people rather than with things. This is reflected in their evaluative attitude profiles (Allport, Vernon, & Lindzey 1970). Furthermore, females show more interest in and positive feelings toward others (Oetzel 1966) and generally rate higher on nurturance and affiliation items (Kelly 1979). In 1973 such findings led to the first program run by SMPY that catered especially to girls (Fox 1976). This was an accelerated algebra program for an all-female class that emphasized social elements. The teachers were female; problems were solved cooperatively rather than via the common independent and competitive approach; problems were rewritten to be more appealing to girls; and several role models were brought in to show by example how careers in fields using mathematics can be appropriate and enjoyable for girls. The major goal of the program was to increase the number of years of mathematics taken in high school and college by these girls. This in turn should have made it more likely for the girls to enter careers with a quantitative emphasis. Although the program was successful in recruiting moderately gifted girls to attend, the long-term effects appeared small as judged from the evaluation by Fox, Benbow, and Perkins in this volume. Apparently the social and academic elements of the program were not strong enough or were not continued long enough for girls of the ability levels involved.

Perhaps the short duration of the program was a critical factor. Two months of effort after the seventh grade may be insufficient to have long-lasting impact. Perhaps encouragement and attention are needed throughout the high school years; this hypothesis follows because girls perceive themselves as being less independent than boys and exhibit less confidence in their abilities (Maccoby & Jacklin 1974; Pedro et al. 1981). Moreover, women tend to attribute their success to luck or chance while men attribute their success to their abilities. Clearly, with such outlooks, girls need more encouragement and attention than their male counterparts if they are to succeed. This may be especially true before precedents are made for girls to enter quantitatively oriented fields. Modified replications of Fox's experiment with abler girls are needed.

ENTERING COLLEGE EARLY

Fast-paced classes are only one accelerative option offered to students in the talent searches. Skipping grades and thereby entering college early, perhaps also with advanced standing, is another. The justification for this approach, discussed by Robinson in this volume, has already been summarized in this chapter. Is this approach effective, however? Does educational acceleration harm students' social and emotional development? In chapters eight and nine the results of the evaluation of SMPY's use of educational acceleration are presented. The late Professor Halbert B. Robinson of the University of Washington discussed the success of "radical accelerants" (i.e., students who have skipped several grades) in his and SMPY's programs. The introductory chapter also provides clues to the later success of radical accelerants, as do Stanley and Benbow (1982b, in press a). In general, the radical accelerants experience academic success without encountering much other difficulty. The early signs of creativity in this group are being detected as some of these students begin publishing their research articles.

Opposition to acceleration of gifted students is justified primarily by concern for the possible effects of acceleration on social and emotional development. Previous research on this topic was compiled and published in an earlier volume of this series (George, Cohn, & Stanley 1979). The main emphasis of that volume was to compare acceleration and enrichment approaches to facilitating the education of gifted students. Yet Keating (1979, p. 218) in that volume concluded that "as for the social-emotional concerns, it seems time to abandon them unless and until some solid reliable evidence is forthcoming that indicates real dangers in well-run programs." The results of the studies reported by Daggett and Robinson in this volume support that conclusion. Neither Daggett nor Robinson found any detrimental effects of acceleration among radical accelerants; nor did the accelerated students voice any detrimental effects (Benbow, in this volume).

Although acceleration can be appropriate for many gifted students, it is not for all. John F. Feldhusen (in this volume) makes that point quite clearly when he argues that one must be eclectic when setting up programs for gifted students. Acceleration and *selective* enrichment are vital elements of any program. This was the main conclusion of the earlier volume (George, Cohn, & Stanley 1979). Feldhusen carefully delineates guidelines for when acceleration and enrichment are appropriate and provides working examples for the professional interested in the subject. His key point, however, is that the best programs for the gifted embody both acceleration and enrichment.

Adaptability of the Programs

A major desirable feature of a program is its transportability. No matter how effective a new program is, if it cannot be adapted or duplicated in another setting, its impact is diminished. John Lunny and Joyce Van Tassel-Baska, both in this volume, provide useful evidence, and so do Sawyer and Daggett (1982). The talent-search model and its associated educational programs can be adapted, cost-effectively, in a variety of settings.

To date the success of SMPY students has been remarkable. This may lead one to wonder if the success of the students is not due entirely to the programs but instead in some measure to "halo effect." Although we doubt that this is true, even if it was, this should not be considered detrimental. If telling students that they have great academic potential will help produce the results SMPY has experienced, telling them should be encouraged. It is virtually certain, however, that without the SMPY and CTY special programs the students could not have achieved nearly as much as they have to date. For example, without the program few would have been able to enter college early. Colleges would not have accepted them.

Stronger, long-term tests of SMPY's effectiveness will come when the talent-search students reach their professional midlives, about age 50. Then we should be able to judge the effects of SMPY's procedures better. From now until at least then the staff of SMPY will attempt to monitor the students' progress with questionnaires at important points.

In this book we have examined the validity of SMPY's identification and educational facilitation procedures by means of longitudinal research. These principles, practices, and techniques were shown to be effective and transportable to various settings. If there is a special lesson to be learned thus far, it is that curricular flexibility, augmented by special fast-paced courses, can work wonders for young, able, highly motivated students. Educational systems should provide those precious ingredients.

Notes

1. One need not wait until SMPY's protégés reach midlife in order to find evidence of their creativity. A number have already been the author or coauthor of an original contribution to the professional literature, e.g., Chien in O'Rourke et al. (1982) at age 15, Camerer (1977) at age 16, and Stark at age 23 in a forthcoming issue of the *Journal of the Association of Computing Machinery* and previously, at age 16 (Stark & Stanley 1978).

2. During the summer of 1983 there was a total of more than 1,000 9–16-year-old registrants in CTY's two three-week residential programs on each of two college campuses. All of these young students, who came from across the country, had scored in the top 1 percent of their age group verbally or mathematically.

References

Allport, G. W.; Vernon, P. E.; and Lindzey, G. 1970. *Study of Values.* Boston: Houghton Mifflin.

Astin, A. W. 1965. *Who goes where to college?* Chicago: Science Research Associates.

Bartkovich, K. G., and Mezynski, K. 1981. Fast-paced precalculus mathematics for talented junior-high students: Two recent SMPY programs. *Gifted Child Quarterly* 25(2, Spring): 73–80.

Benbow, C. P. 1979. The components of SMPY's smorgasbord of accelerative options. *Intellectually Talented Youth Bulletin* 5(10): 21–23.

————. 1981. Development of superior mathematical ability during adolescence. Ed.D. diss., The Johns Hopkins University.

Camerer, C. F. 1977. A proposal for regional adjustments to the minimum standard allowance in financial need analysis. *Financial Aid News* 6(2): 7–8.

Durden, W. G. 1980. The Johns Hopkins program for verbally gifted youth. *Roeper Review* 2: 34–37.

Fox, L. H. 1976. Sex differences in mathematical precocity: Bridging the gap. In *Intellectual talent: Research and development,* ed. D. P. Keating, 183–214. Baltimore: Johns Hopkins University Press.

George, W. C.; Cohn, S. J.; and Stanley, J. C., eds. 1979. *Educating the gifted: Acceleration and enrichment.* Baltimore: Johns Hopkins University Press.

Hunt, J. M. 1961. *Intelligence and experience.* New York: Ronald Press.

Keating, D. P. 1979. The acceleration/enrichment debate: Basic issues. In *Educating the gifted: Acceleration and enrichment,* ed. W. C. George, S. J. Cohn, and J. C. Stanley, 217–20. Baltimore: Johns Hopkins University Press.

————, ed. 1976. *Intellectual talent: Research and development.* Baltimore: Johns Hopkins University Press.

Kelly, A. 1979. *Girls and science: An international study of sex differences in school science achievement.* Stockholm, Sweden: Almquist and Wiksell International.

Lehman, H. C. 1953. *Age and achievement.* Princeton, N.J.: Princeton University Press.

Maccoby, E. E., and Jacklin, C. N. 1974. *The psychology of sex differences.* Stanford, Calif.: Stanford University Press.

Mezynski, K., and Stanley, J. C. 1980. Advanced placement oriented calculus for high school students. *Journal for Research in Mathematics Education* 11(5): 347–55.

Oetzel, R. M. 1966. Annotated bibliography and classified summary of research in sex differences. In *The development of sex differences,* ed. E. E. Maccoby, 223–32. Stanford, Calif.: Stanford University Press.

O'Rourke, J.; Chien, C.; Olson, T.; and Naddor, D. 1982. A new linear algorithm for intersecting convex polygons. *Computer Graphics and Image Processing* 19:384–91.

Pedro, J. D.; Wolleat, P.; Fennema, E.; and Becker, A. D. 1981. Election of high school mathematics by females and males: Attributions and attitudes. *American Educational Research Journal* 18:207–18.

Sawyer, R. N., and Daggett, L. M. 1982. Duke University's Talent Identification Program. *G/C/T,* no. 22, pp. 10–14.

Stanley, J. C. 1977. Rationale of the Study of Mathematically Precocious Youth (SMPY) during its first five years of promoting educational acceleration. In *The gifted and the creative: A fifty-year perspective,* ed. J. C. Stanley, W. C. George, and C. H. Solano, 75–112. Baltimore: Johns Hopkins University Press.

———. 1978a. Educational non-acceleration: An international tragedy. *G/C/T,* no. 3, pp. 2–5, 53–57, 60–64.

———. 1978b. SMPY's DT→ PI model: Diagnostic testing followed by prescriptive instruction. *Intellectually Talented Youth Bulletin* 4(10): 7–8.

———. 1978c. The predictive value of the SAT for brilliant seventh- and eighth-graders. *College Board Review* 106:30–37.

———. 1979. How to use a fast-pacing math mentor. *Intellectually Talented Youth Bulletin* 5(6): 1–2.

Stanley, J. C., and Benbow, C. P. 1982a. Educating mathematically precocious youths: Twelve policy recommendations. *Educational Researcher* 11(5): 4–9.

———. 1982b. Using the SAT to find intellectually talented seventh graders. *College Board Review* 122:2–7, 26–27.

———. In press a. Extremely young college graduates: Evidence of their success. *College and University* (Summer, 1983).

———. In press b. Intellectually talented students: The key is curricular flexibility. In *Learning and motivation in the classroom,* ed. S. Paris, G. Olson, and H. Stevenson. Hillsdale, N.J.: Erlbaum.

Stanley, J. C.; Keating, D. P.; and Fox, L. H., eds. 1974. *Mathematical talent: Discovery, description, and development.* Baltimore: Johns Hopkins University Press.

Stark, E. W., and Stanley, J. C., eds. 1978. Bright youths dispel persistent myths about intellectual talent: Panel discussion with parents and educators. *Gifted Child Quarterly* 22(2, Summer): 220–34.

Zuckerman, H. 1977. *Scientific elite: Nobel laureates in the United States.* New York: Free Press.

Name Index

215

The Johns Hopkins University Press
ACADEMIC PRECOCITY

This book was composed in Baskerville display and
Times Roman text type by Capitol Communication
Systems, Inc., from a design by Susan P. Fillion. It was
printed on S. D. Warren's 50-lb. Sebago Cream paper
and bound in Sturdetan by the Maple Press Company.